7/11
$26.00

ENCARNACIÓN

SUZANNE BOST

Encarnación

ILLNESS AND BODY
POLITICS IN CHICANA
FEMINIST LITERATURE

FORDHAM UNIVERSITY PRESS

New York / 2010

Library of Congress Cataloging-in-Publication Data

Bost, Suzanne.
    Encarnación : illness and body politics in Chicana feminist literature / Suzanne Bost.—1st ed.
        p.   cm.
    Includes bibliographical references and index.
    ISBN 978-0-8232-3084-6 (cloth : alk. paper)—ISBN 978-0-8232-3085-3 (pbk. : alk. paper)
    1. American literature—Mexican American authors—History and criticism.   2. American literature—Women authors—History and criticism.   3. Diseases in literature.   4. Human body in literature.   5. Identity (Psychology) in literature.   6. Mexican American women in literature.
7. Mexican Americans—Race identity.   8. Feminism in literature.
9. Feminism and literature—United States—History—20th century.   I. Title.
    PS153.M4B67 2010
    810.9'3561082—dc22

                                                                    2009032186

Printed in the United States of America
12 11 10   5 4 3 2 1
First edition

CONTENTS

v

FIGURES

ACKNOWLEDGMENTS

*T*his project has roused in me tremendous passion for my subject, and I begin with my gratitude to Gloria Anzaldúa, Cherríe Moraga, Ana Castillo, Maya González, and Diane Gamboa for so vividly capturing the permeability of our bodies and our identities. I have found in their work models for responding ethically and imaginatively to the worlds and beings with which we are intertwined. I am indebted to all of the critics and theorists who have influenced my response to this material (you can find them named in my bibliography). In particular, I'd like to thank Tace Hedrick, who has been an intellectual sounding board for nearly a decade. I'd like to thank AnaLouise Keating for talking, reading, writing, and sharing some of Anzaldúa's unpublished writings with me. And I'd like to thank Katie King for believing in this book.

Encarnación was formed from years of conversation with my personal community of friends and fellow scholars. I fondly recall the discussions—with Lucy Corin, Narin Hassan, Steve Germic, Karyn Sproles, Annette Federico, Mark Facknitz, and others—that initially sparked the idea for this project in the English faculty research group at James Madison University. The writing of this book owes much to my dear friends and former colleagues in Dallas—especially Rajani Sudan, Stacy Alaimo, Jeannie Hamming, Dennis Foster, Nina Schwartz, Rick Bozorth, Beth Newman, Bruce Levy, and Elizabeth Russ—who read chapters so thoughtfully and asked all the important questions. I'm grateful to Southern Methodist University for providing me with the resources to visit archives throughout the Southwest and Mexico as well as a leave of absence to finish most of the writing. To my new life in Chicago: I thank my colleagues at Loyola University for welcoming me and helping me to celebrate *Encarnación*, and I thank the Office of Research Services, the College of Arts and Sciences, and the Department of English at Loyola for helping with the cost of reproducing the images I analyze. Thanks to Gillian Nelson Bauer for helping with the final stages of proofreading. And thank you, Helen Tartar, Eric Newman, and all of the editorial staff at Fordham, for making this project a book.

The research for this project spawned a number of presentations and articles. An early version of Chapter 2 was published in *Aztlán*: "Gloria Anzaldúa's Mestiza Pain: Mexican Sacrifice, Chicana Embodiment, and Feminist Politics" (*Aztlán* 30.2 [Fall 2005]: 5–31). Two other essays emerged from this work: "From Race/Sex/Etc. to Glucose, Feeding Tube, and Mourning: The Shifting Matter of Chicana Feminism" appeared in *Material Feminisms* (ed. Stacy Alaimo and Susan Hekman; Indiana University Press in 2007), and "Vulnerable Subjects: Motherhood and/as Disability in Nancy Mairs and Cherríe Moraga" in *Disability and Mothering* (ed. Cynthia Lewiecki-Wilson and Jan Cellio, forthcoming from Demeter Press).

Encarnación has also roused in me a more expansive understanding of my own self, which is intertwined most intimately with my husband, Stuart Wick, my sister, Kathleen Bost, my parents, Mary Anne and Jon Bost, and my late grandmother Marian Cassidy—who all influenced this project at every level. I honor all of the yoga instructors and the midwives who sharpened my understanding of embodiment. And, finally, I dedicate this book to Samuel Oliver Bost Wick, whose birth toward the end of this project confirmed every word I'd written about sensation, permeability, and caregiving and who changed my self forever.

ENCARNACIÓN

INTRODUCTION

Illness granted me a set of experiences otherwise unobtainable. It liberated me from the routines which would have delivered me, unchallenged and unchanged, to discreet death. Illness casts you out, but it also cuts you free. I will never take conventional expectations seriously again, and the clear prospect of death only makes living more engaging.

Inga Clendinnen, *Tiger's Eye*

*I*nga Clendinnen, historian of Aztec and Mayan cultures, turned to self-representation when she found herself disabled by liver disease. Her memoir, *Tiger's Eye* (2000), relates an incident in which her nose began to bleed uncontrollably while guiding students through an analysis of Aztec bleeding practices (Clendinnen, *Tiger's Eye* 5). Predictably, once the professor's body began to act unpredictably, it became the center of attention, an object of analysis quite different (or perhaps not quite different enough) from the historical sources that were the subject of the course. One imagines that, as the boundaries between subject and object shifted, the matter being taught shifted, too, making historical data and professorial authority less untouchable.

Unlike other texts, bodies are never static. Once they fail to assume their familiar shapes, they become something else: a source of embarrassment, a medical problem, a theoretical provocation, or an emotional provocation. A body that bleeds elicits reactions that go beyond objective reason: fear, disgust, pain, pleasure. Clendinnen argues that to feel pain, to lose control over one's body, to hallucinate from chemical imbalance "is to suffer an existential crisis, not a medical one" (1). Her own sick body posed a problem for her class and for herself that was more than academic and, thus, likely more difficult to talk about. *Tiger's Eye* reflects

1

this shift in discourse, but it also restores the boundary between the author's personal experience of illness and her work as a historian by quarantining the personal within its own binding, apart from Clendinnen's better-known academic publications.

The writers I am most interested in here, Chicana feminist writers for whom the personal is political, do not similarly quarantine their messy bodies. For this reason, theirs is some of the most provocative writing about identity today, redrawing the boundaries between the personal matter of bodies and the political dimensions of identity. For instance, Ana Castillo's account of childbirth in a 1990 poem, "Since the Creation of My Son and My First Book," dissects identity at multiple levels.[1] Pregnancy is obviously an existential problem, one reflected in the poem's shifting pronouns, but the problem is not contained within the body of the patient(s). In the context of contemporary medicine, the woman's body becomes someone else's object when she becomes a patient: "They tested us, tried to drug / us. They took blood from us, / stuck tubes in every orifice, put us / in isolation and watched us for five days" (Castillo, *I Ask the Impossible* 63). Hospitalization provides a new perspective on one's body, isolating the body from its "natural" context, hooking it up to medical communications networks, measuring its inner pulsations, and injecting it with outside influences. This sort of experience redraws the boundaries around identity and makes new "data" meaningful. (Body temperature and heart rate, for instance, become visible and all-important, while race and sex, noted on the chart as relevant factors, become secondary.) After the birth, Castillo's poem shifts for nine lines to the third person, as "I" and "we" become "his mother" with "swollen belly and painful breasts," defined in relation to the fetus that is no longer a fetus but now a separate identity (64). Mother and baby part, with tissues severed and sewn up in new configurations.

Motherhood shifted the writer onto a different axis—"I spoke in plural like God in Genesis" (64)—changing the shape of her identity. By narrating the "creation" of her son and her first book in the same poem, Castillo explicitly shows how these autobiographical details are intertwined with her identity as an author. Being a mother certainly reshaped her writing practice, likely changing its hours, its content, and even its

---

1. Cherríe Moraga has also published an autobiographical account, *Waiting in the Wings* (1997), about childbirth and writing. Coincidentally, both Moraga and Castillo gave birth prematurely to sons. I discuss *Waiting in the Wings* at length in Chapter 3.

physical positions. And being a writer shapes her practice of mothering: "For the reception of my first book, I stopped breast-feeding / and flew to Texas. Our second separation" (64). Which autobiographic details should matter in our interpretation of an author's work? To my knowledge, no published scholarship analyzes this poem as an important component of Castillo's *oeuvre*.

Of course, to put the experience of childbirth at the center of our analysis of Castillo's writing would be reductive and risky, potentially reinforcing the sexist notion that motherhood is all defining for women and potentially conflating the author with the persona in the poem. In fact, this poem might be less useful for helping us to understand Castillo's work than it is for helping us to understand something about identity in general. From the beginning, Castillo's writings have revolved around questions of identity (in particular, race, class, sexuality, and nationality), but "Since the Creation" opens up a different set of questions about the relationship between body and identity, between one body and others, as well as between an individual body and itself. These questions raised by corporeal upheaval are both more fundamental to our thinking about identity than are sociopolitical categories (race, class, sexuality, and nationality) and more complicated, in the sense that they challenge the individuality and the predictability (indeed, the identity) of identity. These questions also move beyond conventional modes of sociopolitical inquiry to the degree that our experience of our own physical instability does not obey the laws of reason. These are the questions that *Encarnación* will take on.

In a videotaped 1988 interview with Castillo, Cherríe Moraga commented on her own writing, "Jesus . . . there's so much damn body imagery." When Castillo asked her if this body was a metaphor, Moraga admittedly "sweated" the question, embodying its difficulty: "How can the body be a metaphor? It's not a metaphor. It just is. I don't know how to explain it. I write about anything and it's a body. So, yeah" (Moraga, *Cherríe Moraga Reads*). This disordered response captures the ways in which the body can metaphorically communicate non-corporeal ideas (like "a pain in the neck") but is also too fundamental ever to be only a metaphor. It mediates all of our thoughts and changes beyond our control. I would argue that identity markers like race, class, sexuality, and nationality—those subjects central to early writings on Chicana feminism—work like metaphors: communally significant ways to express personal experiences that are really too variable to be generalized. If you can't quite pin down the quality of a feeling, slip a metaphor in its place.

3

When our self-recognition is suddenly altered—as by pain or corporeal transformation—our identifying practices initially fail to keep up, until we can assign a recognizable label to our new experience: pregnancy, broken bone, diabetes. The body, however, often has more to teach us than does the metaphor, which works because it is already assimilated into prescribed ways of understanding the world. The metaphor limits our perception to familiar horizons, like sociopolitical identity categories, but the body is more often unfamiliar. I theorize the distinction between the materiality of bodies and the sociopolitical formation of identities throughout this introduction.

Gloria Anzaldúa describes an experience of corporeal upheaval that defies conventional understandings about identity—so much so that critics generally ignore it.[2] In her 1981 essay "la prieta," she explains the early onset of her menstruation: "When I was three months old tiny pink spots began appearing on my diaper." The doctor declared her, improbably, a "throwback to the Eskimo" whose "girl children get their periods early" (Anzaldúa, "la prieta" 199). She considered herself to be thereafter "marked" by this difference from other children: a "secret sin I tried to conceal" (Anzaldúa, *Borderlands* 42). In *Borderlands*, she writes about this experience in the third person, indicating how early menstruation alienated her from herself: "She felt shame for being abnormal. The bleeding distanced her from others. Her body had betrayed her. She could not trust her instincts, her 'horses,' because they stood for her core self, her dark Indian self" (43). This memory is also linked to internal racism, shame for the "Indian" she carries within her identity. But that which makes her "prieta" [dark] is more than race: it is "*la seña*, the mark of the Beast," transgressing accepted forms of human identity. After the bleeding, she sees herself as a visible oddity; no longer a "normal" girl, she relinquishes her personal boundaries: "her soft belly exposed to the sharp eyes of everyone; they see, they see" (43). As with Clendinnen's in-class bleeding, this experience represents a loss of control over the manifestation of one's body, an inability to conceal private corporeal

2. A notable exception is Carrie McMaster's recent essay, "Negotiating Paradoxical Spaces: Women, Disabilities, and the Experience of Nepantla" (2005). McMaster cites her reading of "la prieta" as the moment when she first came to realize that "The framework I had been given for understanding Anzaldúa was too narrow. Although I viewed Anzaldúa as a feminist, a Chicana theorist, and one of the founders of queer theory, I had not learned also to think of her as a woman with a chronic illness, a person with a disability" (McMaster 102).

processes, a failure to maintain one's expected public persona. It poses a problem for our systems of identification.

It makes sense to look away from other people's "medical problems"—to protect their privacy or our own comfort. (I put the term in quotation marks because "problem" is, of course, subjective; it is also not clear what bodily matters should be considered "medical," versus spiritual or existential, concerns.) In *Invalid Women* (1993), Diane Price Herndl examines why Americans refuse to consider invalidism as a valid identity: "Americans, the celebrants of robust heartiness and self-sufficiency, are suspicious of illness as a manifestation of laziness or willful attention seeking" (Price Herndl xiii). Illness undermines our expectation that successful identities are self-sufficient and self-governing, so in our "normal" everyday lives we, deliberately or blindly, ignore it (unless we are forced to experience it ourselves or are momentarily dwelling on the perverse). Pain, illness, and disability are assumed to represent corporeal failure because they challenge our standards of how bodies should work, look, and feel. Yet these very same qualities usually assumed to be negative also have positive (theoretical and political) implications. Illness links individuals with others (including caregivers and those with shared suffering) and forces us to think about how we interpret bodies and sensations. The bodies of the sick cannot be mistaken as static, essential, or seamless; rather, they bear the marks of history (their individual bodily histories as well as shared histories that create, remedy, or reproduce illness). And, often, illness makes political demands: for better healthcare, different treatment, different placement in the world. In a world that seems to be increasingly numb to feeling—through the proliferation of painkillers, technological reproductions of human functioning, or a postmodern love of simulation—pain and illness remind us about the needs of bodies. In this book, as in the books this book analyzes, illness leads to new forms of identification based on the permeability, suffering, and interdependence of bodies. Foregrounding pain, illness, and disability undermines the myth of self-reliance and demands more expansive ways of understanding individual agency. Bodies become significant not as individual models of socially recognized identifications but for the often unpredictable ways in which they interact with their environments and with others around them.

Celeste Olalquiaga, in a cultural study of the current popularity of sadomasochism, interprets the desire to feel or to inflict pain as an effort to recapture corporeal experience in the face of postmodern de-materializing: "Physical experience now stands for both an evanescent material reality and a long-lost spiritual sense of organic connection" (Olalquiaga 258). Today, in popular culture, in the burgeoning health and fitness industries, and in academic writings, it is clear that "the body is back with a vengeance" (257). But whose body is "back" (if indeed it ever was "gone"), and what shape is it taking? Is it a body that feels sensation (as are those in Olalquiaga's study), or is it an artificial ideal? In the last two decades of feminist thought, poststructural psychoanalytic and Foucauldian feminists like Luce Irigaray and Judith Butler have made "the body" academically fashionable.[3] Many very exciting studies have emerged in their wake, but my fear is that the bodies in feminist theory are losing their "matter" to rhetorical frameworks. In Irigaray and Butler, one does not see actual bodies but, rather, universalized principles like "indefinite otherness" or performativity (Irigaray 28; Butler, *Bodies that Matter* 94–95). Janet Price and Margrit Shildrick, feminist disability theorists whose work is influenced by postmodernism, similarly worry that recent feminist theories of the body "seemed to foreclose on the capacity to engage with the 'real' body, and to sideline any concern with the substantive issues of bio-medicine, or indeed other areas of materialist interest" (Price and Shildrick, "Vital Signs" 7). Though my work is certainly influenced by poststructuralism, postmodernism, psychoanalysis, and Foucault, I foreground culturally, materially, and politically grounded accounts of particular bodies' movements rather than revolving my study around culture-blind theoretical discourses. Anzaldúa's, Moraga's, and Castillo's writings on pain and illness critique the institutions (political, medical, and intellectual) that manipulate bodies in the interests of the dominant culture and outline (or, rather, fill in) detailed Chicana feminist models for resisting, and overflowing the boundaries of, these institutions.

Chicana Feminism and Disability Studies

During her illness, Clendinnen describes her "old panoply of self-representing devices" as being "in full mutiny" (Clendinnen, *Tiger's Eye* 14).

3. Evidence of this theoretical trend can be found in the number of anthologies published on the subject of feminism and the body (particularly after Judith Butler's work took hold in the mid-1990s), including *Writing on the Body*, edited by Katie Conboy, Nadia Medina, and Sarah Stanbury (1997); *The Politics of Women's Bodies*, edited by Rose Weitz (1998); *Vital Signs: Feminist Reconfigurations of the Bio/logical Body*, edited by Janet Price and Margrit Shildrick (1998); *Feminist Theory and the Body*, also edited by Janet Price and Margrit Shildrick (1999); and *Feminism and the Body*, edited by Londa Schiebinger (2000).

Such a statement reflects an acute awareness of the self as a strategy that requires constant effort. When illness disrupts these efforts, one can no longer take identity for granted. As someone interested in identity—cultural constructions of identity, in particular—I have long been thinking about how our experience of our bodies shapes and is shaped by our sense of identity, the way we perceive and define ourselves. Visible race clearly influences how people are judged and rewarded, as do visible cues of sex, gender, and sexuality. Most identity theory assumes that these are the primary axes around which identity revolves, relegating other corporeal forms—like illness or pain—to the margins of meaning. Critical work in Chicano Studies has tended to revolve around these primary axes, as well. Chicano Studies was founded in ethno-nationalism, Marxism, and unifying models of racialization (*mestizaje* and *indigenismo*, for instance), as Chicanos worked to establish an identity from which to speak and clear boundaries within which to organize a political movement.[4] In the 1980s, critiques by Chicana feminists (many of them lesbians) added sex, gender, and sexuality to the shape of Chicana/o identity. All of these understandings of identity privilege sociopolitical forms, identifications that are communal, culturally configured, and politically interpellated. In this light, illness and feeling might seem to be private,

4. Though it might seem contradictory, both *indigenismo* (the celebration of indigenous heritage) and *mestizaje* (racial and cultural mixture) have been invoked at the same time—as in post-Revolutionary Mexico and the 1960s Chicano movement—to unify racially heterogeneous Latin Americans. Tace Hedrick's *Mestizo Modernism* demonstrates how *indigenismo* was central to Mexican modernism, even in works like José Vasconcelos's 1925 treatise, *La Raza Cósmica*, which celebrated racial mixture as a means of solidifying national brotherhood in Mexico. I discuss this tension between the native and the mixed in modern Mexico at greater length in Chapter 1. This same paradox was echoed by Chicano nationalists in the 1960s. In *Mestizaje*, Rafael Pérez-Torres explains: "Identification with the Indian gave birth to a Chicano/a critical subaltern identity in solidarity with other indigenous groups throughout the Americas" (Pérez-Torres, *Mestizaje* 9). Chicana/o nationalists also adopted Vasconcelos's ideal of the "cosmic race" and "*la raza de bronce*" [the bronze race], forming unifying images like Amado Peña's silkscreen *Mestizo* (1974) (which blends three different-colored faces into one), and *mestizo* icons like the Virgin of Guadalupe appeared alongside images of Aztec warriors in Chicana/o nationalist mobilization. Pérez-Torres describes how *mestizaje* both "evokes and erases an indigenous ancestry that is at once a point of pride and a source of shame" (Pérez-Torres, *Mestizaje* 8). Unlike the term "Hispanic" and "Spanish," mestizo acknowledges an indigenous component, but it lightens the native with the European.

7

individual, temporary, and perhaps also trivial, untheorizable, or politically irrelevant. The relative invisibility of these subjects in Chicana/o literary criticism perhaps derives from their ex-centricity to politicized identity forms. Yet I have encountered the most provocative theoretical and political propositions reading Anzaldúa's, Moraga's, and Castillo's writings on illness.

These three writers shaped Chicana feminism as we know it. Anzaldúa and Moraga first collaborated on their tremendously influential book *This Bridge Called My Back: Writings by Radical Women of Color* (1981) at the end of the 1970s, drawing attention to the simultaneity of oppressions experienced by women of color. In the 1980s, Moraga's collection *Loving in the War Years* (1983) received substantial critical praise for its crossing of genres and its thematic focus on the frictions between racial and sexual identification, and Anzaldúa's theories of *mestiza* consciousness and the borderlands, articulated in *Borderlands/La Frontera* (1987), were celebrated and adopted internationally. Both writers also brought the study of Chicana lesbianism, linguistic code-switching, and the "trinity" of Mexican female icons (La Virgen de Guadalupe, La Malinche, and La Llorona) to the forefront of Chicana/o critical analysis.[5] In 1988, Castillo joined Moraga to coedit the Spanish-language edition of *Bridge*, *Esta Puente Mi Espalda*, and, throughout the 1990s, Castillo's well-read novels (including *Sapogonia*, *The Mixquiahuala Letters*, and *So Far From God*) were caught up in the sweep of critical attention to Chicana feminism and read as literary models of critical themes established in the 1980s by Anzaldúa and Moraga. Since then, these three writers have taken center stage as representative voices in discussions about Chicana identity. Though other important Chicana writers also emerged in the same time period (including Sandra Cisneros, Helena María Viramontes, Denise Chavez, Pat Mora, and Lorna Dee Cervantes), Anzaldúa, Moraga, and Castillo arguably changed the shape of feminist and literary studies most profoundly with their groundbreaking stylistic, theoretical, and political interventions.

These three writers gradually moved away from their early collaborations along distinct career trajectories, publishing in different genres, with

5. I discuss all three of these icons at greater length throughout the book. Briefly, the Virgin of Guadalupe is the *mestiza* patron saint of Mexico who appeared to the Indian Juan Diego in 1531. La Malinche is the mestizo name for Malintzin, Hernán Cortés's indigenous lover/translator during the conquest of Mexico. La Llorona is the Mexican "wailing woman" who supposedly drowned her own children and wanders rivers and arroyos at night.

different sorts of presses, and in different institutional settings. Moraga moved from her early mixed-genre publications to work in theater, publishing three collections of plays with West End Press in 1994, 2001, and 2002. Castillo published poetry and fiction (primarily novels, but also a collection of essays, a collection of stories, and a children's book) with mainstream presses like Anchor and Plume, though she turned to small presses for her 2005 publications, a play and a novel in verse (*Psst . . . I Have Something To Tell You, Mi Amor* and *Watercolor Women / Opaque Men*).[6] Anzaldúa published less—after *Bridge* and *Borderlands* only a few essays, interviews, two children's books, and two edited collections—but she left several unfinished/unpublished manuscripts when she died in 2004. Even as they parted ways, however, these writers moved toward similar theoretical and political conclusions. Contrary to the identity politics for which they became famous, all three developed increasingly fluid and inclusive conceptions of identity in the 1990s. It is my contention that, like the experience Clendinnen describes above, pain, illness, and medical treatments played a part in shifting their identity politics, since Anzaldúa was diagnosed with diabetes, and Moraga and Castillo both gave birth (prematurely) to sons, inserting the personal into the political in new, destabilizing ways. Physical and psychological pain has always been wrought in some fashion within these writers' work, but critics have generally avoided this aspect of their arguments in favor of constructing a heroic Chicana feminist paradigm. Recently, however, these writers' dis-ease with bounded and static models of identity has become harder to ignore. Rather than rehearsing the same arguments about *mestizaje*, nationalism, and Chicana lesbian desire, criticism must work to catch up to their new and unfamiliar political forms.[7] Since Anzaldúa's, Moraga's, and Castillo's earliest works were published in conjunction with each other, comparing the three again now teaches us about the

6. Castillo's 2007 novel, *The Guardians*, was published with Random House, defying any clear progression of movement away from big presses.

7. Ana Louise Keating's recent edited collection *EntreMundos/AmongWorlds: New Perspectives on Gloria E. Anzaldúa* (2005) does indeed emphasize the ways in which Anzaldúa's work exceeds familiar sociopolitical frameworks by organizing the essays around themes like "nepantla" (transitions between worlds), "intersecting" identities, "expanding" consciousness, and "new alliances" (Anzaldúa's "new tribalism"). Keating, too, laments: "All too often, scholars focus so extensively on Anzaldúa's identity-based interventions that we overlook other aspects of her career" (2).

ways in which Chicana feminism strained against existing paradigms and ultimately had to create its own.

Reluctance to talk about these writers' corporeal meditations is tied to the shape of the critical discourse about identity in the period in which their major writings first appeared. Anti-foundationalist suspicion about personal experience, bodily authority, or "the real" created an apparent divide between "high theory" (a discourse dominated by predominantly male Europeans and Euro-Americans) versus a supposedly untheorized confessionalist mode (often associated, sometimes denigratingly, with feminists of color). The debate between postmodernism and essentialism led to overly reductive oppositions between theory and personal experience. In this light, Anzaldúa's writings about menstruation, for instance, might seem to fall outside the realm of critical discourse, to be simplistically mired in personal matter. For Anzaldúa, Moraga, and Castillo, however, there never has been an opposition between body and theory. Their political defiance and their commitment to indigenous Mexican philosophical frameworks exceed the terms of Euro-American theoretical debate. Essentialism has always infused their ideas, to the extent that they seek validation and recognition for their own experiences as Chicanas, but it is an essentialism that coexists with a thorough deconstruction of unitary notions of race, sex, and embodiment. I would argue that one key to Anzaldúa's, Moraga's, and Castillo's success in the late 1980s and early 1990s was that their representations of identity were simultaneously "essentialist" and "postmodern," affirming cultural memory alongside racial fluidity, ethnonationalism alongside border-crossing, and undeniable lesbian feeling along with a host of roving desires that crossed between genders, bodies, and spirits. They could be all things to all people, which is why one finds their work studied in terms that range from heteroglossia and *differánce* to nativism and the goddess. It is necessary to attend to all of these strands in their writing and to acknowledge internal contradiction as a crucial component of their ideas.

Another critical trend that has likely obscured the pain and illness in these writers' work is political more than it is theoretical. These three writers have been claimed as "foremothers" of Chicana feminism, and subsequent writers and critics often represent them as heroes. As Paula Moya writes,

> Moraga is an important figure for Chicana feminists in the academy today because she is one of two Chicanas (the other being Gloria Anzaldúa) whose work is more than occasionally taken up outside

10

the field of Chicana/o Studies. As such, she is one of the few Chicanas called on to "represent" Chicanas in women's studies and feminist theory courses throughout the United States. (Moya, *Learning from Experience* 48)

When someone is declared to be an originator of a tradition, analyses of that person's work often become reductive, as critics can see that person only through the tradition she is credited with founding. Anzaldúa, Moraga, and Castillo are Chicana feminists, period. We like to overlook the irregularities, contradictions, and weaknesses in our heroes, since it is more difficult to follow a leader whose path is not clearly demarcated.[8] To this end, Chicana feminists are often reluctant to say anything that might undermine their heroes' public façades. In *Chicana Without Apology* (2003), Chicana cultural studies critic Edén Torres writes about teaching Anzaldúa in different kinds of classrooms and notes the change in her students when discussing their Chicana heroes in a woman-of-color dominant setting:

> While most of the students had read Gloria Anzaldúa's *Borderlands/ La Frontera*, we were able to move beyond talking about it as a rare gift. . . . We were able to stop defending its shortcomings and exploiting its use in the development of a political and personal identity. As we discussed its historical context, we were able to look at its possible limitations without being afraid that our criticisms would be used against Anzaldúa specifically and Chicana feminist theory generally. (Torres 133)

8. Sandra Soto also notes this tendency in criticism of Moraga's work. Her "queer reading" of Moraga, "Cherríe Moraga's Going Brown" (2005), for instance, points out how readers often assume that the identities Moraga writes about are monolithic and self-evident. In going beyond critical studies that merely use Moraga's work as "evidence" (of Chicana lesbian desire, nationalism, essentialism), Soto "queers" Moraga's writing, "dehomogenizing it by noting the ways that her meaning-making speech acts perform radically different functions at various moments; disrupting the teleological narratives and analyses that her work so easily invites; and transvaluing affective work of shame and propensity for confession" (Soto 239). Rather than ignoring these writers' (sometimes graphic) personal confessions or filtering out contradictions within their bodies of work—as many critics seem to have done—I follow in Soto's footsteps by regarding these supposed "faults" as tactical moves central to their radical politics and imaginative visions.

11

In other settings, by implication, her Chicana students would not risk opening Anzaldúa to critique. Particularly in the case of a political movement that is still battling very real sexism, racism, homophobia, and classism (increasingly so in the context of recent immigration debates), identity politics seem to need focus, strength, and coherence. The stigma attached to pain and illness (in a social milieu that is still unfriendly to disability) keeps these traits away from our political heroes. Yet reducing Anzaldúa, Moraga, and Castillo to their identities at the frontline of Chicana feminism disregards the complexity of their writing—of their later works, in particular—and the complexity of their political attachments. I would argue that the more diffuse politics that emerge in their later work could *better* address the globalized context and unbounded intricacies of sexism, racism, homophobia, and classism today.

Anzaldúa's death from diabetes has the potential to shift the terms of analysis in Chicana literary studies because of her critical visibility as, arguably, the most anthologized and most frequently taught Chicana author today and because her illness and death most clearly redefined the author we speak of in Anzaldúa criticism.[9] Her interviews emphasize how her illness slowed down her writing progress and her speaking tours. And her last published essay, "now let us shift" (2002), begins with diabetes as a source of meaning about identity, community, and politics and moves away from identity politics toward an "interplanetary new tribalism" that "step[s] outside ethnic and other labels" to discover that "identity has roots you share with all people and . . . all planetary beings" (Anzaldúa, "now let us shift" 560). The content of criticism about Anzaldúa has shifted somewhat, too, with mourning and personal remembrance intertwined in provocative ways with political and textual analysis. Eulogies tend to reduce an individual to her most famous heroic acts, but Anzaldúa's diabetes also introduced new objects of analysis and new critical affinities for Chicana feminism. We are used to thinking of Chicana feminism in relation to Black Feminism, Chicano nationalism,

---

9. Anzaldúa's essays from *Borderlands/La Frontera* are often reproduced in anthologies for classroom use as (token?) examples of borderlands identity, code-switching, and Chicana feminism. Examples include: *Writing on the Body* (eds. Katie Conboy, et al.); *Issues in Feminism* (ed. Sheila Ruth); *Feminist Theory: A Reader* (eds. Wendy Kolmar and Frances Bartowski); *Feminist Literary Theory: A Reader* (ed. Mary Eagleton); *Ways of Reading* (ed. David Bartholomae); *Literacies: Reading, Writing, Interpretation* (eds. Terence Brunk, et al.); *Crossing Borderlands: Composition and Postcolonial Studies* (eds. Andrea Lunsford, et al.); *The Multicultural Southwest: A Reader* (eds. A. Gabriel Meléndez, et al.); and many others.

queer theory, and Eco-feminism. But we must now also consider its relationship to Disability Studies and medicine. *Encarnación* will demonstrate how these new terms of analysis redraw the subject of Chicana feminism, taking it further away from the nationalism of the 1960s and '70s to more open-ended and fluid identifications.

Eve Kosofsky Sedgwick, a "heroic" figure in queer theory and post-structural identity theory, describes how her personal experiences with cancer (including surgery, chemotherapy, and their aftereffects) measured up to her previous theorization about identity:

> As a general principle, I don't like the idea of "applying" theoretical models to particular situations or texts—it's always more interesting when the pressure of application goes in both directions—but all the same it's hard not to think of this continuing experience as, among other things, an adventure in applied deconstruction. How could I have arrived at a more efficient demonstration of the supposed oppositions that structure an experience of the "self"? (Sedgwick, *Tendencies* 12)

Sedgwick's illness provided a material example of the theories she had long been writing about, deconstructing oppositions between "the part and the whole," "safety and danger," "the natural and the technological" without centering any single axis of identity—unless illness, itself, counts as such an axis—as the defining component of this experience. With the open possibility of metastasis, cancer leaves the body in a "free-fall interpretative panic" (13), unpredictable and unintelligible according to familiar rubrics of self-perception. Sedgwick notes, with some ambivalence, how illness also expands beyond the safe sameness of identity politics, leading sufferers into intimacy with doctors, scientists, and other sufferers, "to entrust as many people as one possibly can with one's actual body and its needs, one's stories about its fate, one's dreams and one's sources of information or hypothesis about disease, cure, denial, and the state or institutional violence that are also invested in one's illness" (261). These instances when bodies surprise us in a "free-fall" of new meanings challenge our familiar modes of self-definition, political action, and relating to others.

The emerging field of Disability Studies has demonstrated how illness is socially structured and politically meaningful, as social spaces, political rhetoric, and medicine assume normative embodiments and stigmatize others. Disability Studies centers on bodies that are ex-centric to normative expectations about how bodies should move and where their boundaries should lie. Disabled bodies often overflow the boundaries where race, sex, sexuality, and gender are culturally and legally mapped out. (For instance, race must signify differently for the blind and the sighted, as must sexuality for a paralytic.) Though this approach runs athwart of entrenched identity categories, there is a tension between the heterogeneity of actual bodies with disabilities and the political content of "disability." As with other identity-based movements, disability activists initially promoted a new identity category, "people with disabilities," by locating an axis of oppression that operates in analogous form to racism or sexism. In practical terms, disability identity politics have helped to identify the ways in which societies exclude people with disabilities and have helped to organize demands for rights around coherent "disadvantaged classes." But, as with all identity-based movements, actually embodied people with disabilities strain against the content of their imagined political condensation. Perhaps this straining is even more dramatic with an identity category like "disability," which is used to describe both chronic and temporary, visible and invisible, mental and physical, as well as both genetic and trauma-induced conditions. Similar to studies of race, sex, and gender, studies of disability—especially those that embrace postmodernism—have increasingly recognized fluidity within the identity they study. The heterogeneity of disabilities defies any singular interpellation, perhaps more radically than the variety of racial, sexual, and gendered embodiment. Lennard Davis, whose work *Bending Over Backwards* finds affinities between Disability Studies and postmodernism, suggests that the "malleable and shaky foundation" upon which disability politics have been built "can be the beginning of an entirely new way of thinking about identity categories" and the relationship between actual bodies and political movement (Davis 5). Feminist and Chicana/o Studies can learn from the recognition in Disability Studies that the identity at its foundation is a political construct based on strategic alliance rather than a shared, natural, or static property.

Like feminist theory, queer theory, and critical race theory, disability theory has shed light on the significance of previously overlooked corporeal markings and has denaturalized embodiments assumed to be universal. It is thus methodologically allied with Chicana feminism, but I have found only one critical study that uses the lens of disability to analyze writings like Anzaldúa's. As Carrie McMaster notes, in her 2005 essay "Negotiating Paradoxical Spaces: Women, Disabilities, and the Experience of Nepantla":

Unfortunately, disability scholars have yet to discover the power of Anzaldúa's poetic and persuasive prose and the relevance and flexibility of her theories. Nor have theorists in other disciplines recognized the crucial roles Anzaldúa's struggles with her hormonal imbalance and another disabling condition, adult-onset diabetes, played in shaping her work. (McMaster 102)

Indeed, Anzaldúa never explicitly identified herself as "disabled." Is it because diabetes falls outside the parameters of "disability," or because Anzaldúa could not identify with the subject?[10] One problem has to do with medicalized perceptions of the body versus individual self-perception. Anzaldúa resisted the label "disabled," and even the label "diabetic," though she acknowledged the ways in which her experience of diabetes disabled certain corporeal functions, because medical labels establish objective and universal parameters around otherwise fluid bodies (Anzaldúa, "Re: you & disability studies").[11] For a writer who believed that "the body doesn't stop at the skin" and that the body includes "the mind, the spirit, the imagination, the soul," terms that define identity based on corporeal limitations would obviously be unappealing (Anzaldúa, *Interviews/Entrevistas* 71, 77). This is one reason that I hesitate to classify the authors, bodies, and texts in *Encarnación* as strictly "disabled."

Another problem has to do with race and culture. After surveying major texts in disability criticism, it might seem that disability is either "white" or culturally neutral, as feminism was assumed to be prior to work like *This Bridge Called My Back* (1981) and Gloria Hull, Patricia Bell Scott, and Barbara Smith's *All the Women Are White, All the Blacks*

10. The ADA [Americans with Disabilities Act] Amendments Act of 2008 has expanded the legal definitions of disability and impairment in such a way that most diabetics would legally count as "disabled." McMaster addresses the relationship between disability and diabetes in more theoretical terms: although "'[d]isease' and 'illness' are not derived from the same theoretical models as 'impairment' and 'disability,' . . . some illnesses do indeed qualify as defective mechanisms of the body and—if chronic or even frequently recurring—can be disabling" (McMaster 106n).

11. I am grateful to AnaLouise Keating for sharing this October 2003 e-mail message. In the message, Anzaldúa further explained that the term "disabled" would reduce her to a "partial identity" just like other sociopolitical terms (Anzaldúa, "Re: you & disability studies"). I was pleased to have access to this personal statement that addresses the concerns of *Encarnación* more explicitly than any of Anzaldúa's published writings do.

Are Men, But Some of Us Are Brave (1982). The dominant culture poses its own understanding of disability as universal, and more work needs to be done on the racial and cultural dimensions of disability.[12] Rosemarie Garland Thomson defines disability as "not so much a property of bodies as a product of cultural rules about what bodies should be or do"; it is a "cultural interpretation of physical transformation or configuration" (Thomson, *Extraordinary Bodies* 6). It is helpful to think about identity markers like "disability" as cultural projections, rather than essential or universal qualities, but we must also know which culture forms these projections. Throughout her groundbreaking interpretation of the function of disability in American culture, *Extraordinary Bodies* (1997), Thomson notes that disability is culturally determined, but she does not consider the ways in which it is culturally relative. Even in her chapter on literary representations of bodies that are disabled, black, and female, she assumes that the African American writers she examines accept the dominant culture's delineation of disability and simply invert the dominant hierarchy by revaluing traits "assigned corporeal inferiority" (18, 105). I would argue, though, that the lines drawn between "disabled" and "normal" are neither static nor universal. (The cultural and historical variability of "disorders" like neurasthenia, obesity, microcephalia, or gout is evidence of this fact.) Perhaps Anzaldúa did not identify as disabled because to do so would mean accepting the corporeal boundaries established by the dominant culture. For her, the boundaries around bodies fall in different places.

The Chicana/o and Mexican roots of Anzaldúa's, Moraga's, and Castillo's corporeal philosophies challenge supposedly universal understandings of corporeality, and their work provides a wealth of material for examining how culture mediates experiences of pain, illness, and disability. These writers' investment in ancient Mesoamerican culture, in particular, establishes a set of corporeal ideals very different from contemporary norms. When compared against the models of Coatlicue (the

12. Medical anthropologists Benedicte Ingstad and Susan Reynolds Whyte's volume, *Disability and Culture*, is noteworthy for its focus on the difficulty of categorizing disability in a global context (as the World Health Organization attempts to do), given cross-cultural differences in how disability is defined and perceived. But most studies of disability in the Humanities, like Sharon Snyder, Brenda Jo Brueggemann, and Rosemarie Garland Thomson's 2002 volume, *Disability Studies: Enabling the Humanities*, still center on European and Euro-American experiences. Even Snyder's brief mention of Frida Kahlo in this volume ignores the artist's Mexican-ness (Snyder et al. 173).

Aztec goddess of creation and destruction whose headless body incorporates snakes) or her daughter Coyolxauhqui (who was cut to pieces by her brother, Huitzilopochtli, and cast into the sky), bodies that bleed, hurt, or require infusions take on sacred connotations that differ radically from the affective and political content of conventional disability narratives. Indeed, in a Mesoamerican context, these bodies would be considered enabled, not disabled. I discuss the Chicana feminist significance of Coatlicue, Coyolxauhqui, and Mesoamerican pain culture at length in subsequent chapters and return to the question of culture and disability in Chapter 4, in my analysis of Castillo's *Peel My Love Like an Onion*. My hope is to keep my terminology as mixed and permeable as the identities in my study, rather than accepting one culture's standards of normative versus marginal identities. For this reason I do not privilege the term "disability" over others in my analysis.

Identity Politics and Permeability

What Anzaldúa's, Moraga's, and Castillo's writings share with much recent disability theory, beyond their shared attention to the physical, psychological, and political impact of corporeal deviation, is a shared commitment to expanding the ways in which we think about bodies and identities. In *Borderlands*, Anzaldúa called us to "seek new images of identity" and to "[break] down the unitary aspect of each new paradigm"; she professed a willingness to "[surrender] all notions of safety, of the familiar" in order to "[d]econstruct, construct" identity over and over again (Anzaldúa, *Borderlands* 80, 82, 87). Though they arrive at their conclusions by way of vastly different theories and methodologies, this surrendering of boundaries allies Anzaldúa's work with that of Margrit Shildrick, whose postmodern feminist approach differentiates her work from earlier disability theories. Shildrick's two books, *Leaky Bodies and Boundaries* (1997) and *Embodying the Monster* (2002), open the parameters of bodies, and thus of identities, in a truly radical fashion, rejecting Western culture's fantasies of "containment" and redrawing ethics based on vulnerability, permeability, and interdependence. Shildrick proposes: "the issue is not one of revaluing differently embodied others, but of rethinking the nature of embodiment itself" (Shildrick, *Embodying the Monster* 2). This is precisely what I attempt to do in *Encarnación*, analyzing the ways in which different bodies overflow the boundaries of familiar identities as they move beyond or shift within their own skins. Following

INTRODUCTION

Shildrick, my analysis seeks out "the unpredictably strange and excessive" (Shildrick, *Embodying the Monster* 78), embodiments that mark "the impossibility of securing" "the successful closure of embodied identity of the selfsame" (25). We must expand what we look at when we see bodies—beyond the boundaries of closed or "selfsame" identities—to understand the particular needs and movements of each. In this "ethical economy . . . our specificities, rather than haunted by, are in communion with the differences between, and internal to, us all" (119). Unless it becomes a codified norm, disability shifts the boundaries around and between bodies, challenging the integrity of the individual and the supposed predictability of identities.

While Chicana/o Studies insists that we ground our understanding of texts in a particular cultural context, Anzaldúa's, Moraga's, and Castillo's particular Chicana visions, like much writing about disability, exceed communally recognized forms. Racial, sexual, or cultural politics (nationalist or not) assume shared identification, but the corporeal variety and variability at the center of Disability Studies resist general claims about identity. (This is not to say that Disability Studies is never essentialist in its separation of the "disabled" from the "normate," but that the content of disability itself defies clear demarcation.) Moreover, and most helpful for my thinking, the emphasis on "equal access" in Disability Studies shifts attention from individual agency to intersections between agents and the material worlds through which they move (a focus I return to at greater length, with the example of visual arts, in my conclusion). It is clear that equality for a wheelchair user is not just a property of the individual but a property of the built environment. This approach shifts political weight from individual culpability toward contextual influence, highlighting how identity is mediated not simply by communities and sociopolitical hierarchies (which identify people culturally and racially) but also by physical structures that limit or enable the functions of different bodies.

My work is invested in identity not as a predetermined entity but as a variable, embodied process. Since identity is constantly challenged by corporeal and environmental changes, it does not present a solid ground for politics. When political organization assumes a static or communally shared form of identity (like race, sex, or even deafness and blindness), it forecloses the real variability of embodiment and limits the horizons of possible identification. I do not mean to imply that political movements that revolve around identity are always misguided or that identity politics do not serve valuable functions. Indeed, without identity politics, the institutional and methodological foundations of my work in Chicana/o Studies, Women's Studies, or Disability Studies would not exist. Yet it is important to notice what possibilities and realities are sacrificed in identity politics. My own education (in the 1980s and '90s) was structured by identity politics but also by postmodern theory, and what I have drawn from this combination is an understanding that identity is built upon multiple foundations that shift and intersect with others depending upon one's situation at any given moment.

As an ethnically mixed "white" woman who was transplanted from the Midwest to the Southwest as a young girl, I began to identify with the Mexican American culture that was not "mine" but that shaped my situation (in New Mexico, in childhood, and then in Texas).[13] I learned Spanish at an early age, I developed shared political commitments with Chicana/os, and my education was grounded in Mexican and Mexican American history, Chicana/o literature, and the conflicts and intersections between cultures in the Southwest. I was a transplant who felt no nostalgia for a lost "home" culture, so I tried to absorb completely the soil of my new context. At the same time, there were always reminders of the socially determinant force of skin color, accent, and family when it came to matters of inclusion or exclusion. There were experiences and traditions I shared with Mexican Americans and those of which I was not a part. I do not mean to suggest that I understood, from childhood, how my white skin afforded me certain privileges or when I needed to respect the boundaries of identity politics and accept my "outsider" status. But I certainly knew that identity was complicated, changeable, and contentious as I chose friends, assumed affinities, and posed myself to fit into different identity groups. Many of the groupings I chose were based on cross-racial identifications: the rebels, the scholarship kids, the feminists. In these settings, race becomes highly visible, but so do other shared needs and concerns. I believe that whichever identification(s) matter(s) most in any circumstance should determine the "identity" of political action, and that most actions require one to juggle multiple identifications.

I include this moment of "autoethnography" with great reservations. I do not mean to put my own "identity" at the center of a project

13. I use the more general term "Mexican American" here to include history that precedes the Chicano movement; to foreground interactions between Mexico, itself, and the United States; and to include the many Hispanics in New Mexico who prefer to identify as "Hispano," "Nuevomexicano," "Mexican," or "Spanish," rather than "Chicana" or "Chicano."

that is, in part, about decentering identity. Though my early cross-racial experiences undoubtedly influenced my developing ideas about race, identity, and politics, I had not initially considered my own identity to be an issue for this book. (In public demonstrations, pedagogy, or personal narrative, it matters in obvious ways, but when analyzing literature and theory in an academic book, does it?) When an anonymous reviewer of the manuscript asked, with regard to my critique of identity politics, "Where is Bost coming from?" and "What are her stakes in this project?" however, I realized how much my own social location, and my ethnically ambiguous last name, do matter in my approach to Chicana feminism. What I identify with politically and intellectually crosses beyond my own apparent or genetic identity. I am not seeking to make Chicana identity more permeable so that I can be included within it. Rather, my interest here is what happened when three Chicana feminist writers found their identities intertwined with others in unexpected ways. My own experience surely feeds into this project, but the likelihood of encountering affinities with those who do not share our visible identities, and of encountering unexpected differences with those who do, seems to be a general truth rather than an insight particular to my situation.

Despite my emphasis on crossing beyond identity boundaries, *Encarnación* has particular resonance for Chicana feminism, in particular. Certainly all marginalized populations (especially the feminists among them) have a conflicted history with identity politics as well as a violent historical connection to ideas like corporeal permeability, but in the context of Chicana feminism—such as Anzaldúa's writings about the U.S.–Mexico border as an "open wound"—margins and permeability are crucial "sites" of resignification. My inspiration for this project draws from two sources with particular significance for Chicana/o culture, Catholicism and my training in pre-Conquest Mexico, for it was from these sources that my rejection of medicalized understandings of bodies as self-contained, culturally neutral, and isolated emerged. And my research on *mestizaje* as a theoretical and political concept has explained how Chicana/o writers draw simultaneously from the multiple worldviews that makeup their cultural history (Native American, Spanish Catholic, and U.S. "New Age") in order to thwart the frameworks of modern Anglo-America. I use the term "Chicana" throughout this book, not to signify a horizon or an assumed genetic or political entity, but as a contextual marker to signal the specific cultural mixture and the specific political history that underlie the literature at the center of my project.

In reading about the ways in which pain and illness opened the borders of identity in the writings of Anzaldúa, Moraga, and Castillo, I believe I have found an accurate way of understanding the complexity of identity and an effective way to shift politics from essentialist, exclusionary, or homogenizing understandings of identity toward a politics based on shared needs, shared vulnerability, and shared permeability. Pain and illness are experiences we can all identify with to some degree, and probably we can all recall how these experiences have altered our self-perceptions. I keenly remember needing to ask for assistance to board buses and needing to find alternate routes across the University of Texas campus when I had to wear a leg brace for several months. Now, in the midst of pregnancy, I am encountering unexpected allies, true estrangement from myself, and altered mobility as I dread the realistic possibility of having my insides erupt in public. Corporeal upheavals like these reshape identity and identity politics, even as our race, sex, and cultural history stay the same.

A number of recent publications—by Linda Martín Alcoff, Paula Moya, and Satya Mohanty, among others—have critiqued the erosion of identity in academic thought and argued for a revitalization of identity politics. Alcoff worries that critics of identity politics fear a world where their own social identity "does not hold hegemony over meaning, value, or creative institutions, where the Other, in some cases, holds the epistemic upper hand even over some truths about" themselves (Alcoff 84). I am certainly not trying to reinforce the hegemony of any identity. Nor am I arguing for a retreat into universalism or trying to suggest that markers of identity like race or sex do not matter, because they most obviously do line up with structural power inequities. My intention, instead, is to show how a limiting focus on sociopolitically scripted categories ignores embodied difference. Though identity politics celebrates *a* difference (or a particular intersection of differences), it does not easily welcome—or even see—unforeseen differences that also matter. I am arguing for a more expansive and more permeable understanding of what it means to have an identity than what race- and sex-based identity politics traditionally allow for.

In *Visible Identities: Race, Gender, and the Self* (2006), a philosophical defense of identity and identity politics, Alcoff uses phenomenology to detach identity from individual agency. I embrace Alcoff's argument that "Individual agency is not intrinsic but made possible through certain kinds of social relations. . . . As Merleau-Ponty says, I borrow myself from others, that is, my confidence, self-assurance, my sense of who I am in the world" (116). In this way, any definition of identity must go beyond the boundaries of the individual to include social, historical, and material context. Yet I don't follow Alcoff's extension of this argument that "the social basis of individual selves" is thus the group (121), because I don't see where one draws the boundaries between an individual's "group" and the world of others in which that individual's identity and agency are situated. Though Alcoff insists that group identities "are not illusions, or reducible to the machinations of power" (121), I would argue that it is indeed the "machinations of power" that demarcate a group called a race, a sex, or a class within the larger social context that shapes an individual. While there is some genetic basis for sexual difference and, to an extent, for racial difference, the basis for group formation is social, not chromosomal; it is an effect of cultural continuity, geographical location, a society's valuation of certain visible traits, and historical oppression or privilege. That is not to say that the group is an "illusion," because power is distributed based on certain group memberships, but that these lines are drawn by power relations, and they are often drawn simply to stigmatize, to exclude, or to cut off a group from others with which it shares many affinities. For instance, in the context of international war, national differences are supposed to supersede racial differences that otherwise keep people within nations apart. These national differences also serve to keep the soldiers of the two warring parties from uniting, as armed members of the economic underclass, to overthrow the leaders and officers who are benefitting from their military service. These groups surely matter, but I think political mobilization would be more effective if we looked beyond these "horizons" (to use one of Alcoff's terms for describing group identities) instituted by those in power.

I have also found Moya's discussion of postmodernism and Chicana feminist identity politics in *Learning from Experience* (2002) particularly helpful in clarifying my views about the relationship between identity and politics. Moya's book offers a way of theorizing identity beyond essentialist or positivist understandings, and her "postpositivist realist" approach accounts for the continuity but also the partiality and fluidity of identity. Yet Moya and I differ in two fundamental ways. The first is our understanding of what counts as "identity." When Moya discusses identity or social location, she consistently defines these terms only through "the particular nexus of race, class, gender, and sexuality in which [an individual] exists in the world" (86–87). Though this "nexus" might change through time, Moya still assumes that race, class, gender, and sexuality are the primary determinants of identity. Since these socio-political categories predominate in our vocabulary for identity, it is impossible to deny that they influence how one chooses to identify (or gets identified by others). But what interests me most in Anzaldúa's, Moraga's, and Castillo's later works is the ways in which other corporeal qualities—ones that are not genetic, visible, or already politically inscribed as an assumed axis of oppression/privilege—upend the familiar forms of identity. The complicated, unpredictable, and fluid tissues of particular bodies, as seen through MRI scans, microscopes, and blood tests, unsettle any notion of shared race, sex, or even health itself.[14] Unexpected and sometimes incoherent embodiments like diabetes, pregnancy, or dependence upon prosthestic devices lead to non-identity-based oppressions, connections, and self-perceptions in the texts I analyze in *Encarnación*. Moya views identities as the link between "individuals, groups, and the central organizing principles of a society" (86)—a view that realistically accounts for, but remains invested in, "the central organizing principles of a society." In contrast, Anzaldúa, Moraga, and Castillo imagine new ways of organizing the links between individuals and groups, such as caregiving or nonrational spirituality. Illness presents them with new modes of filiation. These alternate political configurations resist the commodification, trivialization, and institutional rigidity that neutralize sociopolitical filiations that have been regulated by the dominant culture. (Watching the "Latin Grammy Awards" recently provided me with an excellent instance of how identity becomes commodified, trivialized, and made rigid by institutions.)

The second way in which I differ with Moya has to do with postmodernism. Moya is (rightly) critical of Donna Haraway's and Judith Butler's brief and uncontextualized turns to Chicana identities as models for postmodern fragmentation, but she is also critical of Norma Alarcón's and Chela Sandoval's theoretical fusions and Chicana feminism and postmodernism, arguing that postmodernism undermines "the cogency of their scholarly projects" (3). I value postmodern theory as a tool that *enhances* scholarly projects when it is balanced with grounding in the material world and deployed in the service of progressive politics, and

14. See my article "From Race/Sex/Etc. to Glucose, Feeding Tube, and Mourning: The Shifting Matter of Chicana Feminism" in Stacy Alaimo and Susan Hekman's edited collection *Material Feminisms* (2007) for an extended critique of how analysis based on race, sex, or class often fails to account for the messy interior "matter" that complicates identity politics.

my work is indebted to that of Alarcón, Sandoval, Yvonne Yarbro-Bejarano, and other critics who use postmodernism in the service of Chicana feminism.[15] In *Mulattas and Mestizas* (2003), I present an extended critique of postmodernist celebrations of hybridity and fragmentation when these celebrations disregard the historical and cultural contexts in which hybrid and fragmented identities are produced. My work is inevitably invested in postmodernism—because that is the framework through which I first learned to *theorize* identity—but more fundamentally invested in cultural context and social justice—the foundations of my initial interest in identity. Postmodernism adds to movements for social justice an understanding of how identities are formed in the negotiations between bodies and social structures; of how power and oppression shift, morph, and infiltrate our very identities; and of how identity is thus fluid, loaded with internal contradictions, and sometimes incoherent. This does not mean, however, that identity is arbitrary or purely discursive, and the examples I analyze in *Encarnación* demonstrate how these seemingly "postmodern" qualities are experienced materially as well as how they are socially and culturally embedded.

In the last several years, many disability scholars—like Lennard Davis and Margrit Shildrick—have embraced postmodernism as a framework for understanding how disability challenges conventional understandings

15. In "Anzaldúa's *Frontera*" (2003), Alarcón demonstrates how Anzaldúa's "rewriting of the feminine" is "polyvalent," rather than unified, "differently reorganized as she shifts the targets of engagement" throughout her writing. Rather than assuming that the multiplicity of female icons Anzaldúa embraced throughout her career reflects either indecision or teleology, Alarcón argues that it is the dissonance between these multiple names ("Snake Woman, La Chingada, Tlazolteotl, Coatlicue, Cihuacoatl, Tonantzin, Guadalupe, La Llorona") that enabled Anzaldúa to "deconstruct patriarchal ethnonational" consciousness without restoring another monolithic "oppositional consciousness" in binary relation to it (Alarcón, "Anzaldúa's *Frontera*" 361). Yarbro-Bejarano similarly argues that "it is important to search for alternative strategies to 'difference,' ones that will not reinscribe women of color in a relationship of otherness to the dominant Same," and she finds in Castillo's poem "Esta mano" a relationship between body and writing that defies essentialist identification, without sacrificing the body, by emphasizing internal fragmentation and fluidity (Yarbro-Bejarano, "The Multiple Subject in the Writing of Ana Castillo" 65, 71). I like Alarcón's and Yarbro-Bejarano's work because they see identities as multiple (rather than monolithic), critical (rather than neutral or inherent), and in motion (rather than fixed or clearly drawn); I draw from their writings about Anzaldúa, Moraga, and Castillo throughout *Encarnación*.

of identity, and the 2002 collection *Disability/Postmodernity: Embodying Disability Theory*, edited by Marian Corker and Tom Shakespeare, reflects this trend in "second-wave" Disability Studies. Others in the field are more wary of this trend. Tobin Siebers cites a number of disability scholars, including Susan Wendell, who argue that postmodernism and social constructivism fail to account for "the difficult physical realities faced by people with disabilities" (Siebers, "Disability Studies and the Future of Identity Politics" 13). Yet disability itself shifts determinism from bodies to the social structures that incorrectly assume all people are capable of walking, hearing, reading, or reaching for light switches. Disability thus offers a powerful lesson about the material effects of social constructions. Siebers writes, "Disability seems to provide an example of the extreme instability of identity as a political category, but it would not be easy, I think, to prove that disability is less significant in everyday life for being a category in flux" (11). Hence the frequent usage of the term "disabled" even by postmodern scholars who reject identity politics: the identity term is still a significant marker of social location, though not a totalizing way of understanding subjectivity or political filiation. Scholarly projects that apply postmodern theories of subjectivity to particular examples of "disability" or "Chicana identity," rather than remaining in the realm of ideals, can bring these theories of fluid identification back from abstraction to particularly situated corporeal matter and reveal the actual fluidity of that matter. Indeed, postmodern thought has helped me to embrace conceptual otherness and to question normative assumptions about bodies and feelings, making room for more libratory understandings of Chicana feminist pain, illness, and disability.

Moya is far more suspicious of the postmodern tendency to view identity as disrupted or fragmented. Of Haraway and Butler she writes:

> Their attempts to disrupt gender categories (Butler) or to conjure away identity politics (Haraway) make it difficult to figure out who is "us" and who is "them," who is the "oppressed" and who is the "oppressor," who shares our interests and whose interests are opposed to ours. Distinctions dissolve as all beings (human, plant, animal, and machine) are granted citizenship in the radically fragmented, unstable society of the postmodern world. (Moya, *Learning from Experience* 36)

Because of my own experience and my own "identity," I have always been wary of drawing firm lines between "us" and "them," "oppressor" and "oppressed," as if these lines always fell in the same place and as if oppressors were never oppressed themselves (and vice versa). Moreover, "interests" are never so clearly mapped out, and internal dissent is characteristic of any identity-based group. In my own political work (in feminism, civil rights, the peace movement, or the recent rallies for immigrant rights), I have determined that one of the best tools in activism is locating unexpected shared interests between "us" and "them"— because we cannot change the world without changing "them," too—and showing how "our" cause betters the world for everyone, not just "us." Moya argues that "in theory boundaries are infinitely permeable and power may be amorphous," but "people do not live in an entirely abstract or discursive realm. They live as biologically and temporally limited, as well as socially situated, human beings" (36). I would argue the opposite. *In reality,* boundaries and bodies are infinitely permeable. It is only *in theory* that identity is clearly demarcated and only *in theory* that biology, temporality, and social situations are fixed limitations. Indeed, identity, social location, and the lines between "us" and "them" are abstract and discursive.[16] What's real is the messy and complicated ways in which we are like those we politically despise, the ways in which our bodies fail to adhere to ideal racial and sexual forms, and the instability of our identifications depending upon where we are, whom we are with, and how we are feeling. Instability, in this sense, does not mean that we become someone else entirely (as Moya would object) but that who we are is, as I said, messy and complicated.

My argument responds to the call of postpositivist realists like Alcoff and Mohanty to provide "new accounts of the relationships among our various identities . . . [and] new ideas about how to make common cause across differences of privilege and geography" (Alcoff and Mohanty 3). Illness, hospitalization, and disability force individuals to create more permeable forms of identity and politics—finding "common cause" with medical providers; sharing knowledge across lines of race, class, sex, and sexuality; challenging cultural stigmas about proper embodiment—but this permeability does not compromise the uniqueness of individuals. A Chicana does not lose her cultural history when her identity interpenetrates with another or expands beyond the boundaries of Chicana culture. Likewise with bodies or nations: a body is defined by its interactions with its environment (the places where it moves through space, collisions

16. Tobin Siebers also describes identity as an abstraction invented to explain reality: "Identities are complex theories about the social and moral world" (Siebers, "Disability Studies and the Future of Identity Politics" 18).

with or incorporations of other objects, even the cells and germs it sloughs off and picks up from outside), and nations are defined by differentiation from and commerce with their neighbors. (Clearly one of the by-products of continual border-crossing between the United States and Mexico is heightened nationalism and increased flag-waving, even as cultures, economies, and peoples blend together.) Differentiation is made possible by encounters with something that is other (recalling Alcoff's use of Hegel and Merleau-Ponty to define identity); these encounters give shape to boundaries as identities, bodies, or nations grate against each other.[17] In this way, particularity is formed (and reformed) by permeability. Hence my focus on permeability in the particular context of Chicana feminism.

Methodology and Organization

Chicana/o feminism, itself, is permeable as a "culture" and as a "discipline." Anzaldúa's, Moraga's, and Castillo's representations of illness cannot be adequately understood apart from their *mestizo* identifications, which are grounded in the mixture of Spanish and indigenous cultures in Mexico as well as the dominant culture of the United States that further "mixes" their *mestizaje*. My analysis, therefore, compares the enabling models of embodiment that they draw from sources as varied as the lives of Spanish saints, Mesoamerican archeology, Frida Kahlo, and the New Age movement, crossing cultural and intellectual borders at the same time. Saint Teresa of Avila's stigmata and Aztec sacrifice rituals, for instance, both reflect an assumption that physical pain is a sign of regeneration, communication with the divine, and the crossing of spiritual boundaries. Public demonstrations of pain were used to galvanize communities in early Mexico. This context reveals how Anzaldúa's, Moraga's, and Castillo's incorporations of pain coincide with their *mestiza* feminist politics: a politics that is strengthened by its mixing of cultures and its openness to continual change brought on by incorporating difference. The difference in their newest writings, though, goes beyond cultural *mestizaje* to include contemporary medicine's surgical transformations, spiritual shape-shifting, and the profound connections formed between the ill and their caregivers. This new work transgresses current

---

17. I agree with Alcoff's point that "Hegel's account of the self as open-ended, dependent on the Other, and contextually grounded would be an excellent place to start a serious reflection about identity" (Alcoff 62).

27

academic norms by finding rigorous thought in spiritual beliefs and by letting go of identity politics in order to move beyond the status quo.

Permeability shapes my methodology, too. To better understand the literary works at the center of my book, I draw upon the insights of history, anthropology, philosophy, and the arts. Pre-Columbian Meso-american culture has long been central to Chicana/o writers' rejection of "Modern" or "Western" understandings of identity, but I also draw from approaches—like Disability Studies—that are not traditionally paired with Chicana/o Studies in order to reveal additional modes of identification and sympathy. Some of the scholars whose work I find most useful in this project are traditional historians, while others work in Cultural Studies; some are postmodernists, and some are cultural materialists; some are feminists, while others are not; and some turn to spirituality for guidance, while others are strictly secular. This philosophical dissonance is true to the ways in which those who become ill find their familiar intellectual paradigms upended and the ways in which illness and disability often lead individuals to discover new modes of thought and new sorts of affiliations.

I am a literary critic first and foremost. In literature, we can find traces of the sedimentation of cultural assumptions as well as a record of how writers have strained against "the real" to imagine how bodies and worlds could be otherwise. The interdisciplinarity required of this inves-tigation, however, has forced me to think seriously about what one "does" with literature versus the visual arts, history, philosophy, or politi-cal theory. In this book, I am using the writings of Anzaldúa, Castillo, and Moraga to think politically and theoretically about the meanings of illness for Chicana feminism. I am not trying to pin down the authors' "intent" or to measure their work against "reality." Instead, I am using powerful moments in their work as a point of departure for rethinking what counts as identity. I take their ideas literally (even the strange and the supernatural ones), look at them from various angles to explore their potential meanings, and respond with gestures of my own. I also, inevita-bly, approach the other disciplines in this study as a literary critic, close-reading the implications of their language and examining how they func-tion as texts. Rather than trying to be true to the different disciplines in any pure form, *Encarnación* is driven by a love of language, a commitment to Chicana feminist politics, and a desire to try on new ways of thinking.

The methodological gap between the Humanities and Biomedical fields is probably the greatest one that this book confronts, and in my approach to this gap I am indebted to the models established by Shildrick,

Donna Haraway, Lynda Birke, David Morris, and others whose work approaches biology through the lenses of philosophy, culture, or politics. In *The Culture of Pain* (1991), Morris explains how pain and illness necessarily traverse this gap:

> Certainly we can take comfort in assuming that pain obeys the general laws of human anatomy and physiology that govern our bodies. The fact is, however, that the culture we live in and our deepest personal beliefs subtly or massively recast our experience of pain. Normally the shaping force of culture and belief passes almost unobserved. Like upright posture, our everyday experience of the world seems so natural—so "given"—that we take it for granted. It is less our pain than our culture, however, that draws us irresistibly toward the medicine cabinet, as if pills and tablets held a kind of magnetic, eternal attraction for the unseen torments of a bad back. The story of how our minds and cultures continuously reconstruct the experience of pain demands that we look beyond the medicine cabinet. Medicine, in fact, because of its dominant position in our culture, tends automatically to suppress or to overpower all the other voices that offer us a different understanding of pain, including voices of dissent within medicine. (Morris, *The Culture of Pain* 2)

The methods of literary criticism can shine light on these voices of dissent as well as the cultural and political inflections within the narratives with which people make sense of their embodiment. Material survival depends upon both medicine and personal belief, and the transformations of pain and illness occur at the intersection of these two kinds of knowledge. It is the juggling of different kinds of knowledge that most provocatively pushes at the limits of identity, of the flesh, and of our ideas.

Throughout the book I discuss pain, illness, and disability as related corporeal experiences, but I am aware that there is no necessary connection among the three and do not mean to conflate them. I hesitate to classify all of the embodiments I analyze as "disabled" because of the cultural variability I discussed earlier and because to do so would pin down these experiences with one identity. Pain, illness, and disability are distinct, though often intertwined and often mutually constitutive. Switching between these terms highlights these distinctions and keeps my discussion more open and fluid. "Disability" seems to imply a permanent and coherent identification, though reality defies this connotation.

Illness is conventionally posed as an unnatural and (ideally) curable deviation from the norm, but even deviations as temporary as the flu alter one's physical and psychological attentiveness enough to invite some comparison to disability. Likewise, even when not a result of an identifiable illness or disability, pain has a similar physical and psychological impact, making one's movements ex-centric to the norm. Finally, though not all disabilities involve pain or illness, disability, like pain and illness, puts pressure on our understanding of what constitutes ideal corporeal functioning. My approach is not strictly Disability Studies—indeed, it is not "strictly" anything—but my analysis is deeply invested in how what I have learned from Disability Studies and what I have learned from Chicana/o Studies complement each other. The fact that three of the most important Chicana feminists have written so extensively about pain and illness makes one wonder if these matters are perhaps not central to their theoretical and political visions. And if so, what are they doing there?

The works of Anzaldúa, Moraga, and Castillo enable us to examine how identities are shaped and reshaped by culturally embedded processes of "incarnation." This book turns our attention to aspects of these writers' work that are usually ignored—Anzaldúa's autobiographical writings about diabetes, Moraga's narrative about her premature baby's medical treatments, and Castillo's figure of the polio-afflicted flamenco dancer in *Peel My Love Like an Onion* (2000)—to explore the political and cultural dimensions of illness and caregiving. I develop a model for identity that expands beyond the boundaries of individual bodies and argue that this model has greater utility for feminism than identity politics because it values human variability, sensation, and openness to others. My title, *Encarnación*, itself foregrounds the fleshiness of the material I analyze as well as the national, cultural, and spiritual contingencies of bodies and body politics.

I begin by historicizing Chicano literature's investment in ancient Mexico (since the 1960s) to establish the foundation with which contemporary Chicana feminism is in dialogue, and I conclude with my own propositions for the future of Chicana feminist body politics. At the core of the book, my author-based chapters mirror this turn to the past in order to find new sources for theorizing the future. I first situate close-readings of Anzaldúa's, Moraga's, and Castillo's writings on pain, illness, and disability in the context of the Mexican cosmologies to which they allude. These chapters then probe the political and theoretical implications of the bodies the authors represent. I divide the middle chapters among the three authors and three different locations where physical "disorders" are experienced: the corporeal feelings of pain (the Anzaldúa chapter), the medical institutions where bodies are "healed" (the Moraga chapter), and the movement through the world of bodies that are sick, in pain, or disabled (the Castillo chapter).

Chapter 1, "Feeling Pre-Columbian," responds to Elaine Scarry's oft-quoted assertion that pain is world-destroying. I argue instead that pain opens up new perceptions of the relationship between one's body and the world around it and creates new ways of moving through the world. I defend this argument by using insights from Frida Kahlo, hagiography, and pre-Columbian Mesoamerica. Borrowing Norma Alarcón's insight that Chicana literature inhabits "simultaneous time zones," from the ancient to the contemporary (Alarcón, "Traddutora, Traditora" 127), I analyze Anzaldúa's, Moraga's, and Castillo's historiography: the multiple frames of historical reference that enable them to move outside the taboos of today's dominant culture. In particular, the indigenous Mesoamerican traditions they invoke center on public displays of body manipulation—with masks, tattooing, self-bleeding, intoxication, amputation, and heart excision—to enact the fluid boundaries between men, women, animals, the environment, and divine forces. Unlike their predecessors of the Chicano *movimiento*, who adopted the Aztec warrior as an icon to strengthen Chicano nationalism, Anzaldúa, Moraga, and Castillo worship goddesses, saints, artists, and AIDS victims who represent shape-shifting and openness rather than defended bodily boundaries.

Chapter 2, "Pain," rereads Anzaldúa's work in the wake of her death, putting diabetes at the center of her theories of *mestiza* consciousness, the Coatlicue State, and radical feminist spirituality. I begin with an analysis of Anzaldúa's wide and varied critical reception. Her works have been celebrated as utopian, maligned as untrue to history, and cited as both essentialist and postmodern, nationalist and global. Paying attention, as very few critics have, to her autobiographical statements about pain and illness (particularly in her interviews), this chapter explains many of the counterintuitive and inflammatory insights of *Borderlands* (1987). Anzaldúa turns to the models offered by Coatlicue and Saint Teresa to find culturally grounded meaning for physical pain. After analyzing the Aztec and Catholic contexts that allowed her to accept her own pain as a productive, regenerative sensation, I conclude with a section that follows her risky proposal in her last essay, "now let us shift" (2002), to bridge spirituality and feeling with theory and politics. Though feminism has been, for good reason, committed to rational argumentation and protecting women's bodies, Anzaldúa ultimately asks us to let go of those boundaries. Many of her mourners today, especially at the online altar "Rest in Peace Gloria," have taken this risk, embracing alternative divinities, stigmatized corporeal states, and public expression of feeling. I interrogate critical rejections of sentiment and find new feminist potential in sentient, sensitive theory.

Chapter 3, "Medicine," studies the "new *familia*" Moraga formed with doctors, nurses, and medical technology in her personal narrative, *Waiting in the Wings: Portrait of a Queer Motherhood* (1997). Michel Foucault's insight that modern clinics enforce bodily norms suggests that a Chicana lesbian should resist the clinic's standards of health. Although Moraga's writing has historically opposed the technologies of the dominant culture, she finds, in the neonatal ICU where her prematurely born son begins his life, a home for bodies that defy standardized perfection. During this period of her life, Moraga was also conducting research for two plays, *The Hungry Woman* (2001) (which fuses the stories of Euripides's Medea, the Mexican weeping woman La Llorona, and the dismembered Aztec goddess Coyolxauhqui) and *Heart of the Earth* (2001) (a retelling of the Quiché Maya *Popul Vuh*, in which amputations and death are central to the creation of the human race). Studying the plays with the narrative, alongside Aztec and Mayan understandings of bodies, reveals a reverence for corporeal vulnerability that contrasts with dominant medical, political, and philosophical ideals. I conclude with an analysis of this vulnerability and the ethics of care it inspires, using the insights of disability theorists, including Margrit Shildrick and Nancy Mairs, to redraw the contours of identity and agency.

Chapter 4, "Movement," traces the ways in which fluid bodies actually move through the world. I borrow the shape-shifting corporeality of the Toltec god Tezcatlipoca to interpret the extraordinary mobility of the "crippled" flamenco dancer, Carmen la Coja, in Castillo's novel *Peel My Love Like an Onion* (2000). I draw a composite image of the one-legged trickster god from the few and brief allusions to Mesoamerican culture in Castillo's work, and from anthropological studies of Tezcatlipoca, and argue that this model of shape-shifting inspired Castillo—contrary to the anti-technology stance of her earlier work—to value leg braces, medications, and public transportation as means of moving beyond a body's limits. I then turn to the political content of Carmen's disabled mobility, using Celeste Langan's argument for "just transport" to extend mobility beyond individual bodily capabilities. Pairing disability activism's focus on particularly embodied needs with the abstract lessons about movement from Maurice Merleau-Ponty's corporeal phenomenology enables me to read Carmen's flamenco dancing and her bus rides through Chicago as parallel assertions of post-identity politics based on movement rather than belonging to a racial, national, or sexual group.

"Rethinking Body Politics" concludes by considering what feminist politics might look like if they foregrounded movement and permeability over identity. Chicana feminism offers culturally grounded depictions of bodies that are fluid, and I end this book by close-reading visual portraits by Chicana feminist artists Maya González and Dianne Gamboa that embody the complexity of Coatlicue or Coyolxauhqui in contemporary contexts.

1

FEELING PRE-COLUMBIAN: CHICANA FEMINISTS' IMAGINATIVE HISTORIOGRAPHY

> Third space feminism allows a look to the past through the present always already marked by the coming of that which is still left unsaid, unthought. Moreover, it is in the maneuvering through time to retool and remake subjectivities neglected and ignored that third space feminism claims new histories, Chicana feminist histories.
>
> Emma Pérez, *The Decolonial Imaginary*

*I*n Elaine Scarry's *The Body in Pain* (1985), arguably the most influential work about pain in the Humanities, pain figures as the paradigmatic negative, the horizon of acceptable experience. It is so opposed to our self-understandings as living beings that it cannot be put into language: "physical pain—unlike any other state of consciousness—has no referential content. It is not *of* or *for* anything. It is precisely because it takes no object that it, more than any other phenomenon, resists objectification in language" (Scarry 5, original emphasis). For Scarry, pain is thus an incommunicable phenomenon; unlike hatred or desire, which reaches out to others, pain is intransitive, individual. One problem with this theory is that it provides no avenue for change. If we cannot understand others' pain, how can we eliminate the source of that pain? How can we see the ways in which we, ourselves, are implicated? Pain, in this account, is a closed system, sealed within and destroying the body of the sufferer, with no outlet and no communal accounting.

Another problem is that Scarry assumes a particular cultural understanding of pain as something unspeakable because it is impenetrably

Other. Yet, as I will demonstrate, in some cultural contexts, pain is not necessarily hostile, impenetrable, or individual. From the perspective of indigenous Mesoamerican and Catholic belief systems, the traditions that meet in Mexican culture, pain is wrought within understandings of life. Historically, in Spain and in Mexico, martyrs, priests, and sacrifice victims publicly practiced pain as a means of unifying and revitalizing their communities.[1] In these instances, pain is not just speakable; it is central to spiritual discourse. Its functionality rests on its communicability to others. One of my goals for *Encarnación* is to contextualize Gloria Anzaldúa's, Cherríe Moraga's, and Ana Castillo's depictions of sick, pained, and shape-shifting bodies, outlining the cultural lineage that leads them to incorporate these qualities so demonized by modern reason. Since our conceptions of how bodies should look, feel, and act are culturally grounded, it is important to outline the Mexican cultural understandings about bodies that these writers invoke. The conventions of Spanish Catholicism that were adopted and adapted in early Mexico, like pre-Conquest indigenous sacrifice traditions, consistently objectify pain, illness, and bleeding in sacred representations that take us beyond the bodily norms assumed in studies like Scarry's.

The Body in Pain has nonetheless shaped *Encarnación* in a number of ways, particularly with regard to the questions of where bodies' feelings come from and what visual or linguistic forms these feelings assume.[2] In

1. Scarry describes the ascetic pain of religious rites as a way of "canceling" "the contents of the world" and opening a path to the other world (Scarry 34). I would argue, instead, that even when pain rituals are meant to invoke the divine and reach beyond the material world, they are orchestrated materially, in this world, with the object of effecting material change in this world. The object to which pain is directed in Mesoamerican human sacrifice is the audience and the audience's expectation that the satisfactory enactment of ritual will bring them their desired strength/rain/redemption. And Saint Teresa of Avila achieved power in this world (founding the Carmelite order) by way of the painful raptures that radiated outward from her body through her writings to her followers. I discuss these examples further in Chapter 2.

2. When I say "feeling," I mean to invoke both sentience and emotion, "feeling pain" as well as "feeling blue." But I also mean something larger, a sensibility or a perception of one's place in the world. Raymond Williams differentiates "feelings" from "world-view" or "ideology," which are "more formally held and systematic beliefs." He defines feelings as "meanings and values as they are actively lived and felt" (with "felt," there, meaning something like "experienced") (Williams 132). Feelings are thus more fluid ("in process") and individual than formal identification (though Williams's "structures of feeling" assume

considering the political significance of pain, Scarry argues that "pain's attributes . . . can be lifted away from their source, can be separated from the sufferer and referred to power, broken off from the body and attached instead to the regime" (56). In this way, immaterial power structures—like political organizations or religions—become visible by invoking the material bodies of heroes, opponents, or followers. According to Scarry, the bodies themselves are negated in the process, dissolved into the symbolism of the power structure. Scarry focuses on political structures established by war and torture, but what about more peaceful, counterhegemonic political structures? Feminist thought, which itself often uses bodies to make political statements, has also questioned what "truths" bodies tell. While feminist politics initially relied on first-person narration to serve as evidence of how societies wound women ("the personal is political"), postmodern and poststructural feminist theories have since demonstrated that neither bodies nor experience are self-evident and have focused, instead, on the social constructions that mediate corporeal experience. As "the body" has come to signify a sedimentation of the effects of power, corporeal-based truth claims have come to seem naïve—recalling Scarry's assertion that the sentience of bodies can never be communicated as such. The work of Anzaldúa, Moraga, and Castillo emerged in the era of consciousness-raising, and their autobiographical writings seem to participate in the confessionalist mode of feminist truth-telling, with a particular emphasis on how bodies bear the marks of their political situations. The metaphor of the aching back that opens *This Bridge Called My Back: Writings by Radical Women of Color*, for instance, represents the labor of building bridges between feminists as well as the literal "burden" of survival amidst racism, sexism, homophobia, and classism, which women of color try not to let "break our backs" (Anzaldúa, "Foreword to the Second Edition," *This Bridge Called My Back* iv). Each of the forewords, prefaces, and introductions to *Bridge* mentions personal suffering, "the exhaustion we feel in our bones," "the knife we feel in our backs," "the nausea we feel in our bellies" (Moraga, Preface, *This Bridge Called My Back* xviii). Not simply poetic metaphors or untheorized appeals to corporeal authority, these reiterated expressions of pain communicate the material impact of bodies' histories and interactions with the world. These feelings are thus central to the articulation of Chicana feminism. The writers in *Bridge* claim their own pain—which emerges

---

that they must be shared at some level). Most importantly, as I use it, feeling need not be formalized, objective, or rational.

from friction with the dominant society as well as with (racist, classist, and homophobic) feminist identity politics—and translate this pain into their own stirring political visions. Pain, in this sense, is not simply material evidence of oppression; it is the rhetoric of political mobilization and resistance. "Haven't we always borne jugs of water, children, poverty?" (Anzaldúa, "Foreword to the Second Edition," *This Bridge Called My Back* iv).

In Scarry's account, individual pain is always appropriated by larger power structures, foreclosing the possibility that the feelings of individuals might ever be represented against or outside of the power structure. (This would be as if the identities Paula Moya affirms as articulations of the interaction between individuals and "the central organizing principles of a society" [Moya, *Learning from Experience* 86] were subsumed by the greater force of the "organizing principles.") Even in Scarry's interpretation of biblical texts, depictions of wounded bodies function only pragmatically, lending their materiality to "the object of belief that itself has no content and thus itself cannot be represented" (Scarry 198). I know from my own Catholic upbringing that faith can be visceral. The body is not just an analogy for God; it is the particular place where one feels God, and its own materiality is undeniable. When Scarry assumes the "absolute incompatibility of pain and the world" (50), she also assumes a secular, Enlightenment perception of the relationship between bodies and worlds. This is what led me back to my studies of pre-Columbian Mexico, and back to my days at *Sangre de Cristo*/Blood of Christ Catholic Church, to think about other ways that bodies relate to worlds. In short, Scarry's universalizing assumptions led me to history.

Anzaldúa, Moraga, and Castillo, too, in their efforts to expand identity beyond the limiting parameters of contemporary Euro-America, appeal to pre-Columbian Mesoamerican worldviews in which feeling is sacred and objective reason does not form the horizon of corporeal being. (They also appeal to Catholicism, but they favor pre-Columbian cultures over the beliefs imposed by European conquest. When they do allude to Catholicism, they are critical of its patriarchal gender politics and seek to uncover indigenous beliefs that underlie *mestizo* Catholicism in Mexico.) Ancient Mexican culture provides them with a history of, and an alternate "vocabulary" for, representing pain—in visual images, in writing, and in performance. They do not, however, simply retell this history, which would bracket it in the past; they reenact it in their own representations. It is something that they feel in the present. Their vision of the past is not essentialist but motivated by contemporary political needs (and is thus indigenist, rather than European, revolving around goddesses, rather than gods). As Chicana feminist author/historian Emma Pérez describes it, in the epigraph to this chapter, the past for Chicana feminism is intimately tied to the present and the future, the "coming of that which is still left unsaid" (E. Pérez 127). These writers reject dominant accounts of history in order to uncover ways of being and modes of representation that might better accommodate Chicana feminist feelings.

This chapter considers the question: what does Chicana feminist literature have to do with history? Chicana/o writers have invoked pre-Columbian Mexican cultures (the Aztec, in particular) as a source of meaning since the beginning of the *movimiento* in the 1960s.[3] At that time, Chicano nationalists claimed Aztlán (the territories, now part of the U.S. Southwest, from which the Aztecs migrated southward to Mexico over a thousand years ago) as a homeland.[4] This apparently ahistorical

3. Chicana/o literature is now old enough to have its own history, and the "native" sensibility of contemporary writers differs from that established by their predecessors of the Chicano *movimiento* forty years ago. Critics have been pointing out problematic aspects of the Chicano movement's adoption of Aztec heritage almost since this adoption began, so it would be naïve to assume that contemporary writers—especially Chicana feminist writers, whose work is attuned to the blind spots of the movement that preceded them—would adopt this problematic vision uncritically. My discussion of Chicana feminist literature, then, will examine its critical relationship to history on two fronts, analyzing the ways in which these writers position themselves relative to ancient Mesoamerican and modern Chicano cultures.

4. A brief explanation of my terminology: First, critics respond differently to the engendering of the term "Chicano," using "Chicana and Chicano," "Chicana/o," or, more cutely, "Chican@" to be inclusive. Throughout the book, I use "Chicano" to signify the monolithic and masculinist culture of the *movimiento*, "Chicana" to refer to women in particular, and "Chicana/o" to suggest a culture self-consciously inclusive of Chicanas and Chicanos. Second, the use of the term "Aztec" is also problematic. According to Inga Clendinnen, "The word 'Aztec' has been used to mean a number of things, from the 'empire' which sprawled across much of modern Mexico, to the people of the magnificent lake city who were its masters" (Clendinnen, *Aztecs* 1). Clendinnen uses the ethnic term "Mexica" "to avoid the heavy freight that 'Aztec' has come to bear" (1). Centuries of pre-Columbian Mexican history are collapsed in most Chicana/o understandings of the "Aztec," flattening out the diversity and historical variability of indigenous cultures by privileging Aztec culture as it was found by the Spanish in the sixteenth century. This myopia is partially a function of available archival materials: most textual accounts of indigenous Mexico were

gesture rejects the influence of European colonialism to claim Aztec identity as an empowering cultural inheritance and a defiant political orientation.[5] Identification with the Aztecs is one of the central topics of Chicana/o criticism and one of the most debated aspects of Anzaldúa's, Moraga's, and Castillo's writing (hence my extensive use of footnotes,

---

recorded by Spanish friars and military men, beginning in the sixteenth century, as they dealt with the leaders of the Aztec empire during the military and, later, the cultural conquest. I use the term "Aztec" since it is the one most familiar to non-experts and since it is the term most often used in Chicana/o Literature.

5. The Chicano movement's 1969 "El Plan Espiritual de Aztlán" affirms: "In the spirit of a new people that is conscious not only of its proud historical heritage but also of the brutal 'gringo' invasion of our territories, *we*, the Chicano inhabitants and civilizers of the northern land of Aztlán from whence came our forefathers, reclaiming the land of their birth and consecrating the determination of our people of the sun, *declare* that the call of our blood is our power, our responsibility, and our inevitable destiny" ("El Plan" 1, original emphasis). This language positions Chicanos as both a "new" race and the same race as the Aztecs, the people of the sun. Blood, land, and cultural heritage tie Chicanos to the past, before the "gringo invasion," and to the future, "our inevitable destiny." Rudolfo Anaya is one of the writers most closely associated with the reclaiming of Aztlán and Aztec culture in the service of the Chicano movement. His essay "Aztlán: A Homeland Without Boundaries" (1989) explains his literary investment in pre-Columbian mythology, an investment most apparent in his 1976 novel, *Heart of Aztlán*. He writes that "I came to understand that many of the symbols which welled up from my subconscious were not learned, they were part of my ethos, symbols from the archetypal memory residing in my blood" (Anaya, "Aztlán" 236). He later describes a more deliberate search for these archetypes: "The established Indohispano culture was based in the villages, but by the 1960s the community was largely an urban group, and so to reconstitute our history during this time of crisis some returned to the villages to look for origins. Another meaningful return was into the history of the Americas where we examined our Indian roots, the soul of the Americas. There we found not only indigenous historical time, but mythical time which is continuous; that discovery was to have a tremendous impact on the healing of our social fabric" (237). This preference for mythological continuity over linear history defies historical distance as well as social and geographic distance, creating "a new time of hermandad," "a new era of brotherhood" that would unify, heal, and awaken the community to "a new sensitivity in their relationship to the earth and cosmos" (237, 241). This new type of community, founded on shared consciousness rather than on concrete moorings, is overtly idealistic: "An idealistic, utopian thought? Perhaps, but one we need to dare to consider. Those who deal in competition and the selfishness of the modern nation-state are in control, and

here, to avoid extended digression). Many critics have assumed that they are simply claiming an essentialist connection to indigenous Mexico (echoing their Chicano nationalist predecessors).[6] Others critique their misrepresentations or idealizations of indigenous Mexican culture and history.[7] My interpretation differs from these two approaches. I do not

---

they have falsely named competition and material gain as the true values of the world. Perhaps it is time to think of unity" (241). Historical objectivity is set aside in this passionate search for national identity, privileging cultural validation over the bleak truths set in place by colonial history.

6. When Anzaldúa, Moraga, and Castillo first began publishing in the 1980s, many critics seemed to assume that they were operating in an essentialist mode. For instance, in a 1990 analysis of the poetry of Moraga, Alma Luz Villanueva, and Pat Mora, Kristina Passman focuses on these writers' "connection with the primordial and cultural traditions of Hispanic women" and their "realization of authentic selfhood" on "mythic, atemporal, or eternal ground, using archetypal imagery and narrative patterns that resonate with the common experience of women" (Passman 338). In 1997, Rosaura Sánchez criticized the essentialist tendencies of Moraga's, Anzaldúa's, and Castillo's work, noting in particular the "running thread of biologism" in Castillo's claim to "Amerindian roots," which "would be difficult to construe as other than deterministic and essentialist" (Sánchez 360). Yvonne Yarbro-Bejarano responds to such criticism in her essay on Anzaldúa's *Borderlands* by situating Chicana feminist reclamations of "the Indian woman" relative to the history of the Chicano movement: "This wariness toward the invocation of 'Indianness' and the pre-Columbian pantheon must be contextualized in the contemporary critique of the cultural nationalism of the Chicano Movement, which engineered a romanticized linking between Chicanos and indigenous cultures as part of the process of constructing a Chicano identity" (Yarbro-Bejarano, "Gloria Anzaldúa's *Borderlands/La Frontera*" 17). In this context, these writers' pre-Columbian feelings represent not an original gesture as much as a critical response to earlier practices of invoking an exclusionary, masculinist Chicano Aztec ideal.

7. Rosaura Sánchez is one of many scholars who have critiqued Chicana feminism's romantic appropriations of indigenous culture. In effect, these appropriations reduce indigenous populations to "exotic discourses" pulled out of context in the service of contemporary ethnicity and gender politics (Sánchez 358). Sánchez accuses Castillo of "facile" reconstructions of Aztec mythology and a failure to consider how "notions of 'indigenous culture' . . . have been reified in Mexico in particular and manipulated to serve as cultural artifacts by the ideological apparatuses of the Mexican state, an entity known neither for its sensitivity nor enlightened stance toward either women in general or its indigenous populations" (357–58). It is true that these writers often fail to consider the lives of actual indigenous Mexicans, under the reign of the Aztecs or since the

believe that they are claiming any unmediated access to pre-Columbian Mexico; nor are they trying to rewrite history with alternate truth claims. Instead, I regard their claims to pre-Columbian "memory" as deliberately ahistorical and ideological—what Sonia Saldívar-Hull calls "an Aztlán transformed by a mestiza feminist sensibility" (Saldívar-Hull 64).

Assertions of *indigenismo* (or pride in indigenous heritage) elide centuries of *mestizaje* (racial and cultural mixing instigated by Spanish rule), favoring a precolonial imaginary over postcolonial reality. *Indigenismo*, then, is a political and cultural creation rather than a simple matter of descent. Even when these assertions imply an essential connection to the past, their resistant stance and their self-reflexive defiance of history expose deliberate mediation rather than passive genetic inheritance. In his essay "'Feathering the Serpent: Chicano Mythic Memory,'" Rafael Pérez-Torres likewise sees Chicana/os' invocations of Mesoamerican history as critical and theoretical rather than essentialist, describing Chicana/os' Aztec "memory" in terms of discontinuity. Pérez-Torres's use of the term "counterdiscourse" helps to emphasize the "resistant response to discontinuity and violence, to cultural imperialism and discursive erasure" that is built within Chicana/o recoveries of precolonial indigenous culture. The implication of seamless continuity and essential connection to the Aztec is undercut by the friction between the precolonial past and the present, the strategic recreation of "indigenous cultural practices that have been made marginal," and the politicized foregrounding of "the disrupted, the discontinuous, the devalued" repressed by dominant histories (Pérez-Torres, "Feathering the Serpent" 294).[8] Even in its essentialist poses, claiming an Aztec memory defies essentialism.

Working within and against the tradition of the Chicano *movimiento*, Anzaldúa, Moraga, and Castillo have embraced the counterdiscursive impact of *indigenismo* but rejected its masculinist nationalism. Pérez-Torres, too, traces a historical shift in Chicana/o attitudes toward Aztec culture, and "Feathering the Serpent" takes Anzaldúa and Castillo as its two examples of movement away from the nationalism of the 1960s and '70s

---

Conquest. To assume that this elision is based on lack of knowledge or simple oversight on the part of these writers, however, underestimates their philosophy.

8. In a later essay, Pérez-Torres reconsiders Chicana/os' repeated claims to ancient Mexican memory in terms of melancholia, mourning a lost "national/cultural/racial connection," and he emphasizes the psychological dimensions of evoking ancient Mexico as a "lost ethical order" with potential to transform the world in the present (Pérez-Torres, "Placing Loss" 114).

toward a more fluid, tenuous, and "multiplicitous" sensibility: for the later writers, "to be a Chicano becomes more and more a journey toward a becoming across the multiplicitous borderlands that make up North American contemporary cultural landscapes" rather than "a return to Aztlán" and "some clearly definable cultural identity" (301). Yet Pérez-Torres de-emphasizes sex/gender in his account of this transformation and does not make an issue of the fact that his examples for de-essentializing identity are female and his example of essentialist *movimiento* poetry, Alurista, is iconically male. (Indeed, his decision to use "Chicano" and "Chicana" interchangeably further elides sex/gender as meaningful differences [315n].) I would suggest that it is not simply chronology (or posteriority to postmodern identity theory) that makes Anzaldúa and Castillo less nationalist or less essentialist in their pre-Columbian feelings; it is feminism, lesbianism, and resistance to patriarchal Chicanismo. All three critique Chicano nationalism in explicitly gendered terms. Moraga has consistently, from her essay "Queer Aztlán" (in *The Last Generation,* 1993) to her play *The Hungry Woman* (2001), emphasized the alienation of women and queers within the alien nation of Aztlán.[9] In *Borderlands*

9. In "Queer Aztlán," Moraga writes, "Chicanos are an occupied nation within a nation, and women and women's sexuality are occupied within the Chicano nation" (Moraga, *The Last Generation* 150). "What was right about Chicano Nationalism," she argues, "was its commitment to preserving the integrity of the Chicano people. . . . What was wrong about Chicano Nationalism was its institutionalized heterosexism, its inbred machismo, and its lack of a cohesive national political strategy" (148–29). Almost ten years later, in *The Hungry Woman,* she depicts a futuristic, dystopian Aztlán from which "queer folks were unilaterally sent into exile" (Moraga, *The Hungry Woman* 6). At times, her longing to overcome racial, sexual, class-based rejection leads to an embrace of identity politics that mimics nationalism, but she is self-conscious and self-critical about this mimicking. Sandra Soto's 2005 *GLQ* essay, "Cherríe Moraga's Going Brown," provides an excellent way of understanding Moraga's nationalist postures: in Moraga's critique of Mexican Americans' cultural, linguistic, and biological assimilation, "her work can seem much more closely aligned with the radical positions of the masculine *veteranos* of the 1960s and 1970s than with the feminist critiques launched in response to them by women of color in the 1980s. This irony is not lost on Moraga, who admits that 'I am the worse and best of those macho Chicano nationalists'" (Moraga, *Waiting in the Wings* 39, qtd. in Soto 243–44). The key difference Soto finds between Moraga's nationalism and that of the *"veteranos"* lies in personal confession versus universalizing didacticism: "If Moraga builds her case for queer ethnonationalist politics less through didacticism and more through an elaboration of the ways that her personal expe-

(1987), Anzaldúa claimed the fluid third space of the borderlands be-tween nations as her homeland, a place where "the queer" and "the half-breed" reside (Anzaldúa, *Borderlands* 3). And Castillo mocks the machisto politics of Aztlán in her novel *Sapogonia* (1990): the resident of this fic-tionalized "home" to all mestizos is the Sapogón, which translates to big/macho toad (Castillo, *Sapogonia* 1–2). These writers still embrace pre-Columbian cultures as a source of resistant consciousness, but they do so tentatively, critiquing Aztec warrior culture, emphasizing sexual particularity, and opening their mythology to other cultural influences, from contemporary New Age movements to Black feminism, in order to create a more inclusive symbology.[10]

"Cultural memory" is shaped by sex, gender, and sexuality. Many of the icons of pre-Columbian Mexico embody misogynist sex/gender narratives, ranging from the mutilation of the moon goddess Coyolxauh-qui at the hands of her brother, the war god Huitzilopochtli, to Malintzin (or La Malinche, in Spanish), who is accused of betraying the indigenous peoples of Mexico in her role as translator and supposed lover to the conquering Hernán Cortés. Moreover, the violence of conquest and en-forced *mestizaje* in Mexico was experienced by women in an explicitly sexual manner, since it is through the bodies (and the rapes) of women that *mestizaje* was formed.[11] The "pre-colonial springs of life," which postcolonial populations sometimes idealize as an era of lost cultural in-tegrity (Fanon 237), were often violent, and they were differently violent for warriors, for priests, and for women. Emma Pérez's efforts to write Chicanas into history in *The Decolonial Imaginary* invoke a Foucauldian understanding of archeology to emphasize how bodies bear the traces of

---

riences and desires have been relentlessly circumscribed by racial etiquette, sex-ism, and homophobia, then her writing appears to be everywhere about fessing up" (255). This mode of "fessing up" is far more tentative, individual, and self-critical than the more dogmatic nationalist proclamations of Moraga's predecessors.

10. Laura E. Pérez also differentiates Chicana invocations of pre-Columbian culture from earlier Chicano uses. For Chicanas, Pérez argues, "the pre-Columbian" is neither "dead" nor simply a "shallow" source of symbols but, rather, a locus for "a decolonizing struggle at the epistemological level, where being, existence, meaning, and of course knowledge are defined" (L. Pérez, *Chicana Art* 4).

11. See Suzanne Bost, *Mulattas and Mestizas*, for an extended discussion of the role of sex/gender in the formation and the articulation of *mestiza/o* identities.

history's passing: "The body is historically and socially constructed. It is written upon by the environment, by clothes, diet, exercise, illnesses, accidents. It is written upon by the kind of sex that is practiced upon the body and that the body practices" (E. Pérez 108). This corporeal approach must pay attention to violence, sexuality, childbirth, mothering, and other explicitly sexual ways in which indigenous culture and Conquest were experienced. Pérez's "Third Space" or "decolonizing" Chicana feminism critically recovers the repressed within the repressed: the queer and female voices that were marginalized by Chicanos in the recovery of Aztec nationalism. These Chicana feminist histories are doubly "decolonial" in their resistance to the narratives imposed by Spanish Conquest and in their resistance to the narratives imposed by gender-blind or masculinist Chicano nationalism. From a feminist perspective, the past is not an ideal to return to but a contested terrain of competing truth claims, all of which are inflected by sex, gender, and sexuality. (Indeed, attention to the violence of embodying Mexican history might explain some of the pain and disability in Chicana feminist texts.) Chicana feminist *indigenismo*, therefore, is critical, tactical, and tentative rather than nostalgic, passive, or celebratory.

Moraga explains her journey back to her roots as having begun in contemporary Mexico, where she encountered her own "cultural outsiderhood" as a Chicana lesbian, leading her back beyond the reach of living cultures to the pre-Columbian temples, where it was not the peoples or their visible legacy but "the natural landscape in which those *templos* were placed" and "the buried history" contained within them "that brought a shudder of recognition to the surface of [her] skin" (Moraga, *The Hungry Woman* x). This is a past emptied of people—people who would inevitably judge, exclude, or resist a Chicana feminist understanding of indigenous Mexico—and *felt* through an organic or mystical connection, free from the constraints of history.[12] The connection Moraga feels to ancient Mexico is an ideal, rooted in ideas and cosmology, not a realist genealogy. Though she is generally critical of Chicana feminism's so-called "refashioned *indigenismo*," Marxist Chicana critic Rosaura Sánchez describes it as "the shaping discourse that enables the writers to counter Western rationalism and, more specifically, white Anglo-Saxon Protestant traditions" (Sánchez 358). Sánchez

12. Mary Pat Brady also notes how, for Moraga, "the turn to memory, the attempt to create a structure of feeling through Aztlán . . . involves understanding that the past is not fixed but malleable" (Brady, *Extinct Lands* 152).

suggests that these writers do not "go far enough, for there is no call for a transformation of the capitalist system of production that has generated oppression and exploitation" (358), but perhaps they go farther than a strictly realist political critique. These writers draw from the ancient (or, really, from their own imaginings about the ancient) a way of being, thinking, and relating that differs from the behaviors privileged by modern Euro-America: a way out of the competitive, territorial, and compulsory relations that spring from and reinforce patriarchal and imperialist capitalism.[13]

In "Chicana Feminism: In the Tracks of 'The' Native Woman," Norma Alarcón analyzes the psychological implications of Chicana feminism's investment in pre-Columbian culture:

> For many writers, the point is not so much to recover a lost "utopia" nor the "true" essence of our being; although, of course, there are those who long for the "lost origins," as well as those who feel a profound spiritual kinship with the "lost"—a spirituality whose resistant political implications must not be underestimated, but refocused for feminist change (Allen 1988). The most relevant point in the present is to understand how a pivotal indigenous portion of the *mestiza* past may represent a collective female experience as well as "the mark of the Beast" within us—the maligned and abused indigenous woman (Anzaldúa 1987). By invoking the "dark Beast" within and without, which many have forced us to deny, the cultural and psychic dismemberment that is linked to imperialist racist and sexist practices are [*sic*] brought into focus. (Alarcón, "Chicana Feminism" 375)

I quote this passage at length because it introduces what I consider to be the most important dimensions of Chicana feminism's transhistorical imagination. Alarcón initially downplays the ahistoricity of feeling pre-Columbian by suggesting, first, that many writers do *not* claim a lost utopia or a mystical connection to the indigenous past. The writers I am talking about here, however, sometimes do make this claim, precisely

13. AnaLouise Keating similarly concludes, in relation to Anzaldúa, that "although some scholars have read this turn toward the indigenous as escapism or nostalgia, I disagree. Indigenous Mexican philosophies and worldviews offer Anzaldúa epistemological tools for individual/collective self-definition, resistance, intervention, and creation, as well as additional frameworks or vehicles to develop and convey her own innovative theories" (Keating, *EntreMundos/ Among Worlds* 5).

because of its utopian (or otherworldly) potential. Moraga asserts just this sort of embodied connection, a "collective racial memory that every-thing about my personal biography had rejected, but one that my writer's soul irrefutably embraced" (Moraga, *The Hungry Woman* x). In a March 2004 talk subtitled "The (W)Rite to Remember," she called this mem-ory a "right," a "rite," and something recovered through writing ("Indí-gena as Scribe"). This pre-Columbian feeling is a political "right" and a sacred practice, located in the soul rather than biography. I would argue that it is this deliberately ahistorical and ideological embrace of some-thing "lost" that enables the "resistant political implications" Alarcón emphasizes. These writers feel themselves to be part of a world removed from recorded history, strengthening their resistance to the dominant culture's processes of subjectification.

Incorporating "the maligned and abused indigenous woman" within one's self-understanding, in my quote from Alarcón above, "may repre-sent" something collectively female, and this something, though collec-tive and psychic, is "dismembered," applying very material language to something as intangible as a female feeling. There is a suggestion that history is trauma for women of Mexican descent. Perhaps, then, the work of Anzaldúa, Moraga, and Castillo presents something of a "talking cure," returning to the early "childhood" of indigenous women's history in the Americas, understanding the moments of Conquest and shaming, and trying to recover a more "healthy" feeling anterior to this misogyny. If psychic health and pre-dismemberment are, idealistically and counter-discursively, located prior to the entry of Europeans and the birth of Euro-America, then we might look to pre-Columbian cultures to under-stand what health looks like. It is in this spirit that Moraga *imagines* a time "before shame, before betrayal, before Eve, Malinche, and Guadalupe; before the occupation of Aztlán, la llegada de los españoles, the Aztecs' War of Flowers" (Moraga, *The Last Generation* 72). While many in Chi-cana/o Studies find this imagined "utopia" in the nation of Aztlán, I find it in the bodies and words of Chicana feminism.

I will take up extended analyses of Anzaldúa's, Moraga's, and Castillo's pre-Columbian feelings, and the content of pre-Columbian medicine and pain practices, in the chapters that follow. While these writers turn to history for imaginative purposes, I turn to history as a literary critic: finding culturally specific frames of reference for understanding the liter-ary texts that are my primary focus. I believe that the corporeal ideologies I draw from pre-Columbian Mexico are consistent with Anzaldúa's, Moraga's, and Castillo's invocations of this era, and I have consulted the sources that they cite for their own research, but I am not merely trying to "recover" their sources or to replicate their knowledge. My discussions of history are inevitably ideological. I offer my interpretation of history to present ways of understanding identities, bodies, and corporeal sensation that conflict with the dominant logic governing identities and bodies in the United States today. There is surely some degree of self-fulfilling prophecy in the amount of historical and anthropological "data" I have found to support my claims about corporeal permeability in Mesoamerican rituals and medical practices, but my intentions and my methods are scholarly. I rely on my secondary training in Latin American Studies to guide my understanding of pre-Columbian Mexico, though I don't claim to be making any new interventions in the discipline of Mesoamerican history, and I analyze these sources through my own theoretical and political lenses.

Before exploring the details of these writers' visions of history, it is first important to understand why they invoke history and what it means to feel pre-Columbian. In this chapter, then, I introduce critical frameworks for understanding these writers' sentient historiography. I call their work "historiography" since they are not writing history but critically reflecting on how history has been recorded and how we might view history otherwise. The first section of this chapter uses the work of Norma Alarcón and Michel de Certeau to explore the political and philosophical assumptions that underlie what we know as history and, then, develops an alternate model of "Chicana Feminist Hagiography." This pairing of Alarcón and de Certeau (French philosopher of history, politics, and everyday life) enacts the methodological fusion I discuss in my introduction: grounding the critical insights of postmodern theory with the culturally specific and politically engaged insights of Chicana feminism. The second section places the autobiographies of Chicana feminism in dialogue with the self-portraits of the Mexican artist Frida Kahlo to illuminate the links between self-representation, Mexican history, and pain. As Alicia Gaspar de Alba suggests, despite national and temporal differences, Kahlo has been "heroized" "as a role model for Chicana artists seeking to liberate themselves from the male-dominated structures of both el Movimiento and the Chicano Art Movement" (Gaspar de Alba 50). In a 1978 exhibition by Chicana/o artists at the Galería de la Raza in San Francisco, "Homage to Frida Kahlo," one of the Chicana contributors claimed that "Frida embodied the whole notion of culture for Chicano women. She inspired us. Her works didn't have self-pity, they had strength" (qtd. in Herrera, *Frida* xiii). Beyond their shared Mexican heritage, shared resistance to economic exploitation and U.S. cultural imperialism, and shared aesthetic and intellectual independence, Chicana feminists share many thematic elements with Kahlo. Like Kahlo, Anzaldúa, Moraga, and Castillo view themselves relative to Mexico's indigenous past, and all four rupture their own bodies in provocative self-representations, fragmenting them from within and connecting them to other worlds without to dramatize the pain of women who incorporate Conquest and *mestizaje*. Going beyond their Mexican predecessor, however, Anzaldúa, Moraga, and Castillo present clear political visions about the permeability of identity.

Chicana Feminist Hagiography

Juxtaposing two different theoretical lenses onto historiography helps to clarify what these writers are doing with history. In *The Writing of History* (1975), Michel de Certeau argues that "Modern Western History essentially begins with differentiation between the *present* and the *past*" (de Certeau 2, original emphasis). In this sense, history lies in the perception of the past as "other" than the present. The "intelligibility" of "modern Western culture . . . is established through a relation with the other . . . the Indian, the past, the people, the mad, the child, the Third World" (3). The historiography of Chicana/o literature, however, denies this sort of "progress," claiming the repressed past, the "Third World," and "the Indian" as its present from which it was never ruptured. In speaking of contemporary Chicana writers' relationship to history, Alarcón argues:

> [S]ince Chicanas have begun the appropriation of history, sexuality, and language for themselves, they find themselves situated at the cutting edge of a new historical moment involving a radical though fragile change in consciousness. It is an era in which we live in simultaneous time zones from the pre-Columbian to the ultramodern, from the cyclical to the linear. (Alarcón, "Traddutora, Traditora" 127)

What is the reason for this simultaneity? One answer is that these contemporary writers maintain pre-Columbian sensibilities to counter modern America's unfeeling hegemony. Another answer is that, according to the native sensibilities they adopt, time is cyclical and ritually repeated rather than linear and progressive. This premodern sensibility thwarts the logic of modern historiography by refusing to sever the present from the past.

It is not just that Chicana/os perceive themselves as inheriting their native ancestors' vision. Building cultural strength upon the backs of those whom history has declared vanquished challenges what we think of as "historical" and inverts mainstream processes of historiography. By rejecting the Eurocentric historical narrative established for the last five hundred years, Chicana/o writers changed the rules for evidence gathering, challenged ideas of chronology, and discarded that which has passed as "history." In its place, they have developed new ways of making meaning from the events, cultures, and names of the past. After the first generation of visionaries ruptured Chicana/o history from chronology and exposed the falsifying biases and violent erasures within historical narratives, later writers were freed to move in and around stories from the past and to construct histories with no pretensions about "truth." While the *movimiento* claimed monolithic identities like the Aztec warrior Cuauhtémoc and the Virgin of Guadalupe as new sources of cultural strength and unity, Anzaldúa, Moraga, and Castillo give new life to more contested figures like the supposedly disloyal Malintzin and the dismembered/disobedient daughter Coyolxauhqui—women whose histories are undocumented, diffuse, and mythic and whose identities trespass national, gendered, and familial belonging.[14]

As they created a new historical narrative to empower Chicanos, many of the earlier writers excluded resistant facts and identities as much as the builders of history that preceded them. To break with this history of unself-conscious bias, Anzaldúa, Moraga, and Castillo pose "history" as always subjective, malleable, and ideological. As Anzaldúa wrote in her introduction to *Making Face, Making Soul* (1990), "Our strength lies in shifting perspectives, in our capacity to shift, in our 'seeing through' the membrane of the past superimposed on the present. . . . *Encrucijadas,*

14. La Malinche (also known by her Spanish and Aztec names, Doña Marina and Malintzin) was the translator and, ultimately, lover of Hernán Cortés during the conquest of Mexico. She has come to represent one who betrays one's people. Moraga, along with other Chicana feminist scholars, has reclaimed maligned figures like La Malinche as role models for agency and voice. In her essay "A Long Line of Vendidas," from *Loving in the War Years*, she situates her mother (a Mexican immigrant who married an Anglo) and herself (a lesbian who defies the gender/family ideals of the Chicano *movimiento*) within a legacy of "sell-outs," revaluing the terms "vendida" and "malinchista" as markers of women who take risks, defy tradition, and affirm their own desires. She similarly reclaims the moon goddess Coyolxauhqui (who was dismembered by her brother, Huitzilopochtli, for trying to turn their mother, Coatlicue, against him) as a hopeful figure of the wholeness that follows cyclical waning. I discuss this revision of Coyolxauhqui at length in Chapter 3.

haunted by voices and images that violated us, bearing the pains of the past, we are slowly acquiring the tools to change the disabling images and memories, to replace them with self-affirming ones, to recreate our pasts and alter them—for the past can be as malleable as the present" (xxvii). This passage suggests that we in the present bear the imprint of the past, but that this imprinting is not linear or irreversible. Rather, in the present we are *encrucijadas*, at the crossroads, pained by the past but not disabled, able to see it from different angles, able to see through it as a transparent membrane, and able to transform it.

Through their repeated use of autobiography, these writers also make history personal, removing the mask of objectivity and undressing the relationship between historian and history. De Certeau defines history as a "heterology," a discourse of the other, "built upon a division between the body of knowledge that utters a discourse and the mute body that nourishes it" (de Certeau 3). The writing of history reflects "a will to dominate" the obscure and absent body of the past, in this argument (6). The corporeal metaphor becomes even more literal when de Certeau links the developing field of modern medicine to the developing field of historiography (in the seventeenth and eighteenth centuries) as parallel sciences of "deciphering" the meaning of other bodies (3): "An analogous change takes place when tradition, a lived body, is revealed to erudite curiosity through a corpus of texts: Modern medicine and historiography are born almost simultaneously from the rift between a subject that is supposedly literate and an object that is supposedly written in an unknown language" (3). These are both sciences that elevate the erudition of the scientist while exerting power over the objectified body of the other. The historian and the doctor posture as the only speaking subjects in their work, cloaking the object of their analyses underneath their mantle of scientific expertise, making texts out of bodies (a dynamic that recalls Scarry's argument that bodies are consumed by power structures). Anzaldúa's, Moraga's, and Castillo's newest works, perhaps not coincidentally, take on both medicine and history at once, and both engagements explicitly deny the otherness of their objects by erasing the assumed division between patient and medical professional, Aztec and historian. In writing about themselves, they give body to the sick and the past—often embodying positions usually considered untenable for writing subjects—in literary visions that deny the power dynamics posed by de Certeau as well as those critiqued by Scarry.

It will not be surprising to scholars in Chicana/o Studies to have reached the conclusion that Chicana feminist writers defy the logic of an eminent French male theorist. Chicana/os' resistant relationship to dominant frameworks is perhaps *the* central topic of Chicana/o literary and historical studies (from early text and context studies to today's analytic and recovery efforts).[15] For political reasons, Chicana/os continue to take on both history and historiography in order to expose the fictiveness of past histories and to tell stories that have not yet been told. "History" is thus not a linear genealogy of inherited reality; it is a continuing interplay of stories that are politically deployed in playful or violent debates over truth, moving backward and forward in time to chart patterns helpful for the construction of certain desired futures. Authors like Anzaldúa, Moraga, and Castillo are imaginative historiographers, self-reflexively playing with different pasts to defy the chronologies and the power dynamics established by dominant histories.

The conceptual layer I want to add to this take on historiography has to do with the way that bodies mobilize history. As texts whose colors, shapes, scars, and diseases narrate both personal and communal histories, bodies tell us about how people are shaped by their material contexts, and vice versa. The physical pain that often accompanies these corporeal markings clarifies the violence of historical passing. Moreover, as the literal and metaphoric site of creation and destruction, birth and death, bodies have something to say about genealogy, metamorphosis, repetition, and regeneration. Anzaldúa, Moraga, and Castillo use autobiographical narrative, poetry, plays, and novels to give body to the myths that mark them as Chicanas. Fastening these myths to a body (real or textual) gives them life, voice, and mobility (real or textual) with which to subjectify the myth and to act up against history.[16]

15. In a recent example, at the conclusion of his dialectical analysis of Chicano history and literature, *Historia*, Louis Mendoza describes the histories of minorities as separate from, though intertwined with, the history of the dominant culture, since both are built on a dialogue between shared "real" and "imagined" truths, facts and cultural ideologies: "I think, however, it is useful to vex the categories of 'real' and 'imagined' social relations because so often in attempting to project a better future, we are called to articulate the 'not real' in the same way as alternative histories have had to write against the real and imagined histories of elites who presented their narratives as if they were comprehensive and indisputable" (Mendoza 283).

16. The "matter" of my analysis is these writers' textual productions, not their actual bodies, though one might argue that they pose themselves—for public readings, teaching, etc.—as embodiments of a Mexican past. Frida Kahlo certainly did this in her life, costuming herself in indigenous dresses and indige-

De Certeau describes the relationship between historiography and the past as if it were a freak show. We use strange visions of the past to pose ourselves as having evolved and to displace our anxieties about the present onto another time. Yet these histories suggest inheritance as well as differentiation. "As it vacillates between exoticism and criticism through a staging of the other," de Certeau writes, history "oscillates between conservatism and utopianism through its function of signifying a lack" (85). This statement is true for Anzaldúa, Moraga, and Castillo, whose staging of apparently monstrous or exotic bodies from Aztec mythology alongside sick bodies they encounter in the real world juxtaposes past and present to illuminate the continued (undead?) monstrosity of how cultural norms are grafted onto bodies. In the process of this illumination, they critique the world that makes monstrosity (through violence and judgment) at the same time that they use monstrosity to expand our thinking about bodies beyond cultural or clinical norms. The sometimes perverse dwelling in pain and dismemberment that accompanies these writers' visions is balanced by an almost utopian optimism about how the world and bodies could be other than they are now. The temporal ambivalence de Certeau notes of staging the past to "mak[e] a place for a future" (85) is thus something they would avow, but de Certeau's descriptions of overpowering, repressing, and burying the other/past re-enact colonial violence in a manner that they would surely refute. De Certeau claims that to write history is "to use the narrativity that buries the dead as a way of establishing a place for the living" (100). This vision of the passing of history requires the death of the past, making the writer of history a sort of mortician who must make this passing visible. In contrast, Alarcón describes Chicanas' relationship to historiography as one that "catch[es] stunning insights into our complex culture by taking hold of the variegated imaginative and historical discourses that have informed the constructions of race, gender, and ethnicities in the last five hundred years and that still reverberate in our time" (Alarcón, "Traddutora, Traditora" 127). The verb "reverberate" suggests a dynamic and reciprocal relationship between historical moments—a living and regenerative framework that is more appropriate for these writers' work than burial. Alarcón's language is kinetic, calling to mind the image of a woman "catching" with her body the constructions of the past as they pass through her; she is thus able to transform them along the path of their passing, rewriting their passing as she embodies them differently.

---

nous jewelry and posing with indigenous artifacts. I discuss this costuming at greater length in the section of this chapter entitled "Self-Portraits in Pain."

When Anzaldúa, Moraga, and Castillo turn to the Aztec past, they simultaneously turn to their Chicano past and to the relationship created by *movimiento* writers between Chicano and "native." One of the most famous literary texts of the *movimiento* is Rodolfo "Corky" Gonzáles's 1967 poem, *I am Joaquín / Soy Joaquín*—a bilingual epic retelling of Mexican history that gathers different moments and key historical figures into one "I." The first-person narrator asserts that multiple identities are internal to him—"I am Aztec prince and Christian Christ" (Gonzáles 20), "I am the Maya Prince. . . . I am the sword and flame of Cortez the despot" (5)—and his combination of indigenous and Spanish figures incorporates both sides of Mexico's *mestizo* heritage and gives body to the history of conquest. Yet this history ultimately cuts out Europe and centers on the indigenous, inverting the power dynamics of dominant history to rewrite the future: "The Indian has endured. . . . The Mestizo must yet overcome, / And the Gachupín we'll just ignore" (13). The historical figures Gonzáles chooses to embody in his hero are warriors for the Mexican people, from Cuauhtémoc, Padre Hidalgo, and Benito Juárez to twentieth-century revolutionaries, Zapata, Huerta, and Madero. The adjectives he draws from these figures are "Proud and Noble" (3), "Arrogant with pride / Bold with Machismo / Rich in courage" (15), suggesting that the ultimate endurance of Joaquín as a heroic figure depends on masculine force (17). Other than Tonantzin (the Aztec goddess at whose shrine the Virgin of Guadalupe appeared in 1531), the only woman this "I" takes on is nameless:

> sheltered beneath
> her shawl of black,
> deep and sorrowful
> eyes
> That bear the pain of sons long buried
> or dying,
> Dead on the battlefield or on the barbwire
> of social strife
>
> *(Gonzáles,* I am Joaquín *17)*

The only agency imagined for women in this patriarchal history is that of praying for men.

I am certainly not the first to critique the male bias of movement texts like this one.[17] I choose this poem, though, because of its emphasis on the painful sacrifice of Joaquín's body as it moves through Mexican history:

17. See Chabram-Dernersesian, "I Throw Punches for My Race," for instance.

through the course of the poem, he "bleeds in many ways" (13), on the altars of Moctezuma, under the whips of slave masters, against the walls of firing squads, in prison. Anzaldúa, Moraga, and Castillo also describe the incorporation of Mexican history as a painful process, but the embodiments they adopt thwart the warrior sensibility of both Aztec and Chicano. They give body to marginalized figures who have not been claimed by mainstream or Chicano historical narratives, and they give them bodies that expose, critique, and ultimately defy the violence of both narratives. While Gonzáles's poem takes five hundred years of history into one first-person body, Moraga's *Waiting in the Wings: Portrait of a Queer Motherhood* (1997), for instance, multiplies bodies by giving birth and by building family with a diverse network of allies. Her logic is expansive, while Gonzáles was binding up strength and defending identity politics for Chicano nationalism. There are ways in which Moraga's recovery of the past repeats Gonzáles's historiographical gesture, perhaps more than she intended. As Joaquín takes on the identities of warriors that preceded him in order to strengthen his own rebellion, Moraga incorporates Paul Monette, Audre Lorde, César Chávez, and others into her self-made "*familia.*" By choosing not warriors but the sick and the dying as her heroes, however, Moraga's genealogy deconstructs as it builds, leading to a conclusion that is less heroic—or differently heroic. Gonzáles's poem ends with the line, "I shall endure," but the logic of Anzaldúa's, Moraga's, and Castillo's portraits is less invested in the boundaries of an "I" and open to continued corporeal and political upheavals. Indeed, Moraga's narrative concludes with "This, too, will pass" (Moraga, *Waiting* 127).

Perhaps "hagiography," the lives of saints, is a more appropriate term for the ways in which these writers use the past, since it focuses on mystical bodies and the lessons learned from their lives. Hagiographies reflect on the sacred significance of individuals' everyday experiences, pain, and symbolic illnesses. They are not distinct chronologies as much as they are ritualistic reiterations of already familiar spiritual lessons. They select individual moments and individual lives that embody these lessons and isolate them from larger historical narratives. According to de Certeau, "Unlike texts that must be practiced or believed, the Saints' Lives oscillate between the believable and the marvelous, advocating what one is at liberty to think or do. From both points of view they create an area of 'vacation' and of new conditions outside of everyday time and rule" (de Certeau 274). Rather than being faithful to one chronological account, hagiographies are outside of normative histories and more marvelous than they are true to material facts. Their function is not mimetic but, rather, instructional—"at stake is not a story, but a 'legend,' that is, what 'must be read'" (280)—and cultural—"the productive 'edification' of an image intended to protect the group from dispersion" (272). González's invocations of Cuauhtémoc and Zapata, like Anzaldúa's, Moraga's, and Castillo's invocations of Coatlicue and Coyolxauhqui, are less about their "biographies" than about how their bodies have given life to cultural ideologies. Indeed, as Yvonne Yarbro-Bejarano notes in her analysis of Anzaldúa, Chicana feminist invocations of Mesoamerican goddesses are not historical but analytical, critical, and literary, an "imaginative appropriation and redefinition . . . in the service of a new mythos" (Yarbro-Bejarano, "Gloria Anzaldúa's *Borderlands/La Frontera*" 19).

This "new mythos" is open-ended rather than doctrinal. Much has been written about Chicana feminism's indebtedness to Aztec goddesses, the fertility goddess Coatlicue, in particular, but the writers I analyze here do not elevate any single icon to emulate. Instead, Anzaldúa, Moraga, and Castillo have invoked a cacophonous list of indigenous figures throughout their careers, paying attention to the internal complexity of each. In her account of the Virgin of Guadalupe, Anzaldúa jams this icon with a discordant list of names in Nahuatl (the language used by the Aztecs), which could be read as an inversion of Chicano nationalism's singular self-naming as well as of the conventional, patriarchal iconization of the Virgin.[18] For Anzaldúa, the Virgin of Guadalupe is a *mestiza* icon whose history poses her as neither purely European nor purely Aztec.[19] This brown-skinned incarnation of the Virgin Mary appeared in 1531, to the *indio* Juan Diego, near the temple to the Aztec goddess Tonantzin. According to Anzaldúa, the apparition might have been Cuatlalopeuh, "the one who has dominion over serpents" or "the one who is at one with the beasts," but she was misnamed "Guadalupe," the patroness of West Central Spain, because the name was homophonous with

18. Rudolfo Anaya, in particular, celebrates "the Chicano community's" unifying decision to name itself, in the singular, through nationalist belonging to Aztlán (Anaya, "Aztlán" 230), and the Virgin of Guadalupe was one of the symbols deployed to unite Chicanos during the *movimiento*.

19. La Virgen de Guadalupe is a sort of patron saint of *mestizaje*, a mediator between the indios and the Europeans, between this world and the next. Anzaldúa writes: "*La Virgen de Guadalupe* is the symbol of ethnic identity and of the tolerance for ambiguity that Chicanos-*mexicanos*, people of mixed race, people who have Indian blood, people who cross cultures, by necessity possess" (Anzaldúa, *Borderlands* 30).

Cuatlalopeuh (Anzaldúa, *Borderlands* 29). Anzaldúa explains that Cuatlalopeuh and Tonantzin are both aspects of Coatlicue, goddess of creation *and* destruction, who is represented with a skirt of twisting serpents and a necklace of human hearts, hands, or skulls (27). She then divides Coatlicue into different aspects, Tlazolteotl and Cihuacoatl, and historicizes the split of Tonantzin from Coatlicue as a patriarchal effort to split maternal femininity from natural sexuality. This fragmentation of "the goddess" into multiple names and multiple incarnations is consistent with pre-Columbian cosmology but complicated for nationalist unity. (Indeed, in speaking of this segment of Anzaldúa's work, critics usually cut out the unwieldy list of names and focus on "Coatlicue.") Anzaldúa reinjects this pre-Columbian discordance into the Virgin of Guadalupe. And the "Coatlicue" she worships likewise exceeds any bounded characterization by embodying multiple attributes and by remaining open to renaming.

I appreciate the potential irony of using the term hagiography to describe pre-Columbian goddesses and contemporary Chicanas. Castillo pokes fun at the idea of hagiography in her 1994 novel, *So Far From God*. One of the main characters, who rose from the dead at the age of three, is canonized "La Loca Santa" (the crazy saint) after she dies from AIDS, and the final chapter in the novel describes her mother's formation of the international organization Mothers of Martyrs and Saints, which sells commemorative pens and T-shirts and to which the martyred dead make regular ectoplasmic appearances (Castillo, *So Far From God* 247–52).[20] Additionally, the lengthy and descriptive chapter titles in *So Far From God* parody hagiographies like the *Vida* of Saint Teresa of Avila, whose chapter titles are long enough to summarize the content. Mexican-American performance artist Guillermo Gómez-Peña mockingly embodies hagiography in his performance piece, *Temple of Confessions*,

20. As Rita Cano Alcalá notes: "in *So Far from God* [Castillo] uses the hagiographic genre to canonize everyday women who struggle for political and economic self-determination, environmental protection, and spiritual self-discovery. The pantheon of saints in this *vidas de santas* represents spiritual, physical, and political models typically not celebrated in Church texts. Through their representations as curanderas, locas, putas, and vendidas, Sofia and her daughters retool the concepts of martyrdom and saintliness" (Alcalá 13–14). I don't mean to suggest that Anzaldúa, Moraga, and Castillo all invoke the medieval Catholic tradition this literally but, rather, that their historiography pays attention to the lessons learned from embodied experience and takes seriously mystical and spiritual dimensions that exceed modern notions of verifiable data.

which solicits confessions from visitors to a mock temple that fuses pre-Columbian, Catholic, and Chicano iconography. "El Pre-Columbiano Vato" (with Vato signifying something like "dude" in Chicano slang) and "San Pocho Aztlaneca" (translated, roughly, as the saint of assimilated Mexican Americans of Aztlán) pose in front of a Styrofoam pyramid (whose "in-authenticity" is meant to be visible), alternately drinking blood from rubber hearts, flagellating themselves, inhaling paint, smoking marijuana, and playing with a "ghetto blaster." Two women move through the crowd as "living icons," a "*chola*/nun" and a "dominatrix/nun," urging audience members to confess (Gómez-Peña 15–30). Both of these examples reflect postmodern irony about the relationship between Chicana/o, Aztec, and Catholic traditions. The Chicana feminist hagiographies I analyze here are different, are serious about their cultural fusions, their faith, and the power of iconography. "Our faith," Anzaldúa argues, "is rooted in indigenous attributes, images, symbols, magic and myth" (Anzaldúa, *Borderlands* 30), privileging pre-Columbian understandings of gender, nature, iconography, and spirituality over European ones. I take such claims seriously, examining how the sensibility of Anzaldúa's, Moraga's, and Castillo's writings jars against modern understandings of humanity and the universe.[21] The bodily matter of their work resonates with otherworldly possibilities. A Chicana feminist hagiography thus links materiality to spirituality and ancient icons to contemporary political needs.

Self-Portraits in Pain

In 1993, Moraga vowed to recover the body of the "Mechicana" who was "wounded" or "broken" by history in order to "create a portrait of la Mechicana before the 'Fall'" (Moraga, *The Last Generation* 72). In a 1994 essay, "Saintly Mother and Soldier's Whore," Castillo similarly sought to uncover the spiritual "undercurrent" "which has been with woman since pre-Conquest times and which precedes Christianity in Europe" (Castillo, *Massacre of the Dreamers* 95). She proposed a new Xicanista "myth-making" "to guide us out of historical convolution and de-evolution," reaching back before "history," as it has been written, "to write our own story: *In the beginning, there was Eva*" (119). In these

21. Emma Pérez might view these claims in psychoanalytic terms, as "the buried desires of the unconscious," where "desire rubs against colonial repressions to construct resistant, oppositional, transformative, diasporic subjectivities that erupt and move into decolonial desires" (E. Pérez 110).

proposals, both Moraga and Castillo eschewed even the terms "Chicana" (with its indebtedness to the Chicano *movimiento*) and "feminist" (with its European and Euro-American history), adopting the terms "Mechicana" and "Xicanista" to ground their politics in an idealized vision of pre-Conquest, pre-patriarchal Mexica values. ("Mexica," a broad cultural descriptor for the ancient peoples of Mesoamerica, is one of the terms often meant to invoke the pre-Imperial ancestors of the Aztecs.) Adopting this pre-Conquest framework in autobiographical writings enables them to decolonize their own bodies and identities. In tracing an inheritance from Coatlicue, Anzaldúa, too, reached back to a mythic pre-patriarchal *indigenismo*, before "the male-dominated Azteca-Mexica culture drove the powerful female deities underground by giving them monstrous attributes and by substituting male deities in their place" (Anzaldúa, *Borderlands* 27). Unlike the longed-for era before European colonialism, which is well documented, the longed-for era before patriarchal domination lacks historical evidence (and is perhaps therefore laden with more possibility). These historiographic gestures are visionary rather than conventionally historical. This is the foundation of Chicana feminist hagiography.[22]

Moraga claims Frida Kahlo as an ally in the process of recovering indigenous women's broken image (a comparison that asserts Moraga's "right" to and ritual enactment of Mexican identity).[23] Kahlo's use of self-portraiture to recreate Mexican femininity in her own body provides another way of understanding Chicana feminism's repeated return to autobiography. "We too ultimately seek the divine in the beauty we create," Moraga writes; "Sometimes that beauty is merely a portrait of mutilation in color or language. This is something Frida Kahlo understood" (Moraga, *The Last Generation* 72). The use of "portraiture" as a metaphor is significant, since portraits record history through the human

22. José David Saldívar's analysis of *Borderlands* in *Identity Politics Reconsidered* is also helpful, here. He argues that Anzaldúa's investment in *nepantilism*, which he defines as "violent cultural in-betweenness," creates an alternative epistemological ground. These writers' choice to structure their knowledge around pre-Conquest cultures, while residing in the contemporary United States, accentuates what Saldívar describes as the "anti-colonial" posture of border writers' new cultural formations (Saldívar 160–62).

23. Castillo also quotes Kahlo when describing her disabled heroine in *Peel My Love Like an Onion*; indeed, Carmen la Coja might be modeled after Kahlo, since both Castillo's heroine and Kahlo herself suffered from childhood polio and both have a disabled leg. I discuss this comparison at length in Chapter 4.

figure. Kahlo's self-portraits force viewers to reimagine the contours of the female body, masking it with costume, incorporating trees and animals, splitting it in two. The fact that these portraits depict *her* body, not just an abstract feminine, makes these intra- and intercorporeal reworkings very literal. She attaches surreal, monstrous, or absurd qualities to the apparent "real" of her own body, thereby denormalizing, critiquing, or spoofing the historical legacies she, herself, embodies: her family's genealogy, Catholic and Aztec images of women, the spinal injury suffered in her accident, her several miscarriages, the amputation of her leg. Since the body in these images is always recognizable as Kahlo's body, analysis of her work often conflates biography with artistic analysis and forgets to comment upon formalistic techniques, as if her self-portraits were as mimetic as the photographs often displayed alongside them. This slippage between artist and text happens in much criticism of Anzaldúa's, Moraga's, and Castillo's texts, too. Hagiography, as a genre, is about this slippage. Hagiography is also about the slippage between the text/canvas and the reader/viewer who is driven to sympathy, discomfort, confession, or emulation.

Pain is an obvious link between the works of these writers and those of Kahlo. The current popularity—or hagiography—of Kahlo revolves around pain. Attention to her crippling accident and her injured body often dominates over attention to her painting.[24] People are fascinated by her body in pain in the same way that they are fascinated by others' car wrecks: seeing the suffering of others reminds them of their own health and security. Or perhaps they are simply fascinated by the otherness of pain and injury. Pain and suffering are romanticized and fetishized when associated with "others" (like women, slaves, or prisoners of war). In *Devouring Frida*, Margaret Lindauer contends that "characterizations of Kahlo's physical and emotional health exemplify how medical diagnosis

24. In September 1925, a streetcar crashed into a bus Kahlo was riding. The accident broke her spine, her collarbone, her ribs, her pelvis, and her leg (in eleven places) (Fuentes 11). According to the account given by Alejandro Gómez Arias, the friend sitting with her on the bus during the accident, "she rather bizarrely had been stripped of her clothes and covered with gold glitter that another passenger had been carrying" (Lindauer 55). Her body was impaled on a handrail that purportedly entered her back and came out through her vagina (Fuentes 12). This image has largely defined Kahlo's identity in the American imagination, especially after Julie Taymor's 2002 film *Frida* paused over it, longer than other scenes, with a prolonged aestheticizing gaze. I leave this information in an endnote to avoid repeating that lingering gaze.

colludes with social prescription to maintain gender dichotomies" (Lindauer 54). The illnesses and injuries attributed to Kahlo "collude with" misogynist myths about women's pathology. And the images sold in curio shops—now decorating the refrigerators, mouse pads, and earlobes of her fans—iconize Kahlo's blood, tears, and mutilation and reinforce the mythic image of the suffering Mexican woman.

In her study of women's illnesses in Mexico, anthropologist Kaja Finkler argues that pain dominates Mexican cultural discourse about women, where the central role of the Virgin radiates outward to measure all women by the "suffering mother" ideal: "The culturally legitimated ideology of the suffering woman pervades Mexican society and is continually reinforced by women's experience in their daily life. In fact, the ideology of sacrifice sustains women in their daily lives," valorizing self-abnegation and pain (Finkler 56). This "ideology of sacrifice" might also derive from pre-Columbian Mexico, where sacrifice was a sacred public performance of culture. Regardless of its origin, I would argue that part of the romance that Mexico holds for those North of the border is its association with suffering: hence the commodification in the United States of the Day of the Dead, of the tools of human sacrifice, and even of the spiciness or potential harmfulness of Mexican food and drink.[25] So it is with some reservation that I embark upon this discussion of the ideology of pain in Mexico and risk reinforcing the myopic fascination with Frida Kahlo as a site of injury rather than artistic agency.

One of the central tensions in Kahlo criticism is the extent to which her self-portraits are personal (and thus to be viewed through the lenses of biography or psychoanalysis) or political (and thus to be viewed through the lenses of Marxism and Mexican cultural nationalism).[26] This

25. Though Mexican culture embraces death in a playful manner—with dancing skeletons, for instance—I worry about how this playfulness translates across the border. See Bost, "Women and Chile at the Alamo: Feeding U.S. Colonial Mythology," for a discussion of U.S. tourism, sadism, and pain in Mexico.

26. Hayden Herrera, who is best known for her 1983 biography, *Frida* (which has become more influential, particularly in the United States, in the wake of Julie Taymor's 2002 film based upon it), is perhaps the most "guilty" of employing a strictly biographical and psychological approach. Her analysis of Kahlo's work, *Frida Kahlo: The Paintings* (1991), reads the paintings alongside a chronological biographical narrative, identifying paintings as they emerge from traumatic events in Kahlo's life, including the loss of her mother, her husband's infidelity, her inability to bear a child, and her increasing pain, illness, and dis-

debate within Kahlo criticism is highly gendered as well as reflective of debates among Kahlo's political and artistic contemporaries. To assume that Kahlo's self-portraits are merely personal assumes that political art must transcend the individual and move out into public, where Kahlo's male contemporaries (and fellow Communists and cultural nationalists)

---

ability. For Herrera, "the palpable energy that radiates from Kahlo's small, meticulously observed self-portraits comes from the ferocity of her dialogue with herself and the directness with which she told her story. . . . For Kahlo, painting self-portraits was a form of both psychological surgery and denial" (Herrera, *Frida Kahlo* 3–4). Herrera attempts to depoliticize even Kahlo's most overtly political paintings, arguing that Kahlo "tried to politicize her still lifes by inserting flags, political inscriptions, and peace doves. But Frida's paintings remained a hymn to herself and to life" (212). Margaret Lindauer (*Devouring Frida*, 1999) rejects this conflation of author and corpus, which assumes a "one-to-one association of life events to the meaning of a painting" (Lindauer 2), and critiques (implicitly sexist) approaches like Herrera's that limit Kahlo's work to a narrative of her physical and emotional health, her pain, her love, and her mourning—all "prescribed" feminine roles (116). For Lindauer, "texts that most powerfully relegate Kahlo to a feminine sphere of apolitical art and private life uncritically and insidiously sequester the artist from broader social contexts" (5). Janice Helland, in 1991, likewise critiqued psychological approaches that "whitewash" Kahlo's works "of their bloody, brutal, and overtly political content," which she described as "a romantic nationalism that focused on traditional art and artifacts uniting all *indigenistas*" (Helland 8). In Helland's interpretation, images like the wounded heart "may also relate to [Kahlo's] emotional and physical suffering," but the indigenous cultural sources of these images make them not personal but culturally nationalist (10, 12). Lindauer suggests that Helland did not take Kahlo's politics seriously enough either: merely identifying Aztec elements in the paintings "without discussing relationships between Kahlo's symbolism and the particular philosophies she had outlined briefly" and assuming a universal and "romantic" nationalism in post-revolutionary Mexico rather than differentiating Kahlo's positions from that of her (male) contemporaries (Lindauer 115). I appreciate Lindauer's analysis, in particular, since her metacritical approach considers "the language of interpretation and veneration through which the popular persona 'Frida Kahlo' has been constructed" (2). This approach foregrounds the terms in which Kahlo is discussed, terms that reflect the political and cultural interests of art critics, art collectors, and cultural consumers. In this light, the debate between personal versus political approaches to Kahlo's work can be said to reflect tensions in feminist thought, since Kahlo's recent popularity owes much to feminism and feminists' interest in her pain, her boisterous self-assertiveness, and the modern "art world's" tendency to see her only in the shadow of her husband.

were ironically earning expensive commissions and becoming famous (as individuals) for their gigantic murals and one-man shows. This rift between personal and political art is mirrored in the assumed disjuncture between feminist politics and Marxism or cultural nationalism, which Marxist feminists and women-of-color feminists have been battling for generations. This rift is based on an assumed disjuncture between self and community, which my study hopes to challenge. In my view, the personal and the political are one: for the Chicana feminists I study as well as for Kahlo, herself, the self is the site where politics are experienced and self-portraits are a place in which to embody political vision, to portray alternate ways of being in the world, and to explore the relationship between self and others. For feminism, the female body reflects "larger" political concerns, ranging from global economics to the environment, and representations of the female body are thus not simply self-reflective.

Paula Cooey overtly addresses how the personal and the political are mapped onto each other in Kahlo's work, writing, in *Religious Imagination and the Body*, that "Kahlo would probably have espoused in a later time that the personal is indeed political" (Cooey 102). Cooey reminds us that Kahlo's "personal" reflections foreground gender, class, and ethnicity, all of which are inseparable from politics. Cooey critiques "critics and scholars who interpret [Kahlo's] paintings in light of her diaries" and who "sometimes tend toward psychological reduction that denies or diminishes her politics" (99). "Psychologism" is particularly problematic for Cooey, since it "privatizes and domesticates Kahlo, thereby making her more acceptable to an ideology of individualism" (102). Yet Cooey is not trying to frame Kahlo as a spokesperson for any one political movement:

A Mexican Euro-mestiza, whose parents were Catholic and cultural Jew, a Marxist woman who saw her pain and pleasure, represented by multiple projections of her body, as metaphor for her country and its relation to an oppressive neighbor, she deliberately sought to bring into interrelation differing and, in some cases, conflicting religiopolitical images and religious genres of those she viewed as most dispossessed by Mexico's history, those she viewed as dispossessing, and those most celebratory of Mexico's possible future. Her body projected came to represent many cultural voices in tension within her, holding in common only a detouring of any religious and political tendencies to de-materialize human values.

Her images became no longer simulation, but flesh itself, groaning with value. (128)

In this way, the projection that Kahlo's body became, dispersed throughout her multiple portraits and self-portraits, was a conglomeration of the multiple bodies she identified with throughout her life, a combination of different interests that assumes its own "flesh" in the feelings of its viewers and the actions of those moved by it. Though this language depersonalizes Kahlo's body, it maintains materiality and feeling; it also fails to assimilate the body into any coherent symbol. As Cooey suggests, Kahlo's work "sustain[s] sufficient ambiguity and tension to resist oversimplification and thereby avoid ready use for totalitarian interests" (99).

One of the most obvious and most remarked-upon layers of political content in Kahlo's work is a celebration of indigenous culture, which her paintings express not through a retelling of the conquest of native peoples in Mexico's history (as portrayed in Diego Rivera's murals) but by adorning her own living body with indigenous artifacts and imaginatively locating herself in culturally indigenous worlds.[27] Her self is the place where she explores the relationship between nations and natives, the cultural past and the cultural future. Kahlo's self-portraits situate pre-Columbian symbols in a multifaceted context that alters these symbols' significance in light of the artist's personal experience, her Communism, her modernism, and her movements between Mexico and industrial "gringolandia." In this way, Kahlo's *mestiza* body is a nexus for reconfiguring the relationship between different worldviews.

The idealization of indigenous culture in the Chicano movement echoes that of Mexican modernists, and the creation of a new Chicano identity mirrors, in many ways, the *indigenismo* of artists, writers, and philosophers in Revolutionary and post-Revolutionary Mexico. In the 1920s and '30s, many Mexican intellectuals intent on continuing the spirit of the Revolution (Kahlo, Rivera, and José Vasconcelos among them) sought regeneration, redemption, and cultural revolution from their indigenous heritage. This seeking was often posed as a recovery of something lost, ignoring the present of indigenous Mexicans. (The dominant culture might have repressed the indigenous components of its *mestizaje*, but many indigenous Mexicans maintain continuity with their pre-Columbian cultures.) While the state sought to re-center indigenous Mexico in museums and school curricula, indigenous peoples remained

---

27. See, in particular, Helland, "Aztec Imagery in Frida Kahlo's Paintings."

(and still remain) on the margins of power and the margins of the Mexican economy. Moreover, much of the cultural elevation of the Indian, in Mexico as in the United States, has been figured through distorting, romantic, misogynist, and primitivist lenses.

In *Mestizo Modernism*, Tace Hedrick regards the marketing of Kahlo's image in modern Mexico as "indigenous drag." The daughter of a Hungarian Jewish father and a Mexican mother, Kahlo adopted what would be recognized as indigenous dress and indigenous jewelry, regardless of her own ethnicity, after marrying Rivera (Hedrick 165–67). Hedrick argues that the *indigenismo* at the center of Mexican modernism was based on these artists' and intellectuals' longing for cultural authenticity. In the early twentieth century, "Like Europeans, Latin Americans too were looking—and more often than not it was a look backwards—for sources of personal creative energy, a refuge from urban life, for the origins of a national history, or all these combined. But growing nationalist sentiment demanded that such sources be indigenous, and even regional, rather than far away" (45). Latin Americans found "primitive" creative origins right in their own backyards and, often, right in their own bloodlines, though centuries of *mestizaje* and recent industrialization increasingly obfuscated these origins. "For these moderns, the assumptions learned from evolutionist and positivist ways of thinking meant that what they thought they saw when they looked at Indians, for example, were both social and political gaps; and their ways of thinking about nation meant that what was wanted instead was continuity" (44). The disjuncture between an increasingly modern and industrial nation and the continuing "primitive" traditions of the nation's natives caused anxiety because it indicated a fracture within the nation. In the spirit of nationalist unity following the Revolution, Mexican moderns sought to integrate indigenous Mexicans within the nation, leading to a simultaneous emphasis on the nation's indigenous origins as well as the *mestizaje* that unified the nation racially—two types of racial thought that, though they might seem opposed in theory, were, according to Hedrick, intertwined in practice (47). As minister of education, Vasconcelos, for instance, "was actively promoting a nationalist-indigenous celebration of authentic Indian and African cultures while advancing the whitening, or at least lightening, virtues of miscegenation," especially in treatises like his 1925 *La raza cósmica* (Hedrick 48).[28]

28. This vocabulary of the "cosmic" race was embraced by *movimiento* Chicanos in the United States and, in 1987, revised by Anzaldúa in her oft-quoted

Like Vasconcelos, Kahlo dressed her *mestizo* modernism with a mask of *indigenismo* and surrounded herself with artifacts of the pre-Columbian cultures that were increasingly regarded as Mexico's ennobling patrimony. Hedrick analyzes images of Rivera and Kahlo posed inexplicably with pots and figurines:

> Indeed, because pre-Columbian work did not seem to speak its own social meaning to contemporary Americans, such perceived muteness freed modernist artists to appreciate its stylized and repetitive formal aspects while at the same time assuming that there was an unbroken racial or cultural line between such artifacts, their ancient makers, and contemporary Indian artists and their work. (170)

Unmoored from their historical origins, pre-Columbian objects were powerfully mysterious to modern Mexicans, blank slates upon which they would project their own designs. Hedrick compares Kahlo's "indigenous drag" to popular Mexican calendar art depicting Aztec myths, implying that the modern embrace of indigenous culture was superficial, a gesture of self-promotion in which the modern "voice" assumed indigenous culture to be mute. "Drag," then, assumes a sort of "heterology," a remote otherness of the indigenous (as the) past. The early twentieth century was an era of "modernizing," rather than listening to or learning from, the Indian:

> Even as Kahlo collected hundreds of examples of peasant and Indian arts and crafts and dressed herself in Indian costume, government policy makers under the newly liberalized Cardenas administration sought to modernize actual Indian peasant women, weaning them away from their supposed traditional ways of religiosity, superstition, and poor hygiene. (178)

---

essay, "*La conciencia de la mestiza.*" The first paragraph of Anzaldúa's essay begins by quoting Vasconcelos's idealization of *mestizaje* as a global synthesis, suggests that "from this racial, ideological, cultural and biological cross-pollination, an 'alien' consciousness is presently in the making," and then engenders this alienness as a "*conciencia de mujer*" [consciousness of woman] (Anzaldúa, *Borderlands* 77). Vasconcelos's language, however, is insistently patriarchal, arguing, for instance, that the racial synthesis of *la raza cósmica* was "*más capaz de verdadera fraternidad y de vision realmente universal*" [more capable of true fraternity and of real universal vision] (Vasconcelos 60). It is significant that Anzaldúa appropriates this consciousness of alienation and cross-pollination for feminism, perhaps referring to the ways in which *mestizaje* is formed in the bodies of women as well as to women's marginal position in the body politic.

Whatever it was that Mexican moderns sought to preserve of their indigenous past, it evidently was not religious or corporeal practices.

Today, after nearly a century of additional archeological and analytical work in Latin American studies, pre-Columbian cultural artifacts are less mute than they might have been to Mexican moderns. I believe that Anzaldúa's, Moraga's, and Castillo's invocations of indigenous Mexico go deeper than "drag." As U.S. Chicanas, their greater distance from indigenous Mexico might augment their idealization of the indigenous, but it also augments their desire for Mexican rootedness. In my analyses of these writers' work in the following chapters, I focus on how they attempt to detach their own bodies from the hegemony of Euro-America by situating themselves relative to pre-Columbian cosmography. Rather than borrowing Tehuana dresses or Aztec necklaces, they adopt indigenous understandings of humanity, nature, the divine, and the relationship among all of these elements of the universe. Their perceptions of native Mexico emerge not from daily contact with an indigenous underclass or visible remnants of pre-Columbian culture (which might, in fact, lead to superficial understanding) but, rather, from books.[29] Their native feeling is an intellectual exercise. I will demonstrate how the ways they understand their own bodies, and their sensations of pain and illness, are drawn from interpretations of pre-Columbian culture that have been developed in recent Latin American studies.

Though the photographs of Kahlo in indigenous costume might seem superficial and self-promoting, I believe that her work also reflects a deeper indigenous sensibility. Like Anzaldúa, Kahlo often represented herself as "torn between ways," with a border splitting her body between two worlds (Anzaldúa, *Borderlands* 2, 78), an overtly political vision of Mexico's difficult balancing of cultures as well as its ambivalent relationship to modernity.[30] Kahlo, in particular, was torn between science (her first academic passion), modernist aesthetics, and the indigenous cultures to which she felt politically attached. Indigenous artifacts visibly jar against the modern technologies also present in Kahlo's work, indicating a material and psychological duality consistent

29. Indeed, Castillo is professionally trained in Latin American Studies, with a Social Sciences M.A. from the University of Chicago and a Ph.D. in American Studies from the University of Bremen.

30. Hedrick likewise emphasizes Kahlo's ambivalent historical and political position as a modern Mexican *mestiza* trained in European philosophies and aesthetics (Hedrick 185).

with pre-Columbian boundary states. *The Two Fridas* (1939) depicts cultural conflict at the aesthetic level, juxtaposing indigenous versus European fashion, but also at a more sentient corporeal level, opening the figures' shared heart and giving viewers a detailed (and painful) look at the anatomical fracture that bloodies the European-style dress (see Plate 1a). The heart, of course, recalls both Aztec sacrifice as well as Catholic "sacred heart" imagery, bringing together medical, spiritual, and cultural understandings.[31]

Medicine appears as a distinct epistemology in Kahlo's *Henry Ford Hospital*, a 1932 self-portrait representing one of her miscarriages (see Plate 1b). The ribbons of blood connecting Kahlo to fetus, flower, snail, and machine, in this self-portrait, "show her own body as effecting the (often painful) connection between the scientific and the organic worlds" (Hedrick 189). By linking birth and death, as well as organic and inorganic matter, *Henry Ford Hospital* defies the hierarchical oppositions imposed by modern Western thought. While Sarah Lowe argues that "the medical point of view allows Kahlo some distance from the excruciating surgical ordeals" (Lowe 99), I would argue the reverse, that painting enables Kahlo to subjectify the object of the medical gaze. In defiance of the logic of "heterology," Kahlo's painting assigns a viable subject position to the bleeding patient. Lowe claims that *Henry Ford Hospital* "uses organic metaphors" and "an 'x-ray' vision" gained from Kahlo's study of physiology "to convey the inarticulable" and to "exorcise" her demons (99). Instead, I believe it is medical science that silences (or at least displaces) private experience of physiological processes, and Kahlo's use of self-portraiture enables her to open otherwise concealed or ineffable feelings to the public. Moreover, allusions to pre-Columbian sacrifice

---

31. As Hayden Herrera comments, "the bloodiness and self-mortification [in Kahlo's work] goes back to Aztec tradition, for the Aztecs not only practiced human sacrifice, they also pricked their own skin and punctured their ears to draw blood so that crops would flourish. But it was Christianity that brought to colonial Mexico the depiction of pain in realistic and human terms, with the result that almost every Mexican church has a frighteningly veristic sculpture of Christ, either whipped at the post, dragging his cross, or dead, his body always full of bloody, suppurating wounds" (Herrera, *Frida* 283). Herrera argues that Kahlo borrowed her "poetry of blood" (189) from Catholicism "because her paintings were, in their own way, about salvation" (283). I would argue, instead, that blood is one of the ways in which Kahlo demonstrated—through mestiza Mexican visual rhetoric—the interconnectedness of living things, and of life with death, as well as forcing visceral connections between viewers and her paintings.

traditions sacralize the experience of miscarriage, providing a way for viewers to experience the blood, the pain, and the dread associated with miscarriage as sacred, communal, and meaningful.

This painting filters miscarriage through a distinctly pre-Columbian cosmology. The idea of a miscarriage, itself, reflects the logic of the Aztec fertility goddess Coatlicue, who represented both the creation and the destruction of life. (In numerous paintings and in written works, Kahlo celebrated Coatlicue's embrace of life and death [Helland 9, 11; Herrera, *Frida* 214].) As I will demonstrate further in Chapter 3, Aztec conceptions of health radiated outward from the individual to the community, just as Kahlo's body in this image is linked, by organic and inorganic circuitry, to other beings. This portrait is resonant with human-sacrifice traditions, as the blood of one central body reaches out to regenerate others. Indeed, the industrial machines on the horizon of the painting's landscape resemble grain belts and storage silos, which might signal the Aztec link between blood and food, human and agricultural life cycles. One might even note the triangular arrangement of the horizon's buildings, which frames the artist's bleeding body within the shape of a pyramid.

Kahlo returned to the self-portrait in bed many times throughout her career. *My Birth* (1932), *The Dream* (1940), and *Without Hope* (1945), for instance, all depict the artist in bed, not with a lover, but with death and new life, represented by self-birth, skeletons, plants, and blood. These are conceptual paintings that reflect the imbrication of life and death in pre-Columbian cosmology, and they embody subject positions whose life and blood radiate outward to touch others. In Lindauer's interpretation, *Without Hope* reflects Kahlo's resistance to medicalized containment (see Plate 2a). Though, in this painting, "she is literally enveloped in a biological representation of procreation," pinned down in bed and covered with a blanket patterned in "medical diagrams of sperm, ova, and cellular fission," she fights back against this representation. As food is force-fed into her mouth from above, "the funnel overflows with regurgitated food," and "the force-feeding is ineffective" (Lindauer 70–71). Hayden Herrera interprets this painting as an expression of "violence done to Frida's passive body" and her personal disgust at having to eat pureed foods after an operation (Herrera, *Frida Kahlo* 185, 187), but it is not clear in which direction this food is moving. Indeed, the process of ingestion seems to coincide with projection outward from the body; perhaps the food is an incarnation of voice that flows out of the mouth, a sign of self-assertion and creation. The "food" in this self-portrait includes a whole chicken, a whole pig, two fish heads, and a skull with "Frida" imprinted upon it. Unprocessed and uncensored, this "food" incorporates multiple lives. Herrera quotes the painter's inscription on the back of the canvas: "everything moves in tune with what the belly encloses" (qtd. in Herrera, *Frida Kahlo* 187). This quote suggests that the artist's body is an organic machine that both contains and "moves" all, a veritable Coatlicue consuming and regurgitating life, and the image itself, with twin fish heads on the top of the pile, recalls the twinned serpents that form Coatlicue's head (see Plate 2b). This painting, too, has a prominent pyramid shape in the back (a volcanic rock formation), with both sun and moon in the sky, again positioning the painter at the crux of an Aztec-style sacrifice and at the juncture of life and death, day and night.[32]

Like Kahlo, Anzaldúa, Moraga, and Castillo use self-portraiture to represent their feelings of pain and otherness as sacred boundary states and to identify these feelings as emanating from Mexican history. Moraga, in particular, has devoted much of her work to self-representation, beginning with her early poems and essays that examine her own white skin (inherited from her Anglo father), recalcitrant mouth, and metaphorically amputated hands and tongue.[33] In her essay "A Long Line of

32. Herrera interprets the simultaneity of sun and moon as a reference "to the Aztec notion of an eternal war between light and dark, or to Christ's crucifixion, where the sun and moon together indicate the sorrow of all creation of the death of the savior" (Herrera, *Frida* 348).

33. A poem from Moraga's collection *Loving in the War Years* (1983), "You Call it, *Amputation*," recalls Kahlo's self-portraits after the amputation of her leg: "You call it / *am pu tation* / but even after the cut / they say the toes still itch" (Moraga, *Loving in the War Years* 82). As with any other loss, Kahlo's paintings of her leg and Moraga's poem still feel the limbs as memory, embodying something that medical science tells them is gone. Elizabeth Grosz cites phantom-limb syndrome as evidence that "our experiences are organized not by real objects and relations but by the expectations and meanings objects have for the body's movement and capacities. They indicate a 'fictional' or fantasmatic construction of the body outside of or beyond its neurological structure" (Grosz, *Volatile Bodies* 89). This interpretation recognizes bodies not as individuated and isolated objects but as products of their movements and their (cultural, social, material) environments. The artist's leg is lost to the degree that her body's functionality contrasts with normative expectations. It is only in the context of the "water" of Moraga's poem that the body is amputated, out of its element, suggesting the possible existence of another world in which such a body might swim more effectively. The poem ends by making this amputation autobiographical: "still, I

Vendidas," Moraga situates her racial and sexual alienation relative to the Conquest of Mexico by comparing herself to La Malinche (a woman who supposedly betrayed the men of her race through sex) (Moraga, *Loving in the War Years* 124). Moraga's lesbianism is rendered perverse by a Chicano nationalist mandate that she choose her *raza* over her sexuality, and this perception is shaped by Mexican history's misogynist condemnation of La Malinche as "la chingada," the fucked one, as Octavio Paz so famously termed her in *El Laberinto de la Soledad*. In the context of her reclamation of La Malinche's sexuality, Moraga recalls the moments in her youth when she first became aware of her lesbianism: "In my 'craziness' I wrote poems describing myself as a centaur: half-animal/half-human, hairy-rumped and cloven-hoofed, como el diablo. The symbols emerged from a deeply Mexican and Catholic place" (Moraga, *Loving in the War Years* 124). As with the paintings in which Kahlo divides her body down the middle to reflect her cultural split, this essay imagines the writer's body as a bridge between ways of being, and Moraga claims these embodiments as "deeply Mexican," a cultural memory that supports her trans-corporeal feelings. When she was twelve, she dreamt a different self-portrait of transgressive sexuality: "*I am in a hospital bed. I look down upon my newly-developing body. The breasts are large and ample. And below my stomach, I see my own cock, wildly shooting menstrual blood totally out of control*" (119, original emphasis). This self-positioning on a hospital bed recalls Kahlo's bed portraits, an isolation of the body as an object to be examined, and this body, too, exceeds medical understandings ("totally out of control"). Moraga later realizes that her dreams reflect a lack of vocabulary to describe her sexual feelings: "The boundaries white feminists confine themselves to in describing sexuality are based in white-rooted interpretations . . . [and] would have to be expanded and translated to fit my people" (126). The corporeal frameworks of "white"

---

feel / the mutilated body / swimming in side stroke / pumping twice as hard / for the lack / of body, pushing / through your words / which hold no water / for me" (Moraga, *Loving in the War Years* 82). Language is the object of struggle here, recalling Moraga's claim in "La Güera" that the hands have been cut off in her printed poetry since she is unable to embody it with the hand gestures she associates with speaking Spanish (55–56). The lack is not a property of the body but of the cultural context, the water and the words that are an inappropriate medium for the Chicana lesbian poet, who is, in this sea, like a fish out of water. It is no wonder that Moraga tries to imagine environments in which bodies belong otherwise. Her 1997 autobiographic narrative *Waiting in the Wings: Portrait of a Queer Motherhood*, which I discuss in Chapter 3, does just that.

culture do not fit her body. From the perspective of the dominant culture, her self-perceptions are pathological, monstrous—a deviance that
Moraga claims as a source of power. She "paints" herself with the most
abject bodies and vows to bring all of the "raggedy edges and oozing
wounds . . . into the light of day" (138). This embodiment exposes the
painful secrets underlying Chicana/o, feminist, or lesbian politics and
oozes beyond the boundaries of any single identity (female or male,
Catholic or indigenous, human or animal). The "deeply Mexican and
Catholic place" she feels in her "writer's soul" gives her images and icons
for representing this corporeal "otherness."

Anzaldúa, too, breaks the boundaries of bodies in her self-character-
izations, like the following passage from *Borderlands*:

> I write the myths in me, the myths I am, the myths I want to
> become. The word, the image and the feeling have a palatable
> energy, a kind of power. *Con imagenes domo mi miedo, cruzo los ab-
> ismos que tengo por dentro. Con palabras me hago piedra, pájaro, puente
> de serpientes arrastrando a ras del suelo todo lo que soy, todo lo que algún
> día seré.* [With images I subdue my fear, I cross the abysses that I
> have inside. With words I make myself stone, bird, bridge of ser-
> pents dragging along the earth all that I am, all that I one day will
> be.] (Anzaldúa, *Borderlands* 71)

In this passage, myth is not just an ideal but an embodiment, a narrative
or cultural history that inhabits one's body. The word and the image of
myth enable her to "make" something of the "palatable energy" of feeling, and what she makes is a shape-shifting self of stone, bird, and serpents. (Kahlo's work embodies a similar metamorphosis into and
connectedness with plants and animals, and she writes in her diary that
all humans are part of a single "current," connected "through millions
of stone beings, bird beings, star beings, microbe beings, fountain beings"
[qtd. in Herrera, *Frida* 358].) Anzaldúa's vocabulary is Aztec—taking up
serpents from Coatlicue—as well as U.S. woman-of-color feminist—
with the bridge recalling the transracial coalitions of *This Bridge Called
My Back*. Importantly, though this "self-portrait" is about one "I," she
incorporates multiple myths and multiple bodies, indicating a fluctuating,
accommodating, and expansive way of being. This multiplicity and fluidity enable her to "cross the abysses."

Finally, Castillo's *Massacre of the Dreamers* (1994)—an essay collection
whose fusion of history, political critique, personal narrative, and poetry
allies it with Anzaldúa's *Borderlands* and Moraga's two collections, *Loving*

in the War Years and *The Last Generation*—includes what is, at the same time, the most and the least revealing self-portrait. Castillo confesses that she is unable to "unearth" the *indigenismo* she feels:

> I was unable to unearth the female indigenous consciousness in graduate school that I am certain is a part of my genetic collective memory and my life experience. Nevertheless I stand firm that I *am* that Mexic Amerindian woman's consciousness in the poem cited above and that I must, with others like myself, utter the thoughts and intuitions that dwell in the recesses of primal collective memory. (Castillo, *Massacre of the Dreamers* 17, original emphasis)[34]

This complicated explanation undermines the distinction between presence and absence ("I *am*" something "I was unable to unearth") as well as between present and past, self and collectivity. As with Anzaldúa's statement about myth, it is through "utterances" that this "primal" consciousness is accessible.

The poem Castillo refers to, about the "Mexic Amerindian woman," is earlier identified as an "autobiographical poem," "*Entre primavera y otoño*" ("Between Spring and Fall"), which she wrote while in graduate school at the University of Chicago (in Latin American and Caribbean Studies), evidently studying both self and history at the same time (8):

> *La india carga su bandera*
> *sobre su cara*
> *manchada de sangre*
> *sus cicatrices corren*
> *como las carreteras viejas*
> *de su tierra*
> *y la india no se queja.*
>
> *(Castillo,* Massacre of the Dreamers *8)*

The author's translation that follows is "The Indian woman carries her flag / over her face / blood stained / her scars run / like old roads through her land / and the Indian woman does not complain" (8). It is significant that this supposedly autobiographical poem is told in the third person, about an *india* with whom the author cannot wholly identify.

34. Sánchez critiques this particular passage, despite its emphasis on the failure to "unearth" indigenous identity, as evidence of Castillo's "deterministic and essentialist" biologism (Sánchez 360).

Unlike Kahlo, Castillo never pretends to be an *india* without problematizing this connection. The performative posture of "drag" is suggested by seemingly romantic and stereotypical qualities attributed to the *india*, such as her stoic suffering and the connection between her body and the land. But the first lines show us that anything we assume about this woman is based on our own inferences, since the woman's face is covered with her flag. Thus we know nothing about her as an individual; we only know her as a representative or subject of a nation. It is also not clear if the blood stains are on the flag or the face, and the comparison of scars to roads allows dual interpretations of the verb "run." Either her face is covered with running sores—her insides leaking to the outside—or her scars run like old highways, crossing the map, connecting different villages, the embodiment of travel. We can never know which it is, though, since her face is covered, and it seems covered not just for readers but for the Chicana feminist poet, too, who will never really know the *india* inside her. What she tells us, then, is qualified, potentially contradicted, and mystified by remoteness and longing. This body will not submit to any single interpretation.

What Kahlo, Anzaldúa, Moraga, and Castillo share is an awareness of how painful it is to be marked by (racial, sexual, national, or medical) power structures and a search for a (visual or textual) vocabulary with which to represent this pain. They find this vocabulary in the cultural frictions of Mexican history as well as a romanticized indigenous worldview anterior to this painful history. Their self-portraits then fuse history and contemporary politics on the landscape of the human body. In an analysis of Kahlo's "visual autobiography," Mimi Yang suggests that self-portraiture allowed Kahlo "to fetishize her wounded, dissociated, and mutilated body and clinically analyze it" (Yang 129). Yang argues that, by recreating her body on the canvas, Kahlo was able to move "from fragmentation to wholeness" and to "transcend" her painful reality: in short, "painting is the artist's path to liberation from pain" (130–31). As my earlier reference to the "talking cure" suggests, self-representation involves finding patterns, frameworks, or narratives with which to illustrate oneself, which could indeed constitute part of a healing process. Yet this "diagnosis" assumes that health lies in self-perception, in "working out" one's relationship to oneself. For the writers I analyze here, the source of unhealth is exterior as much as it is interior. Anzaldúa, Moraga, and Castillo are not simply "confessional" or self-analytical writers; rather, they use their own bodies to make apparent the violence of the worlds that surround and shape them. As Kahlo "fetishizes" her body as the object of injury (polio, the bus accident, Rivera's infidelity), Moraga fetishizes her white skin and her lesbian sexuality as embodiments that test the limits of Chicano nationalism's exclusionary subject. Anzaldúa fetishizes her body as a shape-shifter and a border-crosser, demonstrating how some bodies do not fit the singular ideals of identity politics. And the bodies in Castillo's work are fictionally injured to highlight the damage wrought by multinational capitalism, industrial pollution of the environment, and misogynist violence against women. These self-representations reach outward in overtly political visions that demand that we change the world rather than simply enacting their own solutions. Yang's study reinforces the view of self-portraiture as self-contained, hermetically sealed within the body of the painter, like Scarry's assumption that pain takes no object. The pain that I analyze in *Encarnación* takes an object: the world around it. Anzaldúa's, Moraga's, and Castillo's bodies in pain are not simply private; rather, they mark the places where public cultures and public institutions amputate certain embodiments. Since the source of injury transcends the individual, as I will demonstrate in the chapters to come, their individual bodies never "transcend" pain or realize "wholeness."

Yang's study also provides a good point of departure for a necessary note about genre. My object of analysis in this study is literature, not the authors' lives, but since their own illnesses and injuries provide the occasion for much of the material I analyze, my understanding of their work hovers around the boundaries of (auto)biography and hagiography. Yang wants to expand our understandings of autobiography beyond narrative, which is a necessary gesture for this project, too, since these writers are known for their movement beyond traditional genre boundaries. Anzaldúa published essays, poems, and children's books. Moraga has published essays, poems, and plays. And Castillo has published essays, poems, stories, novels, and, recently, a play and a novel in verse. Much of the early criticism about these three writers has focused on their "hybridization" of each of these genres, challenging what we think of as "essay" or "literature" by fusing prose with verse, fiction with history.[35] This genre-crossing invariably complicates any comparisons one draws between

35. See, for example, Norma Alarcón's "Conjugating Subjects: The Heteroglossia of Essence and Resistance" and Inderpal Grewal's "Autobiographic Subjects and Diasporic Locations: *Meatless Days* and *Borderlands.*" In "Sexual Indifference and Lesbian Representation," Teresa de Lauretis suggests that there is a connection between the problematic of "lesbian (self-)representation" (par-

these texts and their subjects. The closest to traditional "autobiography" in the works I study here is Moraga's *Waiting in the Wings*, a text (or "portrait," as the subtitle suggests) that layers original diary entries with commentary added at the time of publication, in a different font, in which Moraga takes her own diary and her own history as the objects of her analysis. This format leads one to think about how personal history enters representation at the same time that it fragments its subject into two very different narratives. Anzaldúa's interviews could also be read as autobiography, though their narratives are partial and formed in dialogue with the interviewer. The poems and essays of all three writers, which are often grounded in the first-person "I," are also read (including, at times, by me) as autobiography, but the former are aesthetically manipulated and fragmented and the latter are intertwined with history and political critique, providing no unmediated access to the writers' lives.

Castillo's self-portraits are the blurriest of them all. While Anzaldúa and Moraga are best known for their (semi)autobiographical poems and essays, Castillo's best-known works are her novels. Though these novels' overtly political critiques, intertextual references, and ironic allusions to the author's biography (including Chicanas from Chicago traveling to New Mexico, cats named Xochitl, and painters) break the boundaries of third-person fictional narrative, they are still extended meditations on the lives of imaginary people. Castillo's poems provide most of her autobiographic glimpses, but they are often ignored, and the novels are usually studied in isolation from these glimpses. And her interviews are rarely personal. Indeed, when Bryce Milligan broaches personal questions in his 1999 interview with her, she answers with gaps and switches to a neutral second person. When he asks her about her family's tribal affiliations, she answers, "I have not done any personal research to find out exactly what tribe they were closest to, though I am sure I could," and then moves from this unfulfilled possibility to a general discussion of Mexican *mestizaje*, "if you are of Mexican descent, you invariably have

---

ticularly by lesbians of color) and the subversion of conventional forms of writing. She draws attention to the use of "fiction/theory" in Anzaldúa, Michelle Cliff, and Moraga (among others) as "a formally experimental, critical and lyrical, autobiographical and theoretically conscious, practice of writing-in-the-feminine that crosses boundaries (poetry and prose, verbal and visual modes, narrative and cultural criticism), and instates new correlations between signs and meanings" (de Lauretis 165). These new genres are part of the "struggle with language to rewrite the body beyond its precoded, conventional representations" (167).

Indian blood of some kind" (Castillo, "An Interview" 21). When later prodded on this same question, she simply states that her own family was likely not Aztec and, tantalizingly, that her "father's background is a little mysterious" but "we'll hold that thought" (22). This is not to privilege the autobiographic mode as a source of information or to assume that conventional autobiography provides unmediated access to an author's experience. Rather, this is a caution about the "I's" and the authors' names that circulate throughout this work: they must be regarded as literary constructions rather than windows onto actual people: masked, partial, and political more than they are biographical. Just as the pain of these I's bleeds out into their surrounding communities, the I's themselves are not just individual; they are manifestations of multiple histories, cultural collisions, and sexual politics, including my own.

This mediation of the I's that enter into representation (in text, on canvas, or in performance) brings us back to hagiography, back to the representation of corporeal experience, and back to Elaine Scarry. Scarry wonders if "the originally interior facts of sentience" can be made publicly available "through verbal and material artifacts," and her conclusion is "no," that sentience evaporates in the process of objectification, becoming visible or communicable only as a symbol of other power structures (Scarry 22). In the genre of hagiography, however, the primary object of representation is sentience, and that sentience is meant to leap off the page and to affect readers, commanding their belief, their conversion, or their penitence. For hagiographers, this communication matters more than how their representation compares to the "real" of the author's life. This means that the published lives of saints are not about those lives as much as they are about their political effects and, perhaps, that the most palpable feelings in hagiography are those of the reader. Gómez-Peña poses the possibility of communication between author and reader, saint and sinner, in a very literal manner in the text version of *Temple of Confessions*: the book comes with two postcards on which the reader is to write his/her own confessions, to be mailed back to the author. It also comes with an Aztec tattoo that the reader is meant to transfer to his/her own skin. Is Gómez-Peña making fun or is he serious? Does he read the postcards if he receives them? It doesn't really matter, after all, for the reader who confesses, who tries on a tattoo, for the reader's body and psyche are thereby marked, somewhat changed by their history in the *Temple of Confessions*. Whether or not the author's sentience is what the reader feels, s/he surely feels something.

2

PAIN: GLORIA ANZALDÚA'S CHALLENGE TO "WOMEN'S HEALTH"

My whole life was nothing but pain. Pain. Pain. Pain.
Anzaldúa, *Interviews/Entrevistas* 34

*T*o talk about the work of Gloria Anzaldúa is to cross borders, not just national borders but also the lines between biography and criticism, body and theory. Her recent death troubled these borders more radically as her passing and her suffering from diabetes shifted to the center of discussions about her. The passionate mourning that has followed shows how her lifework, and her life, still bleed into the words of those who have incorporated her ideas and the strength of her rebellion. Inés Hernández-Ávila describes her grief as a gradual embodiment of Anzaldúa's absence: "My body is reluctantly registering in every cell that you are physically no longer with us" (qtd. in Gonzales and Rodriguez). At http://gloria.chicanas.com, an online altar of memorials, Alicia Gaspar de Alba writes: "Her passing is extremely personal and painful to me (as it is, I'm sure to many of us), and feels like a loss of a higher part of myself." Elana Dykewoman's offering also captures this dispersal and incorporation of the author: "She is everywhere in the many borderlands we inhabit" ("Rest in Peace Gloria"). True to her proposition that the border is an "open wound" (Anzaldúa, *Borderlands* 3), critical applications of Anzaldúa transgress the boundaries of her texts and of her individual body. At the beginning of *Borderlands* (her first single-authored text), she opened her body to her readers, "staking fence rods in my flesh" (2) to express viscerally the pain of living with barbed-wire fences. As with the back trouble that caused Cherríe Moraga "constant pain" when using "the muscle that controls the movement of my fingers and

77

hands while typing" (Moraga, *Loving in the War Years* v), this first generation of "out" Chicana lesbian writers laid down their own backs for
political work like *This Bridge Called My Back* (1981)—a modern-day
human sacrifice that literally embodies "cultural collision" (Anzaldúa,
Borderlands 78), "rupture with . . . oppressive traditions" (82), and the
open-armed stretching of *mestiza* feminism (79, 88).

My premise about Anzaldúa is that her writings on pain and illness
reveal an expansive body, that her diabetes reinforced her thinking about
the open and shifting *conciencia* of *mestiza* feminism.[1] In her 2002 essay,
"now let us shift," for instance, Anzaldúa proposed a revolution in the
way we think about identity, and this particular redefinition followed her
acceptance of the effects of diabetes on her own self: "you've chosen to
compose a new history and self. . . . Your ailing body is no longer a
hindrance but an asset, witnessing pain, speaking to you, demanding
touch. Es tu cuerpo que busca conocimiento; along with dreams your
body's the royal road to consciousness" (Anzaldúa, "now let us shift"
558–59). Anzaldúa's "ailing body" opened new avenues of consciousness and new ideas for ways of being in the world. The risk in this
assertion is its apparent endorsement of diabetes as a medium of perception. This risk is greater now that diabetes has led to Anzaldúa's death. I
want to make very clear, then, that I am not celebrating pain or illness.
Though I am interested in hagiography as a genre, *Encarnación* is not itself
a hagiography of a lost martyr. Rather, I want to show how the pain that
framed much of Anzaldúa's experience also framed her ideas. In order to
understand her work, I argue, we must take seriously the perspective
offered by pain and the avenues of thought down which it led her. Her
attitude toward pain, in my analysis, emerges from the Mexican cultural
frameworks that underlie her writing and is directed toward particular
Chicana and feminist political ends.

1. Though discussions of pain often separate physical and mental pain, I
would argue that pain always has cultural, psychological, and corporeal dimensions that mutually define one another. As Anzaldúa writes in "now let us shift,"
"Though your head and heart decry the mind/body dichotomy, the conflict in
your mind makes your body a battlefield where beliefs fight each other" (Anzaldúa, "now let us shift" 549). When her body manifests her thinking, and when
her "body's illness has taken residence in all [her] thoughts" (551), she demonstrates what it would mean to live without this dichotomy. David Morris, too,
critiques the attempt to separate physical from psychological pain in *The Culture
of Pain*.

Anzaldúa's *conciencia de la mestiza* is built on a foundation of violence, cross-cultural penetration, and internal fragmentation—from the conquest and rape of Native America at the hands of European colonizers (which first produced *mestizaje*) to racial and sexual marginalization and the personal illnesses and abuses of the author's own body. Yet the demonization of pain and illness in modern Euro-American society—and the puritanical silence about physiological processes and personal vulnerabilities—has led critics to assume that viable models for identity must not be painful. I will return to this assumption, ultimately, to question whether Anzaldúa would have us rethink pain as an embodiment to practice or whether her references to pain are merely intended to keep the violence of history and the materiality of bodies in mind. To evaluate this question in all of its dimensions, this chapter first traces the ways in which pain has been read out of Anzaldúa's work, analyzes the significance that Anzaldúa attributes to her own body's pain, and outlines the Mexican cultural symbolism that enables her to assign pain a productive role in the formation of *mestiza* consciousness.

Mestiza Reception

In the past two decades, feminist theory, critical race theory, and postmodern theory have turned to the concept of hybridity to heal racial and cultural divisions. Yet the corporeal states historically produced by racial mixture are more often pained and fragmented than whole or healed. It is crucial to recognize, as many critics have not, the foundations of the hybridities that are theoretically touted. In colonial Mexico, for example, *mestizaje* was endorsed as a means of solidifying colonial domination by culturally and genetically "hispanicizing" the natives. In this instance, the process intended to close divisions within the nation and to safeguard Spanish colonial authority was historically realized through the bodies of indigenous women. And, as we saw in Chapter 1, after the Mexican Revolution, *mestizaje* was similarly invoked to unify the nation, at the expense of abjecting the unmixed native population. While mixture may literally blend races into a healthy-looking whole, its formation historically involves racialized and sexualized violence, overcoming difference by violating or eliminating those who are different.

This dynamic still shapes racial definition today. In her prose poem "*Cihuatlyotl*, Woman Alone," Anzaldúa describes her ambivalent relationship to "*la Raza*" in terms of corporeal dismemberment to reflect

79

the difficulty of fitting embodied racial experience into constructed racial types:

> And as I grew you hacked away
> at the pieces   of me   that   were different. . . .
>
> Oh, it was hard,
> *Raza*   to cleave flesh from flesh   I risked
> us both bleeding to death. . . .
>
> . . . there's no-
> thing more you can chop off   or graft on me that
> will change my soul.   I remain who I am, multiple
> and one   of the herd, yet not of it.
>
> *(Anzaldúa,* Borderlands *173)*

The heterogeneity of *mestizaje* complicates racial identity politics. Even within a racially mixed identity like *la raza Chicana*, individuals always embody qualities that exceed the *raza* ideal: rebellious or "deviant" embodiments must be "hacked away," and missing "essential traits" must be grafted on. The personification of *"Raza"* in Anzaldúa's poem, a common address in Chicano nationalist writings, attributes agency to race, itself, giving it hands with which to mold identities in order to solidify the nation. In the process of self-definition, *Raza* amputated parts that are feminist, lesbian, or politically recalcitrant.[2] Yet, Anzaldúa insists, where individual difference is censored by communal identity politics, she remains "multiple," apart, "on the ground of my own being" (*Borderlands* 173). The spacing in this poem emphasizes rupture and difference. She inserts gaps both before and after "of me," making the phrase stand out from the line with individual visibility, independence, and integrity, but the speaker is both "of" and "not of" the herd. Sustaining

---

2. This poem critiques the ways in which the Chicano movement, though racially *mestizo*, often rejected other types of heterogeneity in the process of solidifying a nationalist identity. As Angie Chabram-Dernersesian writes in her critique of Chicano identity politics: "It is ironic that while we live in a period which prizes the multiplicity of identities and charts border crossings with borderless critics, there should be such a marked silence around the kinds of divergent ethnic pluralities that cross gender and classed subjects within the semantic orbit of Chicana/o. So powerful is the hegemonic reach of the dominant culture that fixed categories of race and ethnicity continue to be the foundation, the structuring axis around which Chicana/o identities are found" (Chabram-Dernersesian, " 'Chicana! Rican?' " 273).

this contradiction, as Anzaldúa does, breaks down the opposition between individual and community. Elsewhere Anzaldúa labels this compromise "*nos/otras*" (we and us/others): "in *nos/otras* we are them and
they are us and we're contaminated by each other" ("Coming into Play"
11). "*Nos/otras*" reflects this "contamination" by splitting the plural feminine subject down the middle—fragmenting the subject of Chicana
feminism—and by using the backslash simultaneously to divide and to
fuse "us" and "them." The poem invests individual identity with this
same contamination: "I am fully formed carved / by the hands of ancients, drenched with / the stench of today's headlines. But my own /
hands whittle the final work me" (*Borderlands* 173). This identity is work;
it is overtly constructed, produced by history but open to contemporary
interventions, fashioned by the efforts of both self and others. The dominant metaphors that Anzaldúa uses to describe this unbounded process of
identity formation are painful: hacking, cleaving, bleeding, chopping,
and whittling. Permeability is physically unsettling.

Postmodern theories of hybridity have been offered to recognize the
contingency of identity upon outside elements, to incorporate difference,
and to cross borders without violence. These theories, in effect, like the
nation-building strategies of colonial and postcolonial Mexico, neutralize
difference so that it no longer poses a threat to the coherence of the
whole. While hybridity is often celebrated as a means of transcending
racism or colonialism and building internally heterogeneous communities, much is lost in effacing the friction of conflict, the violence of actual
border-crossing, and the unequal power relations between different
components of the mix.[3] In the case of Anzaldúa's *conciencia de la mestiza*,

3. Inderpal Grewal and Caren Kaplan note that "what seems to get *theorized*
in the West as 'hybridity,' remains enmeshed in the gaze of the West. . . . The
dominant Western attitude toward hybridity is that it is always elsewhere or is
infiltrating an identity or location that is assumed to be, to always have been,
pure and unchanging" (Grewal and Kaplan 7–8, original emphasis). In this sense,
hybridity is based on faith in pure foundations and Western-centrism. Indeed,
Homi Bhabha reinforces this perceived permanence of the dominant when he
argues, "Hybridity represents that ambivalent 'turn' of the discriminated subject
into the terrifying, exorbitant object of paranoid classification—a disturbing
questioning of the images and presences of authority" (Bhabha 155). In this
way, hybridity reflects an incursion of the non-dominant upon the dominant,
transgressing the boundary between dominator and dominated while still reinforcing the authority of the dominant as the precursor to and target of resistance.
When Bhabha claims that hybridity "displays the necessary deformation and

mixture is built upon a historical foundation of violence, pain, and physical fragmentation. Postmodern critics have celebrated the "uprooting of dualistic thinking" that *mestiza* consciousness enables, and feminists and postcolonial theorists have celebrated the idealistic conclusion Anzaldúa draws from this breakdown of binary opposition: "the end of rape, of violence, of war" (*Borderlands* 80–81). Yet the painful components of *mestizaje* are often elided in celebratory applications of *la conciencia de la mestiza*, since pain puts a damper on the postmodern fluidity, transracial universality, and post-essentialist utopianism that is so often extrapolated from Anzaldúa's work.

In *The Body in Pain*, Elaine Scarry describes how involving the physical body lends "an aura of 'realness'" to political ideologies: "The physical pain is so incontestably real that it seems to confer its quality of 'incontestable reality'" on the structures of power that produce the pain (Scarry 27). Anzaldúa's references to pain have this effect of grounding her theories in "real" history, "real" bodies, and "real" geographies. The most frequently quoted passages from *Borderlands* locate pain at the center of Anzaldúa's borderlands *mestizaje*:

> 1,950 mile-long open wound
> dividing a *pueblo*, a culture,
> running down the length of my body,
> staking fence rods in my flesh,
> splits me splits me
> *me raja me raja*
>
> (Anzaldúa, Borderlands 2)

> The U.S.–Mexican border *es una herida abierta* [is an open wound] where the Third World grates against the first and bleeds. And before a scab forms it hemorrhages again, the lifebloods of two worlds merging to form a third country—a border culture. (3)

> In attempting to work out a synthesis, the self has added a third element which is greater than the sum of its severed parts. That

---

displacement of all sites of discrimination and domination" (154) and that "the paranoid threat from the hybrid is finally uncontainable because it breaks down the symmetry and duality of self/Other, inside/outside" (158), he assumes—falsely, I would argue—that hybridity itself is antagonistic to nationalist containment and colonialist domination. Chicano and Mexican *mestizo* nationalism are truly decentered and assume cultural dominance through hybridity. Cultural differences in formations of nationhood resist universalizing claims about hybridity in the abstract.

third element is a new consciousness—a mestiza consciousness—
and though it is a source of intense pain, its energy comes from
continual creative motion that keeps breaking down the unitary
aspect of each new paradigm. (79–80)

All three of these passages encode borderlands identity and *mestizaje* as
processes of "intense pain." Yet, in the twenty years of Anzaldúa's critical
acclaim, few critics have analyzed the wounds within them. As these
passages are quoted time and again in studies of hybridity across cultures,
the pain seems to make critics uncomfortable. The violence that haunts
the border is denied its "incontestable reality" when Anzaldúa's theories
are uprooted from the *"herida abierta"* where they emerge and applied
universally to any negotiation with difference.[4]

Anzaldúa's theories have been adopted around the world and described in terms of postmodernism, post-identitarianism, diaspora, and
différance. Critics who love Anzaldúa's work credit *mestizaje* with revolutionary potential to solve a variety of critical problems, but their desire
for a feminist border hero often overlooks the particular context in
which Anzaldúa delineates *mestizaje*. In 1994, Judith Raiskin read *Borderlands* as a postmodern text, and her anti-essentialism idealizes *mestizaje* as
a critique of racial and sexual "categories of identity along with the modernist nostalgia for an imagined lost innocence when everyone knew,
or could know, her or his place" (Raiskin 159). From a postmodern
perspective, Raiskin dismisses unitary subjectivity, racial and sexual coherence, and nostalgia for a place of belonging as bygone modernist relics
rather than experiences dismantled by forced miscegenation, colonialism,
and war. Raiskin attributes to Anzaldúa a "postmodern appreciation for
the chaos that inevitably results from racist and sexist categories and from
their dismantling" (169). Yet this chaos, in the case of Anzaldúa, is not
just theoretical, and her dismantling of categories is not postmodern as
much as it is an inevitable feature of her lesbianism and her *mestizaje*.
Celebrating this chaos risks romanticizing sites of continued oppression,
like the borderlands.[5]

4. Yvonne Yarbro-Bejarano, too, draws attention to "the expense of gener-
alizing moves that deracinate the psychic 'borderlands' and '*mestiza*' consciousness from the United States/Mexican border and the racial miscegenation
accompanying the colonization of the Americas" (Yarbro-Bejarano, "Gloria Anzaldúa's *Borderlands/La frontera*" 13–14).
5. Paula Moya also critiques the romanticization of marginality in postmodern formulations of Chicana identity: "If we choose the postmodernist approach,

Juan Velasco idealizes Anzaldúa's conception of the border to the extent of eschewing conflict: "As an alternative to the theory of the metaphor of the Border as 'conflict' . . . Gloria Anzaldúa's *Borderlands/La Frontera* (1987) not only redefines the space of the Borderland as a more inclusive and conciliatory utopia but also reinvents a different hero, the new 'mestiza' " (Velasco 224). Yet even as she delineates a "new mestiza," Anzaldúa enmeshes this "hero" in conflict and posits utopia as a goal that is always on the horizon, always shadowed by the "thin edge of barbed wire" (Anzaldúa, *Borderlands* 3) that makes home on the border more painful than "conciliatory." Lynda Hall's reverence for Anzaldúa's theories, and her search for a model "home" space that is "both livable and habitable" for lesbians of color, lead her to minimize the final clause of the passage she quotes from Anzaldúa's essay on homophobia, which is: "though 'home' permeates every sinew and cartilage in my body, I too am afraid of going home" (Hall, "Writing Selves" 110–11; Anzaldúa, *Borderlands* 21). Rather than claiming a comfortable lesbian space, this sentence, to me, makes the body itself a fearful place. If Anzaldúa is afraid of going home, and home "permeates every sinew and cartilage" in her body, does this statement not imply a fear of inhabiting one's own body?[6]

From a different critical perspective, Robert Con Davis-Undiano describes Anzaldúa's theories of *mestizaje* as a "retrieval of a scandal," originating in violation but reframed as a "powerful position" (Davis-Undiano 123–24). In contrast to Raiskin, Davis-Undiano shores up this revolutionary identity by selectively quoting phrases from Anzaldúa and pairing them with essentialist claims. For instance, "since the mestiza herself is defined by the situation of 'straddling . . . two or more cultures' in her own nature, the task at hand [of breaking down paradigms and tolerating contradictions] and the mestiza's innate orientation are symmetrically matched" (124). Davis-Undiano describes this "orientation"

---

we run the risk, for example, of theorizing Chicana identity in terms of ambiguity and fragmentation so that the *Chicana* becomes, in effect, a figure for marginality and contradiction in the postmodern world" (Moya, "Chicana Feminism and Postmodernist Theory" 479).

6. Anzaldúa echoes this same theme in "now let us shift," clarifying why "home" must never be safe but rather a process, a bridge to "the next phase, next place, next culture, next reality": "The thrust toward spiritual realization, health, freedom, and justice propels you to help rebuild the bridge to the world when you return 'home.' You realize that 'home' is that bridge, the in-between place of nepantla and constant transition, the most unsafe of all spaces" (Anzaldúa, "now let us shift" 574).

as "innate" to solidify his celebratory claim that Anzaldúa's new *mestiza* possesses the key to liberation. Yet nothing is so simple in *Borderlands*. Indeed, the phrase Davis-Undiano quotes immediately follows my third quote for this section, in which Anzaldúa insists that "mestiza consciousness" is "a source of intense pain," but the future "*depends* on the straddling of two or more cultures" to alter our perception of reality (Anzaldúa, *Borderlands* 80, emphasis added). This passage does not describe an identity already formed, but rather a painful process upon which the future depends. Anzaldúa's emphasis on pain resists easy identification or ready-made solutions, but the impact of her work is so powerful that both essentialists and anti-essentialists credit *la conciencia de la mestiza* with these revolutionary properties. Indeed, her reception is, itself, *mestiza*: critics with divergent political and theoretical investments all claim her work as representative of their ideals.

Embodying *Mestiza* Pain

In 2000, a number of newly published interviews—AnaLouise Keating's collection, *Interviews/Entrevistas*, and a *MELUS* interview with Ann E. Reuman—reopened *Borderlands* with new perspectives from the author. In Reuman's interview, Anzaldúa describes her response to her critical reception:

> I try and get copies of reviews and copies of papers that are given, and conferences about my work and people who are working on theses or dissertations, and so I have a lot of these papers in my file. And I think that for the most part what was missed in their reviews and interpretations was the spiritual/mystical/poetic aspects of my writing. . . . I think what makes them uncomfortable is that I'm practicing what I'm preaching. (Anzaldúa, "Coming Into Play" 7)

One point she consistently stresses in the more personal form of the interviews—and one site where she literally "practiced" her theoretical ideas—is her own "body in pain." Since her writing about this body is intensely personal, spiritual, and often supernatural, critical studies that remain safely within the realm of "rational" inquiry often exclude this important influence. In a 1998–99 interview with Keating, Anzaldúa emphasizes the role of her body in shaping her identity and her politics: "My resistance to gender and race injustice stemmed from my physical differences, from the early bleeding and my early growth spurt" (*Interviews* 288). Her diabetes, moreover, materialized the obsession with fluctuation and balance in writing about identity formation: "I get dizzy and mentally foggy when I'm having a hypo. I lose my equilibrium and fall. Gastrointestinal reflex has me throwing up and having diarrhea. . . . Things like these change your image of yourself, your identity. . . . The whole thing with diabetes is having a balance in your blood sugar" (289–90). That which is abstract in the essays of *Borderlands*—juggling the different racial "bloods" that are internal to the *mestiza*—receives grounding in the author's body, here. Anzaldúa's theoretical impulse to synthesize bloods becomes concrete, imperative, and immediate with syringes and gastrointestinal processes.

When she describes her writing processes, pain and balance dominate Anzaldúa's rhetoric. In the Reuman interview, she states her goal in writing as creating a balance between theoretical propositions and personal, emotional content, but "It's hard when you want to experience a full range of passions to develop a balance. . . . And the difficulty comes in that I have to live these extremes. That if I'm writing a story about some emotional pain, I can't write it from the sidelines. I have to be embodied in it. And it hurts!" ("Coming into Play" 18). Pain refers to both the content of Anzaldúa's writings and the process of inscribing that content, since, unlike more abstract theorists, Anzaldúa does not write "from the sidelines." In spatial terms, the writer must internalize the object she is writing. Three pages later, she provides an opposing spatial metaphor, explaining "the agony of creating" as "literally like taking myself apart" (21). Writing is thus a process of incorporating and dis-corporating.

> For me as I write I create a textual self, which is different from the "me" that lives out in the world. But the textual self that I create also changes the historical "me." And so I'm kind of creating myself as I go along. . . . In order to do this I have to take myself apart and then put myself together . . . and it's very painful, this dismemberment, burial, and then having to look for all the hidden parts of you that have been scattered throughout. And when you reconstitute yourself, or when I reconstitute myself, it's a different me that I reconstitute, and that's where the transformative aspect comes in. But also it's like tearing apart your innards, your entrails, and it's physically painful, and emotionally painful, and psychologically painful. (14–15)

Anzaldúa sees her writing as, ultimately, objectifying her own sentient self (in defiance of Scarry's assertion that such a proposition is impossible). Yet putting a body into representation transforms it, painfully dismantling and differently reconstituting matter by forming it into a text.

Diabetes accentuated the painful shifts involved in this creative process with "mental distraction, chronic fatigue and depression": "I couldn't function as a writer, as a thinker, because I couldn't hold consecutive thoughts" (19). While before the diabetes her depressions came in cycles ("when my sun was going into the twelfth house"), diabetes disrupted this fixed pattern and subjected her body to the unpredictable fluctuations of disease. At times, diabetes presented real physical barriers to the writing process: "The blood sugar in my body and brain descompuso everything! . . . Not enough oxygen and blood were getting into the capillaries around my eyeballs so I was getting these flashes of light and everything would go blank. I couldn't watch TV, read a book, or work on my computer" (*Interviews* 249). Diabetes presents a variety of intrusions upon her body, which the writer inevitably takes into her work. These material challenges to the writing process present an alternate explanation for the internal splits, the shifts in perspective, and the fusion of genres that characterize Anzaldúa's literary forms, and they also correspond with her intention of "doing these kinds of shamanic, shifting, magical other-worldly excursions in my writing" and "not letting [the "serious scholar"] kill the playful trickster/child/*nahual*" ("Coming into Play" 20, 17). Allowing her writing to follow the fluidity of her diabetic body—changing shapes, traveling down multiple paths, and welcoming in other worlds—produced work that is multiplicitous and multifaceted, irreducible to any single interpretation. Although Anzaldúa critiques "the old metaphor about the suffering artist," and insists on creating a "balanced life," she concludes that pain has been central to her writing: "It's still painful!" "I have to actually jump . . . into that pain, and just write from there" (21). This simultaneous emphasis on balance and painful disequilibrium is one of the dominant contradictions that characterize *mestiza* consciousness.

The body Anzaldúa describes in an interview with Linda Smuckler (1982) is, like the *mestiza* identity she theorizes, open to external forces and thus in a constant state of material transformation: "As a little kid I was wide open—like a sponge; everything came in" (*Interviews* 26). In the interviews, then, Anzaldúa describes what it would be like to live the theoretical strategies of *Borderlands'* "new *mestiza*," for whom "nothing is thrust out, the good the bad and the ugly, nothing rejected, nothing abandoned" (*Borderlands* 79). This opening of boundaries and border-crossing are the paradigms from *Borderlands* that are most often celebrated (even though *Borderlands* poems like "*El sonavabitche*" and "To live in the

Borderlands means you" describe the historical violence of such cross-ings).[7] The image of the sponge-like child in the Smuckler interview clarifies the actual dangers attendant with permeable boundaries. Anzal-dúa keeps her body open to the world around her: "I feel a real unifica-tion with people, real identification with someone or something—like the grass. It's so painful that I have to cut the connection. But I can't cut the connection, so instead of putting a shield between myself and you and your pain, I put a wall inside, between myself and my feelings" (*Interviews* 26–27). Rather than reinforcing external boundaries between self and other, she fragments herself internally. Anzaldúa maps onto this autobiographical body the *conciencia* that has been in danger of evaporat-ing into postmodern abstraction, recuperating the painful ambivalence of border-crossing and materializing potential strategies for living with this ambivalence.[8]

Blood forms a key link from Anzaldúa's theoretical race-mixing to actual racialized and sexed bodies. She describes her first awareness of difference as a product of her heavy menstrual periods, which began for her at a very early age: "The bleeding was the main thing. It made me abnormal" (27, 29). Anzaldúa suggests that her "abnormal" menstrua-tion—which gave her "raging fevers," cramps, and tonsillitis—was not just the product of "hormone imbalance" but also of an extraterrestrial spirit that entered her body when she was three months old ("la prieta" 24; *Interviews* 34). This "extraterrestrial" being literalizes the excess that marked her body as pathological. Since her periods were earlier, more

7. "*El sonavabitche*" describes the ways in which migrant workers who are "illegal aliens" are terrorized and exploited in the United States (Anzaldúa, *Bor-derlands* 124–29). "To live in the borderlands" describes *mestiza* identity as being "caught in the crossfire between camps," "stopped by *la migra* at the border checkpoints," where "the mill with the razor white teeth wants to shred off / your olive-red skin" (194–95).

8. While one might protest that there is a limit to how much symbolism we can read into narratives presented as lived experience, the boundary between autobiography and literature, between history and subjective representation, is blurred in genre-crossing writings like Anzaldúa's. As her texts move between personal narrative, philosophy, history, and poetry, she encourages readers to see the bleeding between disciplines and enacts a cross-pollination of their different reading practices. Even if one could isolate a textual moment as "pure" history, Anzaldúa would still have us "close read" it: "I look for omens everywhere, everywhere catch glimpses of the patterns and cycles of my life" (Anzaldúa, *Borderlands* 36).

painful, more bloody than that which a "normal," "healthy," well-individuated body could contain, she required a supra-human explanation: "I mean, the stuff that was going on with me is like seeing a movie or reading a science fiction book, you know?" (*Interviews* 35). She invokes extraterrestrial beings, spirits, and science fiction to describe an identity that exceeds "Western" paradigms of humanity, rationality, and logic. Anzaldúa reports that doctors ultimately "solved" her medical condition with a hysterectomy, but "until the hysterectomy, . . . [m]y whole life was nothing but pain. Pain. Pain. Pain" (34). This procedure, significantly, removes not just the source of reproductive female sexuality; it also removes her pain, her excess, her "illogical" and alien difference. It normalizes. It reflects the struggle of an individual with cultural standards of health and embodiment. Here we are probing the borderlands of embodiment, questioning what is and what is not one's body, internalizing outside influences and externalizing parts of the self (by adopting medical treatments and having organs removed). This extraterrestrial encounter, too, illustrates a lived *mestizaje*: embodying impurity, incorporating alien elements, and exceeding boundaries.

Anzaldúa emphasizes the friction between the spirit that moves into her body and her body itself: "I always think of this spirit as masculine, because he didn't like my body" (34). Both this encounter and the hysterectomy demand a feminist response: they represent masculine, medicalized intrusions on a body that enacts an excess of female sexual processes. In "la prieta," she describes the hysterectomy as a violent expression of colonizing misogyny: "The doctor played with his knife. La Chingada ripped open, raped with the white man's wand. . . . My bowels fucked with a surgeon's knife, uterus and ovaries pitched in the trash. Castrated" ("la prieta" 203, 208). Misogynist fantasy and medical power work in tandem here to disarm and to disembowel the female sexed body, represented in this passage as a modern-day Malinche, "La Chingada" "fucked" by Conquest. The illnesses Anzaldúa describes in her interviews reflect the violation and pathologization of women of color's bodies in America. Her pain and her blood are considered inappropriate and impure. But Anzaldúa's *mestiza* consciousness appropriates the inappropriate and the impure: embracing otherness and contradictions, extraterrestrial spirits, menstruation in children, identification with grass. Indeed, the boundaries of "the proper" are culturally relative, and adhering to more than one cultural tradition (as *mestiza/os* do) might render them fluid, or at least contested. Is Anzaldúa suggesting that these painful, excessive, and paranormal embodiments are proper to the *mestiza*?

Would *not* having the hysterectomy, keeping the pain and the blood, be a proper feminist response? The risks of advancing pain, the supernatural, and "pathological" menstruation as proper embodiments, particularly for women of color (who were often stigmatized, by racist mythology, as excessively reproductive or less sensitive to pain),[9] might explain critics' avoidance of this aspect of Anzaldúa's work.

But pain, for Anzaldúa, is not just a marker of racial/sexual oppression. It is also an extension of *mestiza* agency. Pain reflects her response to external conditions and social interactions. Her last-published and least talked-about essay, "now let us shift," makes overt her controversial argument about the productive potential of pain. By the time of this essay, she had accepted the effects of diabetes as part of her growth as a writer and a thinker: "By seeing your symptoms not as signs of sickness and disintegration but as signals of growth, . . . by using these feelings as tools or grist for the mill, you move through fear, anxiety, anger, and blast into another reality" ("now let us shift" 552). Refusing to demonize her illness, and the depression that resulted from facing a lifetime of pain, Anzaldúa ultimately rejected dominant thinking about physical and mental health: "Though modern therapies exhort you to act against your passions (compulsions), claiming health and integration lie in that direction, you've learned that delving more fully into your pain, anger, despair, depression will move you through to the other side" (553). Instead of integration, "now let us shift" finds agency in the upheavals that constantly remake the body and expand consciousness.

The body that emerges from Anzaldúa's later thinking is neither passive nor static. It is also not the abstract, universal, or culturally neutral "the body" of some theoretical or medical writings.[10] For Anzaldúa, pain

9. David Morris notes that slaveholders often accepted "a paradoxical article of faith . . . that slaves did not feel pain" in order to justify their cruelty; similarly, the myth that Native Americans "were inherently insensitive to pain" was used to justify the suppression and genocide of native peoples (Morris, *The Culture of Pain* 39).

10. In her preface to *Bodies that Matter*, Judith Butler describes how she "kept losing track of the subject" in her anti-foundationalist identity theories, which were beginning to reveal that "movement beyond their own boundaries . . . appeared to be quite central to what bodies 'are.'" When resistant feminist critics demanded, "What about the materiality of the body, *Judy*?" Butler ultimately challenged the "the" in their assumptions about bodily being (Butler, *Bodies that Matter* ix). "The body," as it is commonly invoked, implies that corporeality— across races, genders, sexes, cultures—can be reduced to an already given, uni-

highlights the inscription of her particular Chicana *mestiza* lesbian diabetic identity: all categories that are historically produced and culturally contingent. Her individual pain also marks the intersection of private and public experience of embodiment: personal feeling and public judgment, individual experience and the shared "suffering" of a racial or sexual community. This perspective responds to current theoretical debates about identity politics—by balancing shifting foundations with material specificity—but also refers to a much longer history of Mexican body politics.

The *Mestiza* Meaning of Pain

As for this you will run
[sticks through your
tongue]: not only to
deserve benefits, but
to cast off the dirt,
the trash. You will make
the staves bloody, you
will tear the lower part
of your tongue, you will put them
through the front part. . . . Thus
you will lose your sins, your evil
acts, your faults.
        (*López Austin*, The Human Body and Ideology *381*)

Mira estas llagas, que nunca llegarán aquí tus dolores. Este es el camino de la verdad. [Behold these wounds, that your suffering will never arrive to this point. This is the path of truth.] (Santa Teresa de Jesús 282)

Pain theorist David Morris writes that "modern" pain is "now officially emptied of meaning and merely buzzing mindlessly along the nerves" (Morris, *The Culture of Pain* 4), but many cultures do not abide by this modern logic. Though she wrote from within the most "modern" world power, Anzaldúa instead identified with Mexico's dual spiritual inheritance, indigenous and Catholic, both contexts in which pain is sometimes perceived as having transcendent meaning (cleansing sins or

---

versally shared, circumscribed, neutral entity. Like Butler, Anzaldúa challenges the possibility as well as the desirability of such closure.

revealing truth, in my epigraphs above). Morris argues that all such meaning has been eclipsed by modern medicine: "The secular, scientific spirit of modern medicine has so eclipsed other systems of thought as almost to erase the memory that pain—far from registering its presence mostly in meaningless neural circuits or in the sterile, living-death of hysterical numbness—once possessed redemptive and visionary powers" (125). Secular, rationalist domination of medicine has reinforced the perception that pain is merely a neural stimulus that should be eliminated. Any other valuation of pain—like traditional Native American pain rituals, the agonies of hagiographies, or sexual sadomasochism—has been stigmatized as irrational, "Old World," or perverse.

In the essay "*La herencia de Coatlicue*," we can see how Anzaldúa came to view physical pain as a "redemptive and visionary power" (to paraphrase Morris) in the delineation of *mestiza* identity. As a child she wondered what was pulling her body/self apart—why "*la vida . . . me araña y me golpea, me deshuesa* [life scratches, hits, and de-bones me]" (Anzaldúa, *Borderlands* 44)—but ultimately she claimed her painful friction with *la vida* as the shape of her *mestiza* lesbianism:

> *Despierta me encuentra la madrugada, una desconocida aulleando profecías entre cenizas, sangrando mi cara con las uñas, escarbando la desgracia debajo de mi máscara. . . .* [The early morning wakes and finds me, a stranger howling prophecies amongst the ashes, bloodying my face with my fingernails, scratching out the shame beneath my mask. . . .] Alone with the presence in the room. Who? Me, my psyche, the Shadow-Beast? . . . And there in the black, obsidian mirror of the Nahuas is yet another face, a stranger's face. *Simultáneamente me miraba la cara desde distintos ángulos. Y mi cara, como la realidad, tenía un carácter multíplice.* [Simultaneously I looked at my face / my face looked at me from different angles. And my face, like reality, had a multiple character.] (44)[11]

This provocative image internalizes the other and exteriorizes the self: she believes she is prying out something shameful that has gotten under her skin, and the "Shadow-Beast" in the room is "me, my psyche." The sentences in untranslated Spanish represent greater ambiguity of identity

11. It is significant that the sentences describing the speaker's encounter with the mask, multiplicity, shame, prophecy, and blood are in untranslated Spanish, reserving these spiritual or metaphysical references for Spanish-language readers.

and agency since the subjects of the verbs "wake," "howling," "bloody-ing," "scratching," and "looked at" are unstated and unclear. When her mask is scratched (by herself or by the early morning), her own face is bloodied, and this painful self-revelation illuminates a crucial *mestiza* ambivalence. After looking at her face from different angles, she realizes the interior other and exterior alien as components of her "*multíplice*" self.[12] This topological inconsistence is consistent with other labels Anzal-dúa embraces, like "half and half" or *atravesado* (cross-eyed/crossed over), each of which breaks down unity of identity, unity of position, or unity of vision.[13] In response to the encounter above, she writes that, at first, "*quiero contenerme*" (I want to contain myself), but then she rejects the impulse and "*desbordo*" (I overflow), spilling out of the boundaries of her own skin (44).

This passage supports readings from a variety of cultural perspectives. Face-scratching seems to beg a psychoanalytic reading: the speaker is awakened (by a dream, by pain) to an unconscious presence in her own psyche and is forced to come to terms with the multiple layers of identity and the potential conflicts between the ego's perception and reality. There is always another self repressed behind one's public identity, wait-ing to be found out. This passage has a Catholic confessional aspect, too: probing and then attempting to purge one's sinful inner drives, making them visible to God/priest. Yet the most prevalent references here reflect an Aztec worldview. (As Anzaldúa writes elsewhere, "I know things older than Freud" [*Borderlands* 26].) The view of "strangeness" is pro-vided by the "obsidian mirror of the Nahuas,"[14] and a literal interpreta-tion of the layers of skin has grounding in the Aztec fertility god Xipe

12. In the interview with Linda Smuckler, Anzaldúa similarly describes find-ing "other faces" behind her own when looking in the mirror, and she devel-oped a theory of "Gloria Multiplex," or "the Multiple Glorias" (Anzaldúa, *Interviews* 36–37). (She made this discovery while tripping on mushrooms, a source of inspiration that she attributes to Aztec healing rituals.)

13. In *Borderlands*, Anzaldúa celebrates "half and half" as a supernatural em-bodiment of both male and female, defying binary opposition (*Borderlands* 19), and claims *atravesados* (cross-eyed, cross-bred, stretched across, pierced, treacher-ous, or wicked) as inhabitants of the borderlands (3).

14. According to Nahuatl/Aztec/Mexica cultures, all beings incorporate dif-ferent animistic forces (like *tonalli*) that shadow their identities and potentially cause dangerous imbalances. A confrontation with one of these animas can lead to a transformation in identity, sometimes even shape-shifting (*nahualism*).

Totec ("the flayed one"), who represented the cyclicality of life and death and was honored by a ritual in which priests flayed sacrificial victims and donned their skin.[15] This meeting of skins reflected the intersection of life and death and was charged with regenerative power. Skin resonates with racialized meaning, so uncovering layers of Anzaldúa's skin would expose the transracial conflicts and conquests that her *mestizaje* embodies. This section looks at the significance of pain in the Aztec and Spanish cultural sources between which Anzaldúa's *mestiza* consciousness stretches.

Although she risks minimizing the reality of the Aztecs' violent imperialism in Mesoamerica and idealizing the significance of Aztec goddesses, Anzaldúa's use of Aztec culture extends embodiment beyond "Western" corporeal limitations. She opens identity to continual restructuring in the process she names the Coatlicue state—in honor of the "serpent-skirted" Aztec goddess of fertility and death. Coatlicue makes life from destruction, breaking down binary oppositions by embodying both ends of the life cycle.[16] Rituals dedicated to Coatlicue sometimes included decapitation, and she is represented with serpents' heads in place of her own and a necklace of skulls. As mother, Coatlicue required the destruction of one being before giving birth to new life. Roberta Markman and Peter Markman distance Coatlicue from the misogynist devouring mother of European mythology, since "these seemingly contradictory roles made sense in a culture that saw death as the necessary precondition for birth, a culture that saw bones as seeds" (Markman and Markman 190).

Anzaldúa describes Coatlicue states as psychological processes in which one engages with, rather than resisting, the pain and destruction

15. According to Roberta and Peter Markman, the feast in honor of Xipe Totec symbolized "the dead covering of the earth in the dry season of winter . . . giv[ing] way to the new vegetation bursting forth in spring" (Markman and Markman 175). This festival was celebrated immediately before the time of sowing, and the ritual donning of sacrificial victims' skin demonstrated the release of spirit that occurs with death and produces new life: "The ritual thus makes clear that the return of spirit, now separated from matter, to the realm of the gods is one of the primary functions of sacrifice. That return is the ritual acknowledgment of the essential cyclicity of life" (176).

16. References to smoking mirrors and heart excision at the beginning of *Borderlands'* chapter on Coatlicue also link the Coatlicue state to the Aztec ceremony of Toxcatl, in which a captive warrior was sacrificed to the "god of gods," "Lord of the Smoking Mirror," Tezcatlipoca (Anzaldúa, *Borderlands* 41; Carrasco 118). Since this ceremony occurred during the dry season, Coatlicue's link to fertility and life cycles bears relevance here.

that we fear, rebirthing the self in the process: "Those activities or *Coat-licue* states which disrupt the smooth flow (complacency) of life are exactly what propel the soul to do its work: make soul, increase consciousness of itself. Our greatest disappointments and painful experiences—if we can make meaning out of them—can lead us toward becoming more of who we are" (Anzaldúa, *Borderlands* 46).[17] Anzaldúa thus theorizes identity as an open-ended process of destroying and remaking our lives. The logic of Coatlicue helps her to accept physical pain as a necessary part of this healthy process: "Every increment of consciousness, every step forward is a *travesía*, a crossing. I am again an alien in new territory. And again, and again. But if I escape conscious awareness, escape 'knowing,' I won't be moving" (48). The new context of each crossing transforms the self, but it hurts to cross psychological, corporeal, and geographic borders. "[S]weating," with a "headache," "*voy cagán-dome de miedo*" [shitting myself with fear], Anzaldúa describes "allowing myself to fall apart" as she proceeds through the Coatlicue state (48). Ana Castillo suggests "that Anzaldúa's spiritual affinity for Coatlicue serves as a resonant reflection of her desire for disembodiment that would free her from a tremendous physical and emotional anguish" (Castillo, *Massacre of the Dreamers* 173). While Castillo sees Anzaldúa's Coatlicue state as a desire to escape from her body, I would argue, instead, that these passages indicate the ability of—and the need for—bodies to mutate in the process of life-making, like the serpent with which Coatlicue is associated. The aching body that falls apart in Coatlicue states feels pain as a materialization of increased awareness and expanded embodiment.[18] Awareness of

17. This passage recalls Nietzsche's point in *On the Genealogy of Morals*: "Man, the bravest of animals and the one most accustomed to suffering, does not repudiate suffering as such; he *desires* it, he even seeks it out, provided he is shown a *meaning* for it, a *purpose* of suffering" (Nietzsche 162). Did Anzaldúa turn to Coatlicue only because she *had to* make meaning out of her pain? Would she have developed these ideas if her own body had not suffered? Of course, we cannot answer these questions, but the comparison to Nietzsche helps to explain how pain can lead to philosophical and spiritual inquiry, and how such inquiry can valorize pain.

18. Anzaldúa uses the term "*nepantla*" to explain the liminal crossing out of the Coatlicue State when/where one loses one's location as a subject; she explains, in a 1994 interview with Debbie Black and Carmen Abrego, "When you come out of the Coatlicue state you come out of nepantla, this birthing stage where you feel like you're reconfiguring your identity and don't know where you are. You used to be this person but now maybe you're different in some

Anzaldúa's suffering with diabetes gives new meaning to this process and suggests that it is more than just metaphorical.

The most obvious and most terrifying use of pain in Aztec culture is human sacrifice. The continuation of life, according to an Aztec world-view, required public sacrifice by humans to the gods, exchanging life for life. Spilling blood and scattering bones on the earth represented a promise of fertility (Markman and Markman 180–81). Markman and Markman describe the essence of sacrifice as "transformation, the means by which the realm of the spirit enters human space and man can enter the domain of the spirit. . . ." At the moment of sacrifice, the subject was believed to "incarnate the supernatural" (179). Costumes and masks were used to highlight the subject's embodiment of the "god image." Historian Davíd Carrasco emphasizes the dialogue between the victim and the crowd during the visual spectacle of human sacrifice:

> On the one side of this ceremonial performance we have the human body encapsulating a vibrating, divine force and adorned with sacred images moving, changing, and linking up a ritual land-scape. On the other side, we have the participants and observers seeing a cosmology and social world come to life through the movements and changes of a divine image. (Carrasco 123)

---

way. You're changing worlds and culture and maybe classes, sexual preferences. So you go through this birthing of nepantla" (Anzaldúa, *Interviews* 225–26). Nepantla represents the birth canal, emergent from the womb state of Coatlicue (226): "Suddenly the repressed energy rises, makes decisions, connects with con-scious energy and a new life begins. It is her reluctance to cross over, to make a hole in the fence and walk across, to cross the river, to take that flying leap into the dark, that drives her to escape, that forces her into the fecund cave of her imagination where she is cradled in the arms of Coatlicue, who will never let her go. If she doesn't change her ways, she will remain a stone forever. *No hay más que cambiar*" (*Borderlands* 49). Coatlicue and *nepantla* make evident that Anzaldúa's border-crossings are more than geographical: they describe the con-tinual reformation of *mestiza* identity itself. In a 1991 interview with AnaLouise Keating, Anzaldúa poses *nepantla* as an alternative metaphor to transcend the more limiting ways that "borderlands" was appropriated from her earlier work: "I find people using metaphors such as 'Borderlands' in a more limited sense than I had meant it, so to expand on the psychic and emotional borderlands I'm now using 'nepantla.' With nepantla the connection to the spirit world is more pronounced as is the connection to the world after death, to psychic spaces. It has a more spiritual, psychic, supernatural, and indigenous resonance" (*Interviews* 176).

Like Anzaldúa's own writing, sacrifice involves metaphorical substitutions, shape-changing, and glimpsing other worlds. As a public display, human sacrifice served a practical function: sacrificial victims were made to embody the Aztec worldview and to secure witnesses' allegiance to that worldview.[19] Carrasco describes the Aztecs as "a people obsessed with the structured nearness of death" (190), and central to their power and dominion throughout Mesoamerica was their ability to control death, to call down gods during public sacrifice rituals, and to channel these forces toward the vitality of the community.

As I see it, the sensation of pain, in this context, must signal the regenerative power of the sacrificial victim. Ancient Nahuatl bloodletting rituals were practiced as a means of communication with the spirit world (López Austin 381). According to the Mexican historian Alfredo López Austin, "The object of flesh piercing and bloodletting was to cause physical pain and to obtain the vital fluid to offer the gods" (380). This description reflects an economy of exchange, trading blood for strength, moral purity, or favors from the gods. Some forms of bloodletting, however, seem to be aimed at more than equivalence or barter, valuing the experience itself. Yolotl González-Torres writes that "*pensamos que este estado de unión con lo sobrenatural era logrado más profundamente a través de la pérdida de la sangre, del dolor de la herida, a lo que iban unidos los ayunos y la ingestión de yerbas alucinantes* [we think that this state of union with the supernatural was achieved most profoundly through the loss of blood, of the pain of the wound, to which was joined fasts and the injection of hallucinogenic herbs]" (González-Torres 118). In this way, the psychological state produced by pain is where the spiritual and material realms meet. "Throughout Mesoamerica the bleeding of ears, tongues, and genital organs by members of the priesthood was a daily ritual occurrence," often involving protracted torture, such as passing cords up to fifteen or twenty yards long through the penis (Markman and Markman 180). The

---

19. Carrasco sees human sacrifice as thus serving an imperialist function: solidifying the allegiance of subjugated peoples and committing them to Aztec ways of seeing (Carrasco 121–23). Sacrifice objectified the power of this worldview and forced audiences to experience and to acknowledge this power (155). To this end, the victim was often paraded throughout the empire to be viewed, touched, sometimes even tasted (155–57). Yolotl González-Torres also notes "*el papel de la religión como instrumento del grupo dominante, como forma de dominación ideológica . . . tanto en Tenochtitlan como en las provincias sujetas*" [the role of religion as an instrument of the dominant group, as a form of ideological domination . . . as much in Tenochtitlan as in the subject provinces] (González-Torres 103).

purpose of bloodletting in these prolonged rituals obviously exceeded the function of producing a quantity of blood. Pain must have been valued in its own right.[20] If Aztec society was structured around death, any affirmations of life would have been achieved in combination with the forces of destruction. Perhaps pain signified this tension, the experience of destruction in life, the presence of the divine in the human. In López Austin's translation, the Nahuatl term for agony, *atlaza*, literally means "to cast off the crown of the head," signifying the passing of the agonized person's spirit or *tonalli* from his/her head and its ascension to the spirit world (López Austin 224). It was believed that the person could then live for a short time without his/her *tonalli*, experiencing this other-worldly communication without death. Agony thus provided a temporary intersection between realms.

Certain Catholic valuations of pain are strikingly similar. According to Morris, the pain of medieval saints was read as a sign of contact with the divine and was "transform[ed] from a private sensation into a public spectacle" (Morris, *The Culture of Pain* 48–50). Conferring honor to martyrs used the pain of individual bodies to solidify, metonymically, the body of Catholic ideology. In the case of the Spanish Saint Teresa de Avila, Johanne Sloane argues, "Receiving this privileged signifier of pain [one of the nails from Christ's crucifixion] was a guarantee of Teresa's empowerment as an individual, allowing her to exceed the dictates of

---

20. Inga Clendinnen suggests the opposite. Though, at the beginning of *Aztecs*, she invokes the Plains Indian's Vision Quest in which self-mortification was meant "to force the manifestation of his Spirit through the intensity of his suffering" (Clendinnen, *Aztecs* 70), she ultimately concludes that, for the Aztecs, "what was being offered [in rites in which priests passed rods of wood through their tongue] was not, primarily, pain. While pain was certainly suffered, it was where practicable minimized: that first obsidian blade sliced cleanly, while the wood of the rods was carefully smoothed. Blood appears to be the desired and measurable product" (256). Clendinnen, too, considers the case of passing long cords through the penis, dismissing the interpretation that inducing extreme pain was meant to induce a vision because "fainting was taken as a sign of disqualifying impurity" (256). I would argue that fainting would be irrelevant if producing blood were the endpoint. Fainting interrupts the sensation of pain, so the "impurity" would lie in the failure to experience pain, not the failure to produce blood. Aztec rituals and sacrifices were designed to represent the ways in which the ecstasy and excess of the sacred obliterated the social orders and boundaries created by humans. Pain would be the clearest expression of this transgression of boundaries.

nature, including the 'obstacle' of her femininity" (Sloane 125). Christ's
nail, in this way, endows the mortal female body with divine power.[21]

Writing just after the Spanish conquest of Mexico, and later one of the
most influential saints in Mexico, Saint Teresa describes the "exceeding
beauty" of God's love in terms of pain. Her poem "*¡Oh hermosura que
excedéis. . .!*" embraces pain as the condition for that love: "*¡Sin herir
dolor hacéis, / y sin dolor deshacéis/ el amor de las criaturas!* [Without wounding you give pain, / and without pain you destroy/ the love of crea-
tures]" (Teresa de Jesús 716). In her hagiography, she describes her
raptures as physical and painful:

> *No se puede encarecer ni decir el modo con que llaga Dios el alma y la
> grandísima pena que da, que la hace no saber de sí; mas es esta pena tan
> sabrosa, que no hay deleite en la vida que más contento dé. Siempre querría
> el alma, como he dicho, estar muriendo de este mal.* [One cannot exag-
> gerate or even say the way in which God wounds the soul and the
> greatest pain that He/it gives, so that it makes the soul not know
> itself; but this pain is so delicious/delightful that there is no delight
> in life more contented. The soul would always want, as I have said,
> to be dying of this illness.] (176)

Her narrations of her own experiences with pain, rapture, and illness
reflect not a denial of the flesh but a celebration of these corporeal dimensions of her spirituality. She writes that the faithful should not "*huir
tanto de cosas corpóreas* [hide so much from corporeal things]" (456), and
as she meditates on her multiple illnesses as well as her religious raptures,
her body is the site where her faith is mapped out.

After her death, Saint Teresa's miraculously unperished body, still ra-
diant and free of decay, was disinterred and cut into fragments, her
clothes soaked in her still-fresh blood and magical fragrance, and these
relics were distributed throughout the realm as symbols of the power of

21. Josef Breuer famously called Saint Teresa "the patron saint of hysteria,"
even while noting her "genius" and "great practical capacity" (Breuer and Freud
232). If we agree with the analysis that hysteria is the embodied expression of
personal desires and anxieties, Saint Teresa's martyrdom allowed for the realization of her genius and manifested her desire for the power traditionally reserved
for men in Catholicism. Her status as recipient of Christ's "favors" (most of
which were felt by her as pain) endowed her with vicarious power as Christ's
"bride" and earned her the authority to teach other nuns, to expand the Carmelite order, and to found convents according to her own religious model.

(Spanish) Catholicism to transcend death. According to Carlos Eire, Teresa's imperishable corpse "blurred the lines between heaven and earth or, perhaps even more, served as a nexus between the two spheres. . . . In brief, her body itself *was* heaven" (Eire 504–5). This symbol of transcendence correlates with the Aztec tradition of displaying dead bodies to link this world to the spirit world and to symbolize the imbrication of life and death. Both the Catholics and the Aztecs used the bodies of sacred sufferers as political tools to strengthen their empires. As Aztec and Spanish Catholic cosmologies syncretically fused to form *mestizo* cosmology in "New Spain," during the same time period that pieces of Saint Teresa's body circulated throughout "Old Spain," the association of pain and death with divinity and life likely presented a powerful point of convergence for the two traditions and potentially rationalized the simultaneous death of one empire (Aztec) and birth of another (Spanish).[22]

Anzaldúa invokes Teresa de Avila as a model of sacrificial power in her poem "Holy Relics," which ultimately fuses this cultural reference with Aztec ones.[23] "Holy Relics" retells not the life of the saint but the posthumous dismemberment and "theft" of Teresa's corpse by greedy priests and competing convents—focusing on the dead body, rather than the "Life," as an object of worship. In Anzaldúa's poem, auctioning off Teresa's fingers, bone fragments, teeth, and "pinched off pieces of her flesh" reflects more than a violation of the saint's body for church profit

22. Many interpretations suggest that the Aztecs perceived the Spanish Conquest as the destruction of the Quinto Sol [Fifth Sun] and the rebirth of a new era (Moraga, *Loving in the War Years* 100).

23. Anzaldúa dedicates "Holy Relics" to two lesbian writers, Judy Grahn and Vita Sackville-West. The latter name reflects an affirmation of life—*vida* in Spanish—and invokes the title of Saint Teresa's personal writings, *Vida de Santa Teresa de Jesús y algunas de las Mercedes que Dios le hizo, escritas por ella misma por mandado de su confesor, a quien lo envía y dirige, y dice así.* Anzaldúa's refrain to Grahn and Sackville-West is "We are the holy relics, / the scattered bones of a saint, / the best loved bones of Spain. / We seek each other" (Anzaldúa, *Borderlands* 154–59). Each poet embodies the relics/bones/poems of her foremothers, and each is severed to bits by the conflicting expectations and critical interpretations of sexual and cultural communities. Anzaldúa's poem stretches across time and nation to gather the pieces and to highlight their dispersal. She situates herself in a genealogy of impassioned women-oriented women, from Teresa to Vita to Judy Grahn, who seek each other as allied body parts. Pain and fragmentation inspire, or demand, connection with others.

(Anzaldúa, *Borderlands* 158). It also demonstrates the intensity of her worshippers' commitment to her flesh and the ability of her dead bones to inspire, to build community, and to incite rivalrous passions. Reminiscent of Aztec beliefs, Teresa's bones held creative, generative powers. Indeed, the "mysterious smell" of her disinterred corpse cures one monk's malaria in "Holy Relics" (157–58). By the end of the poem, the saint's body is left with "a gaping hole where her heart had been ripped out" (159), suggesting that the rituals of the devoted priests mimicked the Aztecs' human sacrifice rituals.

The other poems in the second half of *Borderlands* echo this theme of corporeal sacrifice, and several ("Poets have strange eating habits," "Letting Go," "*La curandera*," and "Creature of Darkness," for example) invoke pain as curative.[24] Like the interviews, Anzaldúa's poems often present more radical visions of identity and embodiment than her essays do, making literal many of the ideas that seem metaphorical in the more frequently discussed works. Most of these poems contain autobiographical details, and subtle cross-referencing between the poems intertwines author with "characters." "*Nopalitos*" describes the painful friction between an educated Chicana and the traditions she has left behind: while trying to prepare *nopalitos* (a *mestizo* dish of cooked cactus), she gets "thorns embedded" in her flesh and her eyes sting from the burning mesquite (113). Through this pain she feels her enactment of tradition as well as the incompetence that has come with cultural distance. Another self-reflexive poem, "that dark shining thing," describes the humiliation "the only round face, / Indian-beaked, off-colored / in the faculty lineup, the workshop, the panel" experiences when she allows the faculty or conference organizers to dig fingernails into her flesh and to chop off her hand in order to minimize/accentuate/accommodate her difference. The "life or death" cause in the poem is that of the Chicana lesbian writer, the one who must name "that dark animal" inside the "colored, poor white, latent queer," the repressed "black," "numinous

---

24. In "Poets have strange eating habits," Anzaldúa writes that "wounding is a deeper healing" (Anzaldúa, *Borderlands* 140). "Letting Go" sexualizes the Coatlicue state as a process of "plung[ing] your fingers / into your navel, with your two hands / split open"—a process ultimately credited with fertility as the contents of the body spill out as flowers, lizards, toads, spring rain, and young ears of corn (164). In "*La Curandera*," Juan Dávila's "pain crawl[s] to where [the speaker's dead body] had lain" and brings it back to life (177). And in "Creature of Darkness," thinking "stirs up the pain / opens the wound / starts the healing" (186).

thing" to which "everyone says no no no" (171–72). Publicly saying yes to stigmatized identities is a form of self-sacrifice. This poem, too, fuses Spanish and Aztec cultural references: "the hand you chop off while still clinging to it" recalls both the amputation in "*Cihuatlyotl*, Woman Alone" and the wrist that Padre Gracian severed from Saint Teresa's arm ("hugging her hand to his body") in "Holy Relics" (155), comparing the speaker to sacrifice victims and saints whose bodies are sacrificed for a political cause. The pain in these poems reflects the internal differences and competing alliances that jar within the *mestiza* lesbian and is validated through an intersection of Spanish and Aztec frames of reference.

Although psychoanalysis and postmodernism help to illuminate the multiplicity within the identities Anzaldúa describes, these challenges to singular subjectivity and the pain associated with them take on very specific connotations in the context of Mexico's *mestizo* cultural frameworks. To appreciate Catholic and Aztec identities—both separately and mixed within *mestizaje*—we must have a conception of human life that includes death; that does not fear physical fragmentation; that respects the intertwinement of this world and the heavens; that incorporates other bodies, animas, and spirits within the individual; and that *feels* pain as productive. Anzaldúa's investment in this tradition takes us outside modern taboos surrounding pain and fluid embodiment.

Pain and Feminism

In *El Laberinto de la Soledad* (1947), Octavio Paz famously explains Mexicans' fear of physical openness as a product of the Conquest of the Aztecs and the Spaniards' supposed violation of La Malinche, *la chingada*, the fucked one, the "mother" of Mexican *mestizaje*. Mexican *mestizos* symbolically embody La Malinche's shame for having been open to Spanish invasion:

> *Para nosotros, contrariamente a lo que ocurren con otros pueblos, abrirse es una debilidad o una traición. El mexicano puede doblarse, humillarse, "agacharse," pero no "rajarse," esto es, permitir que el mundo exterior penetre en su intimidad . . . . Las mujeres son seres inferiores porque, al entregarse, se abren. Su inferioridad es constitucional y radica en su sexo, en su "rajado," herida que jamás cicatriza.* [For us, contrary to that which occurs with other peoples, to open oneself is a weakness or a betrayal. The Mexican can stoop/bend, humiliate himself, yield himself, but not split open, that is, permit that the outside world

penetrate in his intimacy. . . . Women are inferior beings because, upon giving themselves (sexually), they open themselves. Their inferiority is constitutional and is rooted in their sex, in their "split," wound that never heals.] (Paz 29–30)

When Anzaldúa writes, at the beginning of *Borderlands*, that the border splits her ["*me raja me raja*"] (Anzaldúa, *Borderlands* 2), I believe it is a direct response to Paz, but Anzaldúa honors the feminine vulnerability Paz demonizes. The wounding and splitting of Anzaldúa's *mestiza* consciousness is that which enables the incorporation of new elements, tolerates ambiguities, and "breaks down the unitary aspect of each new paradigm" (80).

Paz ties this marking of women as "*rajada*" (split) and "*herida*" (wounded) to the engendering of the "suffering woman" ideal in Mexico: "*Más, en virtud de un mecanismo de compensación fácilmente explicable, se hace virtud de su flaqueza original y se crea el mito de la 'sufrida mujer mexicana'* [Moreover, by virtue of an easily explainable mechanism of compensation, their original weakness becomes a virtue and the myth of the "suffering Mexican woman" is created]" (Paz 37). Claiming pain as a normative, indeed valorized, identification for women corresponds to misogynist mythology designed to ensure women's submission. Paz's writings support this mythology by railing against corporeal and national openness as explicitly feminine forms of shame. When Anzaldúa counterintuitively adopts these demonized attributes, is she, in this process, accepting vulnerability as *mestizas'* special responsibility (as female descendants of La Malinche)? I would argue that, though her vision is grounded in *mestiza/o* history, Anzaldúa's body politics are forward-looking, always reconfiguring her cultural inheritance. Unlike the suffering woman who supports the status quo of gender politics, Anzaldúa took pain as the starting point for her theory of agency, the shock that propagates change. She made permeability politically progressive, using that which is illegitimate and painful in *mestizaje* to question our standards of legitimate corporeality. If permeability can be a position of possibility and progress, then women's bodies instantiate an ideal, not shame.

Feminists might recoil from Anzaldúa's sacrificial gesture. From its beginnings, feminism has taken women's physical security as one of its primary goals: defending women from violence, protecting women's health, and strengthening women's place in the world. From this perspective, pain and illness seem counterproductive for feminist body politics. Paradigmatically, Simone de Beauvoir's *The Second Sex* (1949) bemoans the ways in which the burdens of female physiology hinder women's existential transcendence. Although de Beauvoir regards the body as a situation, rather than a fixture of destiny, she describes how women's possibilities are restricted by enslavement to the processes of reproduction, weak and unstable corporeality, and cyclical physiological crises (de Beauvoir 32, 34). These factors make it more difficult for women to transcend "immanence" and thus contribute to their status as the "Other." There seems to be near-consensus that feminists must lift women out of the situation in which they are at risk, in pain, and open to outside intrusions. There also seems to be near-consensus that pain and illness inhibit one's ability to operate as a full political subject (as we see in de Beauvoir's critique of women's physiological immanence as well as those old arguments that women who are menstruating, pregnant, etc., are unfit to vote, to preach, to rule, etc.). Anzaldúa asks us to think otherwise.

Most of us regard pain as something to be eliminated, illness as something to be cured. Modern corporeal logic is thus oriented toward an endpoint of fixity. Indeed, Lynda Hall reads Anzaldúa in this manner, within a framework of "ameliorography": "Anzaldúa connects the act of writing with desires to heal the self and . . . [with] attempts to relieve personal pain as an 'othered' person" (Hall, "Lorde, Anzaldúa, and Tropicana" 113). Yet the quote Hall selects from *Interviews* to support this statement describes "making meaning of pain," rather than healing (Hall, "Lorde, Anzaldúa, and Tropicana" 113; Anzaldúa, *Interviews* 276). I interpret Anzaldúa's phrase as evidence of the potential meaningfulness of pain as a suspended state of being rather than as an attempt to eliminate pain or to repair the "othered" body. The body that Anzaldúa depicts continually elides any illusions of ultimate security. This deferral of health is a political gesture that asks us to rethink the way we interpret certain sensations. It asks us to respect fluidity in defiance of conventional wisdom that seeks to maximize stability. Or, in Norma Alarcón's interpretation, Anzaldúa's *mestiza* feminism "risk[s] the 'pathological condition' by representing . . . [a] break with a developmental view of self-inscription" (Alarcón, "Anzaldúa's *Frontera*" 362). Never fully "inscribed" or "whole," the *mestiza* "becomes a crossroads, a collision course, a clearinghouse, an endless alterity who . . . appears as a tireless peregrine collecting all of the parts that will never make her whole" (367).[25] This

25. Norma Alarcón links the "polyvalent" naming of Anzaldúa's "feminine"—La Chingada, Coatlicue, Cihuacoatl, Guadalupe (and, I would add, Saint

is a "peregrination" with no final destination. In a 2001 interview with Irene Reti, Anzaldúa redefined health itself: "I don't define health as the absence of disease, but as learning to live with disease, with dysfunction, with wounds, and working towards wholeness. If you're human, you don't have to have a whole integrated body" (Anzaldúa, "Daughter of Coatlicue" 51). "Wholeness" remains on the horizon of this disintegrated "health."

Given that women's bodies are "by nature" open, potentially shapeshifting, and sometimes bleeding, this might be a more appropriate framework for feminist body politics (despite our desires to find firm and solid footing in the world). I am suggesting that feminist theory should learn from disability theory ways to separate political strength from corporeal strength. As David Mitchell and Sharon Snyder ask:

> Is it necessary to refuse an acknowledgement of biological fragility or incapacity in order to establish an effective political movement? Can one not recognize the often very real limitations of the bodies that we inherit or acquire without having to give up on revising the politicized reception of the disabled body? The question that disability studies scholars must take up now is whether or not it is possible to acknowledge a physically/cognitively limited body that is not automatically viewed as hopeless, unproductive, or benightedly tragic in the social sphere. (Mitchell and Snyder 247)

It seems to me particularly counterproductive for feminism to condemn weakness and vulnerability as tragic impediments. Gaining equal footing should not require static corporeality.

Susan Bordo's critique of postmodern feminism fears applying theoretical ideals like fluidity and instability to women's bodies:

> To deny the unity and stability of identity is one thing. The epistemological fantasy of *becoming* multiplicity—the dream of limitless multiple embodiments, allowing one to dance from place to place and self to self—is another. What sort of body is it that is free to change its shape and location at will, that can become anyone and

---

Teresa)—to the continual "hunger" of this open-ended identification: "Such a hunger forces her to recollect in excess, to remember in excess, to labor to excess, to produce a text layered with inversions and disproportions, which are effects of experienced dislocations, vis-à-vis the text of the Name of the Father and the Place of the Law" (Alarcón, "Anzaldúa's *Frontera*" 361, 367). Continual dislocation shifts the names of her model.

travel everywhere? If the body is a metaphor for our locatedness in space and time and thus for the finitude of human perception and knowledge, then the postmodern body is no body at all. (Bordo, "Feminism, Postmodernism, and Gender-Scepticism" 145)

In Anzaldúa's representations one can find an answer to Bordo. A *mestiza* body, as Anzaldúa envisions it, does change its form, cross boundaries, and exceed corporeal boundedness, but it is also not "no body at all." It retains material substance, political sensitivity, historical origins, and cultural specificity.

Since biological study confirms physiological fluctuation to be a norm, feminist biologists have been developing new models for analyzing health. Lynda Birke, for instance, proposes medical attention to bodies as constitutionally shifting in dialogue with the outside world, and she locates agency in this dialogue: "[W]hat I seek to emphasize here is an understanding of agency that emerges out of the engagement of the organism with its surroundings; it is thus an agency in relation, not an essential property of the individual" (Birke, *Feminism and the Biological Body* 152). Birke values corporeal fluctuation as a form of self-assertion, rather than a hindrance, foregrounding how organisms dynamically respond to context and contingency, actively transforming themselves (152). Since pain often involves a puncture in the skin or a rupture of tissues, it provides a point of entry for understanding how our bodies respond to external forces. Pain happens where we touch the world. It marks our interactions with context, reorganizations of skin and muscle, and the straining of our bodies against physical limitations. Particular experiences of pain filter this movement through a lexicon of sensation that is culturally grounded, physically alert, and sensitive to affect. Perhaps pain itself is a sign of agency.

Feminist attempts to secure women's health by sealing their boundaries reproduce potentially destructive binary thinking about health/pathology, good/bad, self/other. Bill Burns, Cathy Busby, and Kim Sawchuk's introduction to *When Pain Strikes* (1999), a cultural study of pain, describes the militaristic framework that medical discourses of the body perpetuate:

Pain figures as a force invading the fortress body, smashing against its walls like the hammer that hits the head in a classic Bufferin advertisement from the midseventies. The skin is presented as a thick black line with a definite interior and exterior, rather than a permeable border that continually opens out and into the world. . . . Blockades are deployed to keep pain at bay and to reestablish symbolically the solid black line, that generic picture, of the walled body. Pain in this schema must not only be minimized for the subject but it must also be prevented from escaping one body and moving on to another. (Burns et al. xx–xxi)

The implication of this rhetoric is that bodies, like modern nations, must shore up their boundaries because everything outside (other nations, other people, even the air itself) is dangerous and must be aggressively fought off. Perhaps a conception of bodies that incorporates pain could produce a rhetoric of openness and a politics more suited to feminism and *mestizaje*. Since women's bodies do not fit the militaristic ideal (based on biological and psychological studies of their greater openness, permeability, and receptivity to pain),[26] we need a model, such as that offered by Anzaldúa, that does not require closure for vitality or agency. Anzaldúa's representations of pain embrace corporeal fluctuations and displace the rhetoric of fortresses, defenses, and weapons. A theory of permeable identity—one that includes contact with others—would have no need to be so defensive. Opening subjectivity in this way could have positive political implications, though it complicates the presumably stable subject ("woman") at the center of feminist identity politics.

Margrit Shildrick argues for a postmodern feminist ethics based on "leaky bodies." In resistance to the "illusory closure" defended by biomedical convention, undoing "the binary of order/disorder must result in a very different ethic . . . in which normalisation would be meaningless" (Shildrick, *Leaky Bodies* 214). "[T]he experience of illness or disability" or, perhaps, pain, "might itself constitute new subject positions not just resistant but excessive to the norms of the Western logos," exceeding patriarchal norms that stigmatize all who are "different" (215). Anzaldúa affirmed this kind of thinking in the end:

Although all your cultures reject the idea that you can know the other, you believe that besides love, pain might open this closed passage by reaching through the wound to connect. Wounds cause you to shift consciousness—they either open you to the greater reality normally blocked by your habitual point of view or else shut you down. . . . Using wounds as openings to become vulnerable and available (present) to others means staying in your body. (Anzaldúa, "now let us shift" 571–72)

26. See, for example, Fillingim and Ness.

Accepting wounds as openings to others—to "trigger compassion," she writes (572)—defies all conventional wisdom about affect, sensation, and safety, but perhaps that is because such "wisdom" has been governed so long by the competitive, defensive, and anesthetic sensibility of modern nations. In her theory of radical feminist spirituality, Leela Fernandes similarly endorses "using one's suffering as the guide and basis for activism," using suffering to "break out of the cycle of violence that is inherent in any form of justice based on retribution" and using the sufferer's vision of oppression to "make a fundamental break from the logic of oppression" (Fernandes 72). If the "logic of oppression" assumes solid boundaries to defend, then bodies in pain, with their intimate awareness of oppression's effects, might break the "cycle." But, in reality, most sufferers refuse to accept their broken boundaries, and the oppressed sometimes make the most likely oppressors.

Of course it is dangerous to accept pain—particularly the pain of women of color, which has been historically inflicted through racism, sexism, and colonialism—as a viable alternative to health. Yet perhaps it is more dangerous not to discuss this pain or the identities that have been founded on pain. Cassie Premo Steele suggests that ignoring pain indirectly inflicts it: "Anzaldúa's writing shows that healing comes through the acceptance of pain as a sign. She demonstrates that in order to heal, one needs to recognize the wound and to see what it can teach; one needs to feel the pain in order not to inflict further violence as a way of denying the pain" (*We Heal from Memory* 152). Steele also analyzes Anzaldúa's work through a rhetoric of healing, but she describes healing as an ongoing engagement with trauma, "not a vision of a utopian end to suffering but . . . a process that continues without end" (143). Rather than presenting a finally healed or assimilated surface, Anzaldúa highlights the friction of power inequality, the pain of conquest, and the corporeal contortions required to fit racial, national, and sexual ideals. Her body bears the marks of "la herida de [the wound of] colonialism and the trauma of conquest" (Anzaldúa, "Daughter of Coatlicue" 55). Ideally, this uncomfortable exposure will inspire a transformation of the institutions that violate certain bodies. But there is no guarantee. As Anzaldúa represents it, her body was eternally vulnerable. "*I'm not invincible, I tell you. My skin's fragile as a baby's I'm brittle bones and human, I tell you. I'm a broken arm*" (Anzaldúa, "la prieta" 204, original emphasis). What sort of identity is a broken arm? The tissues of this body are malleable rather than self-defensive. Fragile, as we all are, and injured, as we inevitably become throughout our movements in life, this "I" speaks to some

Plate 1a. Frida Kahlo, *The Two Fridas* (1939). © 2008 Banco de México Diego Rivera & Frida Kahlo Museums Trust. Av. 5 de Mayo No. 2, Col. Centro, Del. Cuauhtémoc 06059, México, D.F.

Plate 1b. Frida Kahlo, *Henry Ford Hospital* (1932). © 2008 Banco de México Diego Rivera & Frida Kahlo Museums Trust. Av. 5 de Mayo No. 2, Col. Centro, Del. Cuauhtémoc 06059, México, D.F.

Plate 2a. Frida Kahlo, *Without Hope* (1945). © 2008 Banco de México Diego Rivera & Frida Kahlo Museums Trust. Av. 5 de Mayo No. 2, Col. Centro, Del. Cuauhtémoc 06059, México, D.F.

Plate 2b. Coatlicue (Museo de Antropología, Mexico City).

Plate 3a. Book cover, *Waiting in the Wings.*

Plate 3b. Coyolxauhqui (Templo Mayor, Mexico City).

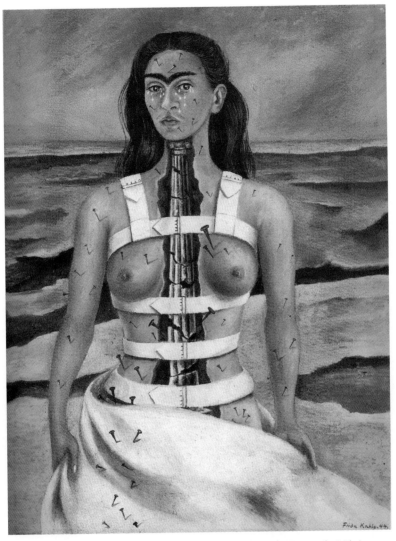

Plate 4a. Frida Kahlo, *The Broken Column* (1944). © 2008 Banco de México
Diego Rivera & Frida Kahlo Museums Trust. Av. 5 de Mayo No. 2, Col. Centro,
Del. Cuauhtémoc 06059, México, D.F.

Plate 4b. Pablo Picasso, *Seated Female Nude* (1909–10). © 2008 Estate of Pablo
Picasso/Artists Rights Society (ARS); courtesy Tate, London, 2008.

Plate 5. Maya González, *Death Enthroned* (2002). © Maya González.

Plate 6. Maya González, *The Love that Stains* (2000). © Maya González.

Plate 7. Maya González, *Switching Rabbits* (2002). © Maya González.

Plate 8. Diane Gamboa, *Little Gold Man* (1990). © Diane Gamboa.

"you" from both the "baby" end and the "brittle bones" end of life (like the fertility goddess Coatlicue). It's not invincible, but it is, nonetheless, "I" enough to identify itself as such over and over. If this "I" is here now and proud, its sense of itself is consciously temporary and tenuous. Anzaldúa offered this gesture toward a new kind of political filiation that draws from our permeability rather than our strength. If all people were to embrace this openness and brokenness in themselves—as many of Anzaldúa's mourners have—there could be a radical reconfiguration of physical interaction outside the dominant logic of anesthetized, isolated, and perfected bodies.

This counterintuitive questioning of "health" coincides with recent thinking in feminist spirituality. Fernandes's *Transforming Feminist Practice* (2003), a book Anzaldúa called "the next step" in feminist practice and "indispensable . . . for activistas and thinkers" (Fernandes back cover), insists that feminists must let go of their search for "a place of safety" and operate instead from "a place of risk" and continual "disidentification" (34). Fernandes defines disidentification as "a process of letting go not just of external social identities but of various forms of often invisible ego-based attachments" (35). In order to welcome difference and to avoid (potentially violent) competition, Fernandes argues that we must continually reject the ego and open our identities to the world around us. Safety is an ego-based, reactive impulse that does nothing to change the world.

Fernandes suggests that spirituality is the key to finding interconnections with other people, with the environment, with the universe:

> Spirituality can serve as a tremendous source of power that can enable us to challenge some of our deepest practices of identification, and can lead us to understand our self as an infinite, unbounded source of divinity, spiritual strength and empowerment. It leads us to question our ingrained assumptions regarding the boundaries of individual autonomy, agency and rationality. It leads us to question the often hidden distinctions we make between mind, matter and spirit. It dares us to disrupt the careful lines which thinkers and activists, both modern and postmodern, both religious and secular, have carved out between the realms of the human and the divine. (37)

I am not interested in endorsing or critiquing the spiritual component of this logic or its perceptions of the divine, but I am very interested in the shape of identity it delineates. Spirituality almost always accepts humans'

vulnerability to forces beyond their individual boundaries and their incorporation of some sort of "spirit" or "soul" that transcends mortal
limits. Those who accept spirituality thus accept some forms of boundary
crossing and relational attachments of the ego: acceptances that could
ideally shift human interactions. Unlike rhetorical appeals to "Christian"
good will and compassion that are missionary or (neo)colonialist in their
intention to reform the rest of the world in the image of Western Christianity, Fernandes's account of spirituality would require a continual re-
linquishing of one's own sensibilities, questioning of one's own beliefs,
and expansion of one's identity to welcome others. And unlike strategic
appeals to religion designed to eclipse material inequalities and oppressions, Fernandes's account of spiritual identity "does not dislodge the
materiality of these identities; rather, it requires a full and complete confrontation with the various sources of power, privilege and oppression
which shape our lives so that this spiritual self can emerge" (37). Spiritual
disidentification leads to continual self-questioning, "radical humility,"
and recognition of a shared spiritual source that crosses boundaries between individuals (44, 41). Idealistic? Overtly so. But isn't that the nature
of spirituality? According to Fernandes, "Transformative action *is* a utopian project. However, a spiritualized understanding of social justice recognizes that utopias are not simply noble goals, they are realizable
possibilities" (76, original emphasis). Fusing a sense of corporeal particularity with spiritual transcendence leads to an analysis of real material
contexts that is willing to think beyond the status quo supported by
Western rationalism.

Though many critics avoid Anzaldúa's spiritual leanings, this avoidance misses the crux of her thinking about bodies, identities, communities, and politics.[27] Her last published essay, indeed, is almost entirely
dedicated to spiritual activism, and her late collaborations with AnaLouise Keating indicate Anzaldúa's belief in the power of "spirit" to expand
our vision beyond competitiveness, self-defensiveness, and anesthesia. In
their Acknowledgments to their collection *This Bridge We Call Home:
Radical Visions for Transformation* (2002), they "give thanks" to the "oris-
has and espiritus . . . for guiding us, whispering words of encouragement

27. Laura E. Pérez argues (rightly, I think) that Chicanas' use of spirituality
"alongside more familiar areas of social struggle" like gender, sexuality, class, and
race challenges "cultural blind spots in mainstream values" as well as "what gets
to count as 'real' or useful knowledge" (L. Pérez, *Chicana Art* 3). The fact that
some scholars regard spirituality as "an embarrassing intellectual faux pas best
ignored" (2) signals the intellectually transgressive nature of spirituality.

that nourished our hearts, energized our bodies, and inspired our vision" (Anzaldúa and Keating xiv). This is what makes *This Bridge We Call Home* "radical," and it's a slightly different "radical" than that of its predecessor, *This Bridge Called My Back: Writings by Radical Women of Color* (1981). I believe that applying "radical" to "visions" in their subtitle is linked to the wider "net" Anzaldúa and Keating cast in including writings by anti-racist white women and feminist men in their collection. "Radical visions" are open-ended, unlike the identity-politics–based "radical women of color" of the original *Bridge*. In the newer *Bridge*, it is not just the writers who are radical (in their feminist, anti-homophobic, anti-racist, anti-capitalist politics). *This Bridge We Call Home* is conceptually radical in that it foregrounds heart, spirit, vision, and body, rather than academic frameworks or identity politics, as political tools.

In the new *Bridge*, Anzaldúa writes that "You use these spiritual tools to deal with political and personal problems. Power comes from being in touch with your body, soul, and spirit, and letting their wisdom lead you" (Anzaldúa, "now let us shift" 570). And, in the same collection, Keating writes that:

> Viewed from the Soul's presence there's no "me" or "you." There's just "us." And yet this "us" has been shattered and fragmented—split into a multiplicity of pieces marked by the many forms our identities take. I believe, with all my heart, that spiritual activism can assist us in creating new ways to move through these boundaries. ("Charting Pathways, Marking Thresholds" 19)

More recently, Keating developed the term "raw openness" "to underscore the painful, vulnerable dimensions" of maintaining this interconnectedness to others in a culture that teaches us "to define ourselves as unique, fully autonomous, rational individuals with permanent boundaries between ourselves and all others" (Keating, "Shifting Perspectives" 248–49). It is radical to suggest that we abandon the individuated subject of Western rationalism, but the subject most suited to Anzaldúa's politics of openness cannot be motivated by the boundaries of individual identities or personal needs. Invoking the spirit enables Anzaldúa, Keating, and Fernandes to push our thinking beyond the boundaries of current ideologies, and reluctance to treat in things of the heart or soul produces friction between these "less-structured thoughts, less-rigid categorizations" (Anzaldúa, "now let us shift" 568) and the rules of academic discourse. Perhaps there is something wrong with existing ideologies if they fail to account for feeling. Anzaldúa offered "soft" material (driven by faith and feeling rather than data) for serious political thinking, and, given current intellectual taboos, hers might be the hardest work of all. This friction brings us back to central tensions in feminist thought of the 1980s: In terms of method, can feminists risk "soft" aesthetic and political practices when women's work has for so long been disregarded for its lack of "rigor"? And in terms of content, can women risk deconstructing a subjectivity that has always been tenuous for them? The fact that Anzaldúa has been so influential, and her ability to maintain material specificity while etherealizing her subject through shape shifting and spirituality, suggest that the answer to both questions is "yes."

My own Catholic grandmother suffered from disabling rheumatoid arthritis, blindness, and a damaged nerve that left one leg numb, encased in a brace, and eight inches longer than the other. Whenever she moved, she winced with pain, and every pain she felt she "offered up" to a particular cause: for the poor in Ireland, for the soldiers at war, even for my final exams. These prayers seemed silly to me until I thought about what it would mean to believe in them. My grandmother perceived her pain as productive, a material gesture like counting off beads for prayers on her rosary. And she was not simply bartering, one spasm for one missed bullet, one prayer for one exam: she really perceived her pain as radiating beyond the boundaries of her body to other worlds. Her religion taught her to feel a corporeal commonality with the various sufferings of others around the world, and she felt it. Whether or not my grandmother's pain directly helped anyone, it has consequences. What matters is that she perceived it, not as the dissolution of her own body, but as a reminder of her spiritual interconnectedness with other bodies—a faith with potential material effects. Her suffering formed webs with others across borders, races, and sexes and shaped her pacifist and feminist politics (my terms, her actions).[28]

Invoking the spirit makes our understanding of bodies and identities more complex by recognizing "thinner boundaries" between individuals and multiple entities within each self: "You sense you're more than one body—each superimposed on the others like sheaths of corn. . . . The

28. Nancy Mairs also talks about learning "to *do* love" from the Catholic Church and from her own disabled body's demands for care: "I really do believe that actively nurturing your fellow creatures through serving them, in what the Catholic Church designates as the corporal works of mercy, develops and disciplines the whatever-you-call-it: the part of the human psyche that transcends self interest" (Mairs 78).

ability to recognize and endow meaning to daily experience (spirituality) furthers the ability to shift and transform" the self (568). Changing "your relationship to your body, and, in turn, to other bodies and to the world" ultimately, in Anzaldúa's thinking, changes the world (574). These shape-shifting gestures are corporeally risky (painful) and theoretically risky (nonrational), but they push us clearly beyond the static forms and defended states of patriarchal racism. I believe that Anzaldúa has had such an impact because she took these risks. Though most critics fail to address the riskier aspects of her writing, they have clearly been shaken (moved, disturbed, or put off) by these risks. Rather than simply rehashing the ideas that preceded her, Gloria Anzaldúa truly did lay down her own body as a bridge "to the next phase, next place, next culture, next reality" (574).

3

MEDICINE: CHERRÍE MORAGA'S BOUNDARY VIOLATIONS

Second day after Rafaelito's surgery. To our relief, no more intestine was lost. "A simple procedure," the doctors told us, simply reconnect the small and large intestine, sew up the stoma. Two days later, Ella holds Rafa in her arms with a respirator down into his lungs, two IV's stuck into the veins of his head, and a tube running down his throat to suck out leakage in his stomach. He has dehydrated, is unable to urinate. And my baby has bloated up to twice his body-size. His face is a monster's—his eyes, black seeds buried into a mass of fluid. When I put my hand to his cheek to caress him, the imprint remains, deforming him.

Cherríe Moraga, *Waiting in the Wings*

*P*ain, illness, and disability are politically significant, in part, because they defy contemporary norms for how bodies should look and act. When Gloria Anzaldúa struggled to find spiritual transcendence through the fluctuations of diabetes, this struggle was always in friction with medical diagnoses and treatments. Similarly, when Ana Castillo's disabled heroine in *Peel My Love Like an Onion* dances flamenco, the euphoria of physical capability lies in direct resistance to institutionalized boundaries for "handicapped" identity and the limited mobility associated with post-polio syndrome. The power of boundary-crossing is partially produced by the boundaries being crossed. This chapter turns to representations of medical treatment to analyze the competing interests that meet in the bodies of the sick.

In *The Birth of the Clinic* (1963), Michel Foucault's "archeology of medical perception" uncovers two ideological dimensions of medicine that are foundational to my argument: first, the awareness that diseases reflect the complex social sphere in which they emerge (Foucault 16–17), and second, the understanding that modern medicine dictates a "normative posture" as it heals. Clinics create "a definition of the *model man*" as they outline "knowledge of *healthy man*" (34, original emphasis). These two dimensions must meet in tension. Medical treatment attempts to "normalize" individuals whose diverse illnesses—since they reflect a complex web of social, cultural, and economic forces—surely resist the limited "model" imposed by the clinic. As with the image of the epigraph to this chapter, there are competing imprints on the malleable bodies of patients.

When Foucault writes, however, that "we have not yet emerged" from the era (dating from the nineteenth century) when disease, pain, and symptoms are perceived to be contained "within the singularity of the patient" (x) and "a science of the individual" (197), his use of "we" does not encompass the diversity of medical perceptions that shape the world. Though I am certainly not alone in noting the limitations of Foucault's pronouns, noting this particular limitation opens the door for seeing bodies and medicine otherwise. If we look beyond Foucault's "we," we can notice how disease and society intersect in ways that deviate from the dominant trends of modern medicine. Many contemporary thinkers—including Chicana feminists and those interested in alternative spiritualities—have adopted Native American conceptions of the links between individual, communal, and environmental health. The Aztecs, for instance, viewed health as a property of the community, negotiated through rituals linking humans to plants, animals, and the gods.[1] If bodies are connected to outside forces, then corporeal forms are subject to continual change, unmoored from individual culpability, and invested in the "health" of others—defying the institution of any singular bodily norms. This opening of corporeal possibilities is perhaps one of the reasons Chicana lesbian writers like Cherríe Moraga have turned to Native American

1. In an extensive study of indigenous medicine in Mexico, Gonzalo Aguirre Beltrán writes: "*La salud constituye parte integrante del proceso social; la imagen del cuerpo, como unidad orgánica, una continuidad con la naturaleza; y la enfermedad, por consiguiente, la expression de una inadaptación social* [health constitutes an integral part of the social process; the image of the body, as an organic unity, a continuation of nature; and illness, in consequence, the expression of a social imbalance/maladjustment]" (Aguirre Beltrán 258).

cultures in trying to define health apart from Eurocentric heterosexist and patriarchal expectations.

Moraga's early work encodes lesbian desire and mixed-race embodiment as painful processes, often using the metaphor of dismemberment—disembodied heads, mouths slit open, one-legged bodies trying to swim—to reflect the difficulty of fitting her body into the normative shapes of identity.[2] In her book on Moraga, Yvonne Yarbro-Bejarano incisively interprets Moraga's poetry as "constantly tak[ing] apart the entire female body, recognizing how it has been appropriated and attempting to reclaim it" (Yarbro-Bejarano, *The Wounded Heart* 5). Yarbro-Bejarano discusses this fragmentation in terms of resistance, as Moraga's attempt to sever her body from patriarchal/white/heterosexist norms and to reconstruct it "from the blueprint" of her own desire (7). In this argument, the poet deconstructs bodies only in the context of possible healing, "with a vision of a new way to be whole" (10) as a Chicana feminist lesbian. Yarbro-Bejarano thus positions Moraga's corporeal sensibility in opposition to dominant "blueprints" and assumes that her writing strives toward a new kind of wholeness.

What then do we make of plays like *Heroes and Saints* (1994), which ends in the destruction of its heroine's disembodied head, or poems and essays that maintain the author's task as one of working with an amputated body? Moraga insists, in *Loving in the War Years* (1983), that the hands have been "cut off" in her poems (Moraga, *Loving in the War Years* 55–56) and that her chronic back trouble gives her "constant pain," especially when she writes: "The spot that hurts the most is the muscle that controls the movement of my fingers and hands while typing. I feel it now straining at my desk" (v). This self-reflexive statement appears in a discussion of the pressures of being a "movement writer" and Moraga's choice to lay down her own back as a bridge in cooperative work like *This Bridge Called My Back*. The suggestion here is that physical suffering is both inevitable and integral to her work. Her poem "For the Color of my Mother" expresses the pain of voicing radical politics that explode beyond the boundaries of her individual body: "at two / my upper lip split open / clear to the tip of my nose / it spilled forth a cry that would not yield" (*Loving in the War Years* 60). Is this cry simply a sign of oppression? Or is the cry, itself, the expression of radical politics? Do radical politics flow from wounded bodies or from healthy corporeal resolution?

2. See, for example, the poems "For the Color of My Mother" and "You Call It, *Amputation*," both in *Loving in the War Years*.

The force of Moraga's writing, I would argue, resembles and maintains the "screaming mouth . . . sewn back into a snarl" (60), scorning healing and making pain visible in a gesture that reaches out into public like an Aztec heart excision. In this sense, pain is the measurement of political resistance, tearing flesh beyond normative containments.

Moraga's newer works continue to be preoccupied with the body as a site for conflicts over identity politics, but the added themes of childbirth, motherhood, and illness expand the identity she embodies. Each of these states necessarily trespasses the boundaries of the individual, complicating the ideal of wholeness. And, for Moraga, each elicits the conflicting imprints of modern medicine, Chicana lesbianism, and native Mexican cultural traditions, pulling the "sick" body and its identity in multiple directions. This is not, however, a matter of simple opposition, as the three worldviews also intersect in surprising ways. Nor is it a matter of choosing one avenue of medical "treatment" over another, as the patient's experience is inextricably situated at the intersection of the communities in which she is immersed. Indeed, both "choice" and "community" are permeable once one becomes somebody else's "patient."

Waiting in the Wings: Portrait of a Queer Motherhood (1997) is an autobiographical account of Moraga's experiences with motherhood, including lesbian insemination, the pre-term delivery of her son Rafael Angel, and the baby's torturous three months of surgeries and recoveries in the hospital's neonatal intensive care unit. This narrative violates personal integrity as one body becomes two and all bodies are subject to clinical processes. Rather than focusing on one body's negotiation with norms, intertwined stories of family and friends' mortal illnesses extend the text's exploration of fragile bodies to consider the communal level of "public health" as well as the friction between institutionalized medicine and human variability. In the clinic, scared, angry, hurting, culturally and sexually heterogeneous humanity becomes dependent upon a supposedly objective science. Within their mismatched marriages to clinical culture, individuals find strategies to humanize the clinic and to rewrite their medical conditions with frameworks that defy the standardized "neutrality" of modern medicine. Illness, itself, locates people "in the belly of the beast," from whence their toying with clinical norms transforms the face of "model man."

Moraga wrote two plays during her pregnancy and new motherhood: *The Hungry Woman: A Mexican Medea* (2001) and *Heart of the Earth: A Popul Vuh Story* (2000) turn back to Aztec and Mayan creation stories as if looking for historical meaningfulness for the Chicana mother's suffering. *The Hungry Woman* investigates ambivalent maternal feeling through mythic figures of murderous motherhood (Medea and La Llorona) and the Aztec goddess of birth and death (Coatlicue). *Heart of the Earth* retells, with contemporary Chicano allusions, the Quiché Maya story of the initial failed and dismembered creations that ultimately formed the human race. Both plays use indigenous cosmologies to conceive pain and dismemberment as part of larger creative processes, allowing us to view Moraga's medical journey as a recovery of ancient corporeal sensibilities. As with Anzaldúa's use of Coatlicue to theorize the link between creation and destruction, the plays remove wounded bodies from the context of institutionalized healing as we know it today, asking us, perhaps dangerously, to accept illness as an expansive gesture of Chicana feminist politics. When she critiques modern medicine, however, Moraga does not simply favor native medicines in its place. Her invocations of Aztec and Mayan body practices also reject the historical violence of these ancient empires. She does not submit to any system of body management, keeping the bodies in her writings open to her imagination.

Resisting institutions at the level of the body is painful. Though Elaine Scarry asks us to think of pain as "world-destroying" (Scarry 29), Moraga sifts through Mexican cultural references that enable her to experience pain as world-creating. In order to understand the shape of Moraga's new "world," this chapter analyzes her writings through Aztec and Mayan cultural lenses, as well as through the lenses of disability studies. The first section provides a close reading of Moraga's account of "queer motherhood," highlighting the ways in which her representation of illness opens up both bodies and clinics beyond institutionalized boundaries. At the same time, her dependence upon institutionalized medicine challenged Moraga's identity politics and led her to form new sorts of (transracial, transcultural, transpolitical) *familia* with doctors, nurses, and other patients. The trajectory of healing is "queered" by reciprocity between caregiver and patient and by the continual deferral of "health." The next section situates this "queering" in the context of Aztec and Mayan corporeal ideologies to show how Moraga's challenge to institutionalized medicine reflects not just a contemporary critique but an alternative framework that predates and has not been subsumed by modern "Western" institutions. I conclude with an analysis of the political dimensions of the health that Moraga defies, rethinking how bodies should be treated, in the clinic and beyond. Ultimately, Moraga's work suggests that we shift our desires from the self-defensiveness of health to the permeability of caregiving.

Queer Motherhood

Pregnancy and motherhood are among the most familiar narratives in literature. In the context of Moraga's opposition to normative gender identities and family structures, pregnancy and motherhood are thus an unexpected undertaking. "I imagine most people would think it radical to take it upon one's lesbian self to make such a proposal" (Moraga, *Waiting in the Wings* 16), she writes. "Having babies was something 'real' women did—not butches, not girls who knew they were queer since grade school" (20). This section will explore what happens when this extraordinary writer engages with one of the most ordinary narrative traditions. As Della Pollock writes in *Telling Bodies, Performing Birth* (1999), birth stories "(re)produce maternal subjects" and "rehearse the body politics at the heart of debates" over reproductive technologies and the construction of families (1). After having garnered international attention for her radical politics in *Loving in the War Years* and *The Last Generation*, Moraga's desire to be a maternal subject and to publish a birth story might seem like a conservative turn, reinforcing the centrality of motherhood as the ultimate subject position for women. Sandra Soto notes this apparently teleological aspect of Moraga's movement from cultural outsiderness (in *Loving in the War Years* and *The Last Generation*) to cultural belonging as a mother (Soto 244). Yet Moraga's writing troubles all simple conclusions, and her birth story does not reproduce conventional politics. As Soto describes it, she engages with essentialist identification primarily through "disavowal" (258). Not only does Moraga's birth story disavow the normative shape of motherhood; she also challenges the conventional affective responses associated with it, taking readers through a painful and nonteleological encounter with illness and death.

In *The Last Generation* (1993), Moraga claimed that one of her motivations as a poet is to write what has been missing in other visual and textual accounts: "An honest portrait of our pain" (Moraga, *The Last Generation* 71). I believe she subtitled *Waiting in the Wings* "Portrait of a Queer Motherhood" to link this text to the portrait she proposed earlier. Unlike her earlier books, whose covers feature abstract images and goddess figures, the cover of *Waiting in the Wings* features two portraits that uncharacteristically foreground the author herself as a "real" referent for the text; see Plate 3a. A photo of Moraga sitting in a lawn chair, wearing sandals and sunglasses, holding her son in her lap, partially obscures another photo underneath it, a family portrait with several generations of heterosexual couples, children, and a baby in baptismal clothes held in the center. The image of the queer mother and child is sharply in focus, while the heterosexual family portrait is digitally altered to blur the image. Yet, if it seems that Moraga poses her queer family as an ideal, the narrative behind the cover unsettles all notions of progress, health, and family making. An unresolved tension remains between the author's self-posturing as a new queer ideal and her narrative confessions of the pain that underlies the mythic surface of motherhood. This is a story that centers on the gap between the picture and the suffering maternal body.

The "queerness" of the motherhood whose portrait Moraga outlines in *Waiting in the Wings* goes beyond the mother's lesbian sexuality (and the "queer" process of insemination involving two female lovers, one male friend, a mason jar, and a syringe) to "queer" understandings of birth, life, family, body, and medicine.[3] Rather than repeating the narrative of childbirth as the painful but noble sacrifice women have endured throughout time to produce healthy babies, Moraga writes of her preterm delivery: "my body is engulfed in pleasure—an animal pleasure, a pulsing, an aliveness like nothing I've known. I am a girl and a woman and an animal, and estoy temblando like the best of sex" (Moraga, *Waiting in the Wings* 53). In birthing a baby her body not only expands and multiplies but also crosses boundaries between human and animal, girl and woman, pain and pleasure. This shape-shifting exceeds the boundaries and sensations assumed to govern maternal subjects. The image is also more self-indulgent than self-sacrificing.

When Rafael Angel is born at just twenty-eight weeks of gestation, his life is initially regarded as a failed creation, with a "revolving door of neonatalists, residents, interns, and nurses aides" at first unable to predict what it means for a baby to be born so early (50). What it means, in this story, is three months in the hospital, wavering between life and death, infections, surgeries, and intense pain for baby and mothers. His life hurts more than his delivery. The baby's early life is intertwined with machines as his body's sustaining exoskeleton changes from womb to incubator in

3. In an interview with Rosemary Weatherston, Moraga distinguishes between her self-identification as "lesbian" and her use of "queer" to encompass a greater range of identities, "not only a range of sexualities but also a position of opposition to heterosexual dominance" (Moraga, "Queer Reservations" 66–67). "Queer" ultimately comes to signify, for Moraga, a basis for cross-cultural and cross-sexual alliance between resistant and marginalized groups—a framework distinct from but intersecting with her specific needs as a lesbian.

the Intensive Care Nursery (ICN) after birth. The surface of the baby's isolette developed steam from his breathing (70), likely filtering his view of the isolette through a veil of his own breath. The contact between baby's breath and isolette, like the mother's milk flowing through the plastic tubes that feed the infant, leads Moraga to rethink the boundaries between body and plastic, mother and machine. She ultimately senses a "seamless connection" between "those incubator walls and [her] milk-hard-breasted body," pressing against the incubator to touch her baby (57, 62). She surrounds the incubator with symbols of her *mestiza* spirituality—holy cards, healing stones, arrowheads—providing a cultural context to defy the neutral and scientific isolation of the isolette. This is no alien technology; from the perspective of the baby, the machines breathe, guard, pray, nurse, and mother after the pre-term delivery. This intimacy of life with machine further "queers" the "queer motherhood" Moraga narrates, unmooring maternity from "natural" reproduction, heterosexual intercourse, and mother-father pairings.[4]

As Moraga delineates Rafael Angel's queer family, she incorporates a legacy of Chicana/o activists, gay and lesbian writers, and feminist thinkers into his spiritual parentage. The making of this "familia from scratch" (Moraga, *Giving Up the Ghost* 35, qtd. in *Waiting in the Wings* 14) involves more than birth. Moraga explains that "my own queer story of pregnancy, birth, and the first years of mothering" is a story of "struggle for

4. Many feminists decry artificial means of reproduction as a displacement of women's bodies by patriarchal science—as "the long-term triumph of the alchemists' dream of dominating nature through their self-inseminating, masturbatory practices" (Braidotti 88)—but, as Rosi Braidotti notes, apparently monstrous fusions of mother and machine also help to transgress "the barriers between recognizable norms or definitions" (82), to imagine "new ways of relating" (93), to redefine "what we have learned to recognize as being the structure and the aims of human subjectivity in its relationship to difference, to the 'other'" (94). The history of mechanized reproduction is intertwined with racism and misogyny, but these very technologies could be used to counter their own oppressive origins by reconceiving motherhood apart from racist or misogynist norms. Medical technology can separate motherhood from domains that romanticize reproduction according to nationalistic, patriarchal, homophobic, or religiously governed ideals. Allowing technology into motherhood and motherhood into technology welcomes conceptual "otherness" into both, adding deliberate choices to motherhood and emotionally and corporeally grounded humanity to technology—a feminist gesture with the ability to redraw the boundaries that have circumscribed femininity, family, and motherhood.

survival/for life in the age of death/the age of AIDS" (*Waiting in the Wings* 22). The parallelism in this description emphasizes how birth is experienced in tension with death, particularly in an age when (and in a city—San Francisco—where) living happens against the backdrop of AIDS. This narrative is thus intertwined with illness and impending death—not just the baby's but the death of César Chávez, memories of Audre Lorde's cancer and funeral, the deaths of Chicana-dyke Myrtha Quintanales's mother and father, poets Ronnie Burke's and Tede Matthews' deaths from AIDS, the deaths of Moraga's uncle and the birth father's father, the aging of Moraga's parents, her partner's mother's gradual "crippling" from Parkinson's disease, and Moraga's own seemingly constant battles with pain, depression, anxiety, colds, flu, and allergies (ironically caused by the "seeds of life," "pregnancy happening everywhere" around her in the springtime [38]). These multiple illnesses unsettle the boundaries of the "portrait" in this narrative, making it about communal illness and shared mortality more than the queer mother and her new baby. Sickness and dying take up far more narrative space here than conception, pregnancy, and birth, so most of the text is (appropriately) set in hospitals, focused on the ongoing processes of sickness and treatment. "It is not the death that frightens so," she writes, "it is the slow humiliating dissolution of the body" (32–33). Rather than focusing on the endpoint of birth or death, this narrative is taken up by the continual reorganization of tissues and the erosion of bodily boundaries that both pregnancy and illness involve.

Of course it is not really extraordinary to mention physical pain and fears of death in a birth narrative. As Pollock writes,

> [Birth] stories and the performances of these stories offer us a peephole onto the hazy presence of danger. They play with disaster, knowing it will be cast out or contained within the comic structure of the story. They tease us into a kind of freak-show confidence in our own normality and, in turn, invite a sense of superiority to death, disaster, and deformity, as if all it takes to avoid such ends is the proper exercise of courage and technology, as if death were a moral failure and abnormality were the cost of betraying the social order. (Pollock 4)

Pain is exposed in birth narratives in the context of an expected "good outcome." Sometimes pain, fear, and danger are elaborated in the spirit of "improving the climax, of ensuring relief in the final orderliness of all things" when birth "deliver[s] order from disorder and pleasure from abandon, transgression, and pain" (4). Birth stories that emphasize pain and fear are expected to serve the same kind of function as freak shows: transgressions are contained in the order of the temporary or the anomalous, reassuring audiences that the production of a well-ordered subject is the proper conclusion. Though, as Pollock notes, "taboos against talking about birth are beginning to erode," the "narrative script [still] simply lacks room for stillbirth, miscarriage, abortion, all deformity—aberrations in the 'normal' scheme of things apparently too embarrassing or too grotesque to mention" (5). The subtext of these narratives is that there is an assumed norm that birth must reproduce, and deviation must ultimately reinforce our confidence that medical practices will restore the norm in the end.

Moraga's narrative, however, installs no such norm and is framed in the context of no such confidence. She promises nothing but further "deformation" of the norm. Though Rafael Angel does ultimately survive, his survival is a continual embodiment of death. Moraga describes the first years of his life as "the road taken toward life . . . and death" (Moraga, *Waiting in the Wings* 85). The baby is alive, but the mother's experience has trained her focus on the pain and dying that accompany life. The two sections written after bringing the baby home from the hospital continue to focus on illness. On his first visit to the sacred tree in Watsonville (where the image of the Virgin of Guadalupe appeared in 1992), the author's attention is consumed not by her own son—who remains "unnoticed" under her rebozo—but on a six- or seven-year-old child in a tall stroller with "spaghetti legs," unable to walk: "And I am there in that mother's skin, as I pull Rafaelito into me, holding on for his dear life, his dear health. Knowing I could've been her. Still can" (89). Fears of crippling "deformity" did not end with birth, and the real possibility of disability structures Rafael's life. The mother's life, too, continues into the second year as "the haze of a prolonged and private illness, an acute exhaustion," fearing each time she lies down that she "may not rise up again" (105). The painful illness of life extends beyond bodies to the author's perceptions of nature, seeing in her garden "the giant cedar split vertically at its peak after a harsh winter's storm, the bald spot of exposed fence where once a tree sprawled diseased and beautiful. It was uprooted and carried away in a dumpster. To my left, the skeletal frame of a fruit tree, never bearing fruit. To my right an avocado, also childless" (126). It is important that Moraga finds beauty in these "childless," "split," "diseased," and absent tree-bodies, and this imagery displaces any idyll of Edenic fertility with an aesthetic of pain and vulnerability. The concluding theme of *Waiting* is the ongoing process of dying: "each day there is a birth and a dying of this time in our lives together" (126). There is no finality to birth or death. If there is an order installed in the end of this text, continual disordering is its governing logic:

> Rafael Angel is a messenger of death, not in the negative sense of the word, but in that he brings the news of the cruel and sudden miracle of the cycle of our lives. I could write he is a messenger of life, but I know it is truer to acknowledge that my sometimes quiet sadness at the deepest moments of joy with my child has to do with this complete knowledge of impermanence. (127)

This order of dissolution, of the cyclicality of cruelty, is reflected in the final words of Moraga's narrative: "This, too, will pass" (127).

While recounting the convergence of her pregnancy and her research for the plays, Moraga rhetorically asks readers why it is that she "must write the story of killing a child," of Medea and La Llorona, when she is about to give birth to her own child (33). In a 1997 interview with Rosemary Weatherston, shortly after becoming a mother, Moraga explains this "dangerous" decision to write a play about lesbian child-killing, and she links this decision to her preoccupation with "female wounding":

> I know that, as women, we have been deformed, by not being allowed full humanness. With this play [*The Hungry Woman*], I have picked one of the most taboo, antisocial acts a woman can commit as the essence of the plot. The only role women are given sanction for in society is motherhood, right? I mean, a good woman is a good mom. And so, what's the worst thing you can do against society, i.e., against patriarchy? Kill motherhood. The child killer is a greater aberration to society than is a dyke. (82)

This response suggests that one of the ways of freeing women from the "deformation" of patriarchy is by assaulting patriarchy's most treasured role for women: motherhood. In this context, *The Hungry Woman* and *Waiting* can be read as the "passing away" of patriarchal motherhood.

One of the tasks of Moraga's personal narrative is to provide a feminist framework for valuing women's experience of childbirth and motherhood in a new way, as more than a reiteration of mythic female suffering for the sake of reproducing the status quo. "This sickness es una limpieza," she concludes (*Waiting in the Wings* 33), sweating out inherited stigma to clear the way for creating new meaning. The word "wound" is used throughout Moraga's work to signify the racial/sexual/homophobic deformation of Chicana lesbian bodies—"the festering places in Chicano culture" produced by "the interconnected forces that inflict both psychic and physical damage on women" (Yarbro-Bejarano, *The Wounded Heart* 151). In *Waiting*, the birth narrative transforms this wound. Moraga experiences a new sort of female legitimacy as "mother" in the eyes of family and hospital staff (Moraga, *Waiting in the Wings* 76), but she does not give birth in order to assimilate her body into the iconic mother role. Instead, she projects the wound onto motherhood, itself, "killing" the idyllic birth narrative. She is still a queer mother of a sick child, wounded rather than healthy.

When clinics market themselves, they often draw upon the mystification of motherhood with billboards depicting smiling babies, eclipsing the reality of corridors full of sick people. They represent themselves as the origin rather than the potential endpoint of life. Moraga rejects the clinic's erasure of sickness and death by regarding her son's new life as already wounded rather than a perfect clean slate: "He is all wound, and he is my son," she seems proud to proclaim (65). In this way she frames her child's life with her own rhetoric of deformation and physical vulnerability. She "infects" the hospital ideology with her own queer understanding of health and demystifies the icons of blissful motherhood and bouncing baby boys. Though born in Hollywood, Rafael Angel is "all wound," hairy, "indio," "monkey," and unfathomably fragile in his "birdweight," not like the newborns placed on their mothers' stomachs "in the movies" (53, 54, 65).

In Moraga's account, the hospital is not simply a place where one goes to be made well. Because of Rafael's extended stay, his isolette becomes an "apartment" (81), and the hospital becomes a home that his mothers furnish according to their spiritual and cultural traditions, a place where they stay not as patients but as mothers. Yet this "home" is sometimes hostile. Moraga and her partner are met with homophobic harassment from security guards who try to block their entry after hours (75). The supposed neutrality and objectivity of the hospital are uncovered as a mask for the sexual politics of the larger society. Beyond simply treating the baby, the hospital "treats" the mothers according to dominant-culture judgments about sex and family. But they cannot free their "home" in the ICN from this hostile exoskeleton, just as they alone cannot keep Rafael Angel alive. Networks of respirators and IVs are physically more important to the baby's life than his mothers are, so they must take the medical equipment, like the security guards' homophobia, into their motherhood. They begin to incorporate qualities of the baby's machines as they share their parenting with them: "Daily we have watched fear's venom pass through plastic tubes, in and out of open veins and miniature organs. I know fear's scent pressed into the industrial detergent of my baby's doll-sized sheets and blankets. We carry its odorless indifference home with us on our clothes, in our skin" (66).

Illness and disability often demand that bodies incorporate medical technology. Disability studies have shown us how romanticizing the body as something purely natural, bounded by its own flesh, and independent of other entities stigmatizes people with disabilities. Bodies that depend on machines to stay alive or bodies with prosthetic devices must incorporate these instruments as part of their own identity, agency, and mobility. Rosemarie Garland Thomson adopts Donna Haraway's cyborg as a way to reconceive bodies that are "merged" with prosthetics, wheelchairs, or hearing aids as "survivor[s] of cultural otherness, ready to engage the postmodern world on its own terms," rather than grotesque outcasts (Thomson, *Extraordinary Bodies* 114–15). Of course, needing these technologies deprives bodies of many pleasures. As an infant, Rafael Angel cannot nurse from his mother's nipples. But focusing only on the loss that accompanies dependence on prostheses assumes that disabled embodiments are only pathetic, failing to value nonnormative ways of being. One of the ways in which Moraga's narrative "kills" romanticized notions of motherhood is by integrating machines into mothering, learning to feel through plastic.

The workings of the clinic remain integral to Moraga's motherhood because her son embodies them: "Does he remember awakening at 3:00 A.M. under the hot glare of hospital lamps, no mama in sight, a sharp pain piercing his gut? I wonder where in his small body he has put all that suffering, what traces of it will reside in him as a grown man" (106). Though she initially "resent[s] these white male pediatrician-types with their nurse wives and seven kids 'bonding' their way into my Mexican psyche," she cannot expel the corporeal traces of their operations or the memories of their lamps and scalpels—a boundary-crossing that turns out to reinforce her politics of corporeal openness. While Moraga has conventionally positioned herself in binary opposition to the institutions of the dominant culture, she cannot fully oppose the clinic. The hospital turns out to be more than a place of homophobic, patriarchal, and anglocentric norms. The staff of caregivers—"Rose, Stacey, Bobbie, Sue, Gurline, Donna, Terry, and others whom we never met"—"watched

[Rafael] throughout the night while we slept" and treated him as more than work. Their clinical labor is also mothering. "Some of them have even come to love Rafa, thinking of him as 'their baby'" (78). At first Moraga is afraid of her dependence on these women, but, in later reflection, "it is not our dependence on the nurses that I fear, so much as the loss of the connection. These women have become our family" (78). The nurses' guidebooks and gifts to the baby go home with them in the car. As the hospital rooms are transformed by Moraga's kind of motherhood, so she too must accept clinical medicine into her private life and become intimate with doctors, nurses, and machines that she would have opposed before. The cultures of queer *familia* and hospital interpenetrate and infect each other.

These tensions Moraga experiences reflect tensions embedded within the clinic itself. Clinics attempt in vain to draw a line between sickness and health, to install a norm that its patients continually defy with their illnesses. The hospital is a place where pain, vulnerability, and illness are, in fact, the norm. Moraga has perhaps found a home for her extraordinariness in the clinic, along with Alex, who has sleeping limbs, Simone who is blind, Freddy who has Downs, and other "one- and two- and three-pound human animals with swollen brains and strokes and weak hearts and drug addictions and troubled families," "mirroring Rafa's own embattled state" (69). At the same time that Moraga was creating a queer and Chicana/o *familia* for her baby, the hospital created another *familia* based on shared pain and vulnerability. Letting this *familia*, and the hospital itself, into her life expanded her identity, her politics, and her motherhood.

Other Medicines

Moraga writes that after being rushed to the emergency room during her pregnancy for "heavy bleeding due to polyps sloughing from the cervix," she turned to her daily readings of "Maya ritual bloodletting" (Moraga, *Waiting in the Wings* 39), linking her bleeding to her literary work (writing *Heart of the Earth*). This narrative turn also moves Moraga's bleeding from the interpretive framework of the emergency room into the realm of sacred sacrifice; or perhaps it converts the emergency room into a sacred Mayan space, where the bleeding body carries dual significance as both in crisis and transcendent. Feeling pre-Columbian in contemporary California multiplies Moraga's cultural resources and takes her body beyond any single diagnosis.

Moraga concludes that her pregnancy brings her closer to the Maya: "somehow my giving birth involves me in this trajectory, this continuing history of conquests and culture clashes, of the regeneration of raza and the creation of new razas" (38). As with Anzaldúa's Coatlicue states, childbirth is part of a cycle of destruction and regeneration, ritually repeated by women throughout time, across cultures. Moraga's writing about childbirth is self-reflexively a ceremonial performance, but she creates something new rather than regenerating a tradition: "I shape these letters onto the page as tiny steps in a dance circling circling circling until I arrive at the heartbeat, a pulse, a place from which the writing stirs new life" (47). She "stirs" up, or perhaps she conquers, the oldest female role with the new vulnerable life she has created, the new *familia* she has forged, and the new narrative she has written. This is not to imply that there is only one role or one static form of motherhood that Moraga ruptures. Rather, her plays invoke a cross-cultural cacophony of birth narratives to expose the contextual variability of motherhood. This variability contradicts the assumption of one "continuing history of conquest" and "regeneration," and the "new life" Moraga stirs into each history she invokes destabilizes the reproduction of any status quo.

As she searches for alternative forms of motherhood, and alternative forms of medicine, Moraga turns to the indigenous cultures she believes form her "deep racial memory" (*Loving in the War Years* 136). She explains her preference for ancient Mexico in the forward to *The Hungry Woman*: contemporary Mexico presented her with "a painful reminder of my own cultural outsiderhood."

> But the templos of México—Monte Albán, Palenque, Tulum, Teotihuacán—told me something different. As I ascended those temple steps, I unwittingly descended into the visceral experience of a collective racial memory that everything about my personal biography had rejected, but one that my writer's soul irrefutably embraced. . . . Those templos to the gods were the edification of a history lost to me. Thus began my (re)education process and my (re)turn to Mito in hunger for a true god and a true story of a people. (*The Hungry Woman* x)

There are several questionable leaps in this passage. The assumption that the indigenous past is still there, a forgotten memory embedded in the "writer's soul," defies history and *mestizaje* with a seemingly essentialist link between pre-Columbian native and Chicana.[5] She "hungers," "viscerally," for a lost but recoverable native feeling, which becomes manifest in her body as she repeats the step-climbing of her ancestors at Monte Albán and Palenque. This preference for pre-Columbian ruins idealizes the indigenous as a time/place before pain and cultural alienation, as if the people of these templos were not themselves misogynists and violent imperialists. Moreover, this list of native places, and Moraga's writings themselves, tend to collapse different indigenous traditions, apparently confusing ethnicity with historicity in an undifferentiated pre-Conquest culture. Perhaps this sense of the native as a "*lost* history" (in ruins) enables it to seem more "true" and welcoming than living populations that can reject, exclude, or dispute.

One could conclude that Moraga is simply not sensitive to history, but I would argue instead that her sensitivity is finely tuned and mobilized with a writer's skill beyond unimaginative, one-dimensional histories. In Moraga's writing, the ancient past is a realm of possibility; the cyclical time of pre-Columbian Mesoamerica points to alternate ways of passing time and making history. When she describes her recovery of the past as a "(re)turn to Mito," she eschews linear chronology—by turning and returning repeatedly to the same stories—as well as the primacy of veracity. Myths have value not because they occurred in the past but because they are continually and powerfully relived in a culture's imagination. "Native" Mexico in Moraga's work is imaginary, not in the sense of being untrue or immaterial, but in the sense that it is truer to the author's beliefs than it is to historical fact. This approach enables her to think about bodies beyond the parameters of both contemporary and historical medicine.

The "other medicines" in this section are multifaceted. I first offer my own interpretation of how Mesoamerican body practices differ from modern Euro-American conceptions of health, healing, and physical integrity. I then examine how *The Hungry Woman* and *Heart of the Earth*

5. When this critique was raised after Moraga's lecture, "Indígena as Scribe," she responded that she knows claiming "racial memory" is essentialist and that this is exactly why she claims it. She also rejected "Western" binary thinking that does not tolerate contradictions. Instead, the way to "think the unthought" is to adopt multiple different ideas at once. We cannot, therefore, assume that Moraga's essentialist claims position her on one side of the essentialist/constructivist binary. Instead, she would ask us to imagine how politics could be both at once.

adopt, fuse, and revise the cultural legacies that Moraga feels herself involved in. In these plays, conceived during her pregnancy and Rafael Angel's early life, she foregrounds traditions that would value her son's vulnerable body not as a failure or "other" to health but as a vehicle for understanding humans' place in a larger cosmological context. Her imaginative appropriation of Greek, Aztec, Mayan, Mexican, and contemporary U.S. mythologies is disorienting, providing no singular, coherent image of health but, rather, exceeding every framework she invokes.

It was believed by ancient Mesoamericans—and, to a degree, is believed by many of their descendants today—that all elements of the universe converged in man and that illness signaled disequilibrium among these elements (López Austin 255). Illness was not an enemy intruder to be kept out but, rather, a sign of imbalance between the body and its environment.[6] For both the Aztecs and the Maya, health was thus not a property of self-contained bodies but a matter of restoring balanced interface between bodies and the elements of the universe. Vulnerable bodies, in this context, might signify human intertwinement with the rest of the world and the continual cycles of dissolution and regeneration that maintain the universe. In this light, permeability would be a healthy ideal. In his comprehensive study of Aztec and Spanish medicine in colonial Mexico, Gonzalo Aguirre Beltrán writes about the interdependencies established in Aztec society based on religious beliefs and the communal organization of private life: "*Esta relación de dependencia que responde a la ansiedad resultante de un sentimiento de desamparo, de una sensación de limitación de recursos, de falta de fortaleza y capacidad y que es una actitud de solicitación de ayuda, de apoyo y protección, tiñe todos los apartados de la medicina azteca* [This relation of dependence that corresponds to the anxiety resulting from a feeling of disempowerment, of a sensation of limited resources, of lack of strength and capacity and is an attitude of seeking help, support and protection, affects every aspect of Aztec medicine]" (Aguirre Beltrán 42–43). Bodies must signify differently in a culture that values community and divine intervention more than individual men. Incisions of the skin, like tattooing, piercing, and bleeding, were

6. Some "unnatural" diseases, though, were brought on as punishment by the gods or from "hexes" cast by ill-wishers (Aguirre Beltrán 43–45; Orellana 27–28), and some accidents, like battle wounds or scorpion bites, were likely experienced as boundary violations (Ruiz de Alarcón 296–99).

prized—perhaps because they point out the permeability of flesh. Transfiguration through *nahualism* (or shape-shifting) enabled humans to externalize their animas/souls and to incarnate other beings (López Austin 368–74; Ruiz de Alarcón 33). This respect for boundary crossings could form relationships based on fluidity and interpenetration rather than individual self-interest. Moraga's focus on the processes of giving life to Rafael Angel presents a vivid example of this possibility: incorporating another being, physically dividing, removing pieces of body in surgery, and linking bodies to networks of machines and caregivers.

Hernando Ruiz de Alarcón (a Spanish-appointed ecclesiastical judge in Southern Mexico) transcribed Mesoamerican curing rituals in his 1629 *Treatise on the Heathen Superstitions That Today Live Among the Indians Native to This New Spain*. His transcriptions reveal the complex relationship between the pain individuals experienced and its perceived sources and cures. During such rituals, massaging, bathing, puncturing with needles, or the use of medicinal drugs was accompanied by invocations to different priests and gods, often distinguished by different colors, to pursue variously colored pains: "blue-green pain," "dark pain," "yellow pain," "black pain." These "spells," as Ruiz de Alarcón calls them, suggest a complex medical "science" in which varying types of pain sensation corresponded to different natural elements, temperatures, divinities, and regions of the body (different colors were also used to signify the four cardinal directions). For instance, the cure Ruiz de Alarcón records for earaches involved consumption of tobacco, chanting, and breathing into the body of the sufferer: the breath of the curer was projected "within my nine caves" to "go in after / The Blue-green Pain" (Ruiz de Alarcón 238). Plastering bone fractures required a similar interpenetration of bodies:

Please come forth,
White Priest:
Please cradle in your arms
My enchanted thigh,
Which is now being effaced
By Blue-green Pain,
Dark Pain,
Yellow Pain.
The vassal of God—
You will help him;
He is suffering.

Priest who is 1 Water,
You will cradle in your arms
My enchanted thigh.[7]
   (Ruiz de Alarcón, Treatise on the Heathen Superstitions *267)*

Close-reading this chant/prayer reveals that neither the sufferer nor his illness can be reduced to discrete entities. A splint is not enough to "fix" whatever is wrong with this leg. The powers of the appropriate gods and priests must be called upon to transform the "suffering" body in an extended ritual. The suffering itself is described as three different-colored sensations, which together "efface" the body of the injured one. In this way, the patient's leg is transformed (or, rather, taken over) by the sensation of pain and again by sacred intervention in the healing process. The leg penetrated by suffering and healing is "enchanted," a possession that seems more empowering than disempowering as various natural elements and sacred forces converge around and within the injured body part. The image of the priest cradling the injured thigh in his arms represents healing as an intimate interaction—more intimate than what we expect of clinical medicine today.

One of the most impressive aspects of the indigenous civilizations the Spaniards found in sixteenth-century Mexico was an advanced culture of medicine. In fact, they were so impressed by the varieties of herbal cures available in the New World that, in the early years of the Conquest, many Spanish soldiers (including Hernán Cortés) preferred indigenous curers over their own doctors (Aguirre Beltrán 25, 36; Flores y Troncoso 83–84; Ruiz de Alarcón 38), and medicinal plants were one of the primary indigenous commodities studied, catalogued, and sent back to Spain to be used there.[8] Yet Aguirre Beltrán warns that most studies of

7. This is Michael Coe and Gordon Whittaker's English-language translation of Ruiz de Alarcón's original transcription in Nahuatl, so it is filtered through the latter's Catholic repulsion by the "pagan" practices he was studying as well as the contemporary historians' interpretation of these spells as "powerful" poetry (Ruiz de Alarcón xvii). My analysis, however, revolves around the multiple ways of referring to pain and the invocation of divine assistance, qualities that should be apparent in any translation.

8. By the 1530s, Spain was regulating medicine in New Spain. Once the Spanish established hospitals (and the Inquisition) in Mexico, indigenous healing methods were deemed heretical and were, in fact, one of the most common crimes prosecuted by the Inquisition in its cultural colonization efforts (even though Indians, themselves, could not be tried by the Mexican Inquisition) (Anzures y Bolaños 55–56, 75, 82; Aguirre Beltrán 261, 264). In their introduction

indigenous medicine have missed the emotional content upon which Aztec healing depended:

> ¿Cuál es la característica principal de esa medicina [azteca]? Evidentemente su pathos constituido por el clima místico en que se desenvuelve. En efecto, los hombres de la medicina azteca participan de los atributos sagrados de los sacerdotes; la ira incontrolable de los dioses es causa de enfermedad y en el diagnóstico y en el tratamiento de las dolencias intervienen fuerzas divinas. [What is the principal characteristic of this Aztec medicine? Evidently its pathos, constituted by the mystical climate in which it evolves. In effect, the men of Aztec medicine share the sacred attributes of the priests; the incontrollable ire of the gods is a cause of illness and in diagnosis and treatment of pains divine forces intervene.] (Aguirre Beltrán 38, original emphasis)

This long passage reveals the ways in which religion and medicine blended in ancient Mesoamerica. Doctors, surgeons, midwives, shamans, diviners, and priests were prominent figures revered for their interventions in life processes. Much of what we know about Aztec and Maya sacred practices centers on the human body: fasting and bathing to purify bodies; bleeding and mutilating bodies to communicate with the gods; painting, sculpting, and displaying bodies in artwork. (Sacrifice rituals must have established precise familiarity with human anatomy, likely exceeding that of the Spanish doctors who battled Church taboos against human dissection.) Religious ceremony was enacted with dancing, bleeding, and costumed bodies. The elaborate choreography of these ceremonies suggests that their value lay in ritualized movements and protracted sensations—the actions that called upon the gods—rather than simply an end product.[9] Moraga engages this ancient sensibility in her

to their edition of Hernando Ruiz de Alarcón's 1629 *Treatise on Superstitions*, Michael Coe and Gordon Whittaker argue that the Indians in Mexico were more advanced than the Spanish in medical arts until medical science was revolutionized in the nineteenth century (Ruiz de Alarcón 38). Those curers who were deemed heretical "sorcerers" had more successful medicinal remedics and superior surgical skills.

9. This sensibility likely carried over to indigenous perceptions of pharmacology. Wouldn't they have valued the altered sensation medicinal plants produced—since this alteration would be taken as a sign that divine forces had entered the patient's body—rather than simply taking "drugs" as a means to an end?

search for a worldview that values communal rites and suffering as integral to life processes.[10]

Drama, like these sacrifice rituals, stages ideas with bodies. As Yarbro-Bejarano writes of Moraga's earlier play collection, *Heroes and Saints and Other Plays*, theater makes overt "the underlying concerns with identity as constructed and open-ended in Moraga's writing as a whole," through its processes of embodiment and role-playing. "Since [the plays] 'live' in the flesh, so to speak, they voice truths the analytical mind rejects, represses, or censors. . . . The voices begin to manifest, from a more conscious level, the 'wounds' the essays analyze" (Yarbro-Bejarano, *The Wounded Heart* 27). *The Hungry Woman: A Mexican Medea* and *Heart of the Earth: A Popul Vuh Story* go beyond the living "flesh" of the earlier plays as they enact Moraga's thoughts about motherhood, birth, and death—ostensibly within semantic frameworks of ancient Mexico but ultimately constrained only by her own imaginative vision. In *The Hungry Woman*, most of the actors play more than one role, detaching identity from corporeal particularity. *Heart of the Earth* uses puppets as actors to explore identities that exceed the limits of our understanding of embodiment. Since the bodies moving on the stage are clearly artificial products of artists' imaginations, and since their identities result from the combined efforts of puppeteer and puppet, human and plastic, the link between body and identity is denaturalized.

The Hungry Woman begins and ends in a multivalently signifying "clinic"—at once hospital, insane asylum, and prison—where the heroine, Medea, is being held for the dual crimes of lesbianism and child-killing (Moraga, *The Hungry Woman* 98).[11] This convergence of functions reflects the normalizing, juridical function of medicine as well as the conflation and demonization of any female role beyond that of the "good" mother. In the beginning, Medea claims that she lives "inside the prison of my teeth" (11), equating her voice, her body, and the space

10. Throughout *Waiting in the Wings*, Moraga searches for and creates new ceremonies, like communal "sweats" and watering her garden with mother's milk, to heal her baby and to cleanse her own body (Moraga, *Waiting in the Wings* 40–41, 58, 64–65).

11. This clinic, too, is more than a sterile place where identity is stamped into normative patterns. The entire play emerges from the framework of the clinic, which forms the stage upon which audiences witness the play. The stage notes indicate that the distinction between "clinic" and "home" is signaled only by changes in lighting and sound; the two scenes occupy the same space (Moraga, *The Hungry Woman* 7).

of narration with the institution in which she has been incarcerated. "My voice can't escape this wall of maize-white tiles sealed shut" (11), Medea claims, but she claims this with a voice that reaches out from the stage to an audience. The entire play thus emerges from within a clinical framework but continually overflows clinical boundaries, just as Medea's expressiveness overflows the barrier of her teeth. The incarceration does not hold.

In her conception of *The Hungry Woman*, Moraga reclaims "the mutilated women of our indigenous American history" (x), along with the tragic Greek icon Medea, to represent the ambivalence of motherhood and the intersection of cultural traditions. By blending Coatlicue, La Llorona, and Medea within her heroine, she frames motherhood within a transcultural pattern of destruction.[12] Coatlicue (Aztec goddess of birth and death), her Mexican counterpart, La Llorona (the legendary wailing woman who drowned her own children), and Medea (abandoned wife and killer of two sons) embody motherhood in terms of life-giving as well as life-taking. Their own mutilation is passed on to their children. During her early motherhood, Moraga explores this intersection between birth and murder and the possibility that her life might be framed within the same pattern.[13] In *Waiting*, the author prays that she will "learn how to raise a male child well, that the wounds men have inflicted on me . . . will not poison me against my son" (Moraga, *Waiting in the Wings* 41). While Medea and La Llorona killed their babies after birth, Moraga fears killing her baby before he is born. During her pregnancy, she worries that the fevers in her body will "burn him out" at the same time that she questions her ability, as a lesbian feminist, to reckon with his maleness (33). The premature delivery is itself an act of potential child-killing, as

12. See Domino Pérez's "Caminando con La Llorona" for a discussion of how contemporary Chicana/o writers have reframed the La Llorona legend in terms of female agency rather than mythic misogyny. I discuss Medea and Aztec murderous mothers at greater length in my reading of *The Hungry Woman* because these references are more prominent in and central to the play.

13. Moraga's Medea is somewhat autobiographical: "broken," afflicted with "a wound . . . found too many years ago," and "thick necklaces of flesh strangling me" as her chin drops "just like all the women in my family" (Moraga, *The Hungry Woman* 12–14). This physical brokenness is both communal and personal to the individual mother. The wound reflects the one that emerges throughout Moraga's work, and the collapsed chin collapses Medea and Moraga into one mother, since Moraga describes her own chin as collapsing in *Waiting* (*Waiting in the Wings* 57).

the mother's exhausted body purges the amniotic fluid and she "cr[ies] her baby's heart out" (49–50) before his lungs are fully developed.

The Hungry Woman depicts a successfully birthed son at age thirteen. Yet, as surely as his mother is named Medea and he is named Chac-Mool (the vessel in which indigenous Mesoamericans placed the pumping hearts of sacrificial victims during fertility rites), his entire life is framed within the context of his own death and sacrifice.[14] Significantly, Medea's occupation is midwife and *curandera*—a healer whose practice occurs outside clinical institutions—and the entire play challenges normative conceptions of medicine and motherhood. From the beginning, childbirth is deromanticized and rendered as a violation, "suck[ing] off the seven pound creations of other women" (*The Hungry Woman* 16). When Medea is about to lose her son to his father and to adulthood, she encodes this loss in the language of birth, culminating in the claim that "I lost my baby. We were splintered, severed in two" (87). Losing him to birth is like losing him to death, and both losses are described as an amputation, splitting the self into parts. It is in the scene after this one that Medea poisons Chac-Mool. Birth and murder collapse into one act. By representing this story through the lexicon of ancient mythology, Moraga provides a validating cultural framework for the shape-shifting of motherhood and the loss of a son.

The narration of Moraga's Medea story comes from a Greek-style chorus made up of "Cihuatateo," who, according to the stage directions, wear skull masks, bare their breasts, and tie up their skirts with snake cords, recalling Coatlicue's skirt of serpents and necklace of skulls. Usually spelled "Cihuateteo," these Aztec goddesses represent women who

---

14. Before his mother can kill him, Chac-Mool inflicts wounds upon his own body, which becomes a stage for sacrifice: "Various small rings of silver hang from his eyebrow, ear, lip and nose" (Moraga, *The Hungry Woman* 19). He makes a ceremony of his own body's pain, going to a tattoo artist to create his own sacred ritual: "I pray as you cut. I pray deep and hard and if it pusses, I pray harder for the pain. In the center of pain, there is always a prayer" (21). As Moraga imagines Rafael Angel's life as being a continued meditation on the pain he experienced in the hospital, Chac-Mool experiences life through pain. He insists that his pain is holy, that he is reenacting an ancient collective memory: "I was never officially taught. . . . Everything relies on memory. . . . I heard about Aztlán and the piercing of the skin as a prayer" (21). In this image, Chac-Mool's sacrifice is a way of communicating with the lost homeland, Aztlán. The tattoo carved in his flesh is the image of a chac-mool, his historical referent, with the bowl in its belly for the sacrificed hearts—a doubling of his identity, a reiteration of his Aztec namesake and destiny.

died in childbirth.[15] Historian Inga Clendinnen describes Cihuateteo as "malevolence incarnate," whose "malice was to choose to afflict rather than to kill outright":

> Their preferred victims were children, whom they struck down with paralysis or convulsions or sudden deformities, twisting faces and limbs, marring and mangling, but leaving them, barely, alive. We glimpse here the classic lineaments of the witch, the inverted image of social woman, implacably malevolent, inexhaustibly envious, inimical to life, who destroys rather than nurtures children. (Clendinnen, *Aztecs* 179)

Clendinnen tries to complicate this image as more than simply the classic "other," from the standpoint of misogyny, by focusing on the power evoked by women in childbirth. The Aztecs considered childbirth to be women's "field of battle," a dangerous (and bloody) boundary state where, like warriors, they faced the sacred intersection between life and death, the possibility of "obliterating the self," and the opening of this world to the divine (204–5). Women who died in childbirth were permanently charged with this energy or "sacred force." Their deaths were treated outside the bounds of social interaction, without traditional mourning, their bodies sneaked out a hole broken into a back wall and buried at night at a crossroads—"most sinister and most marginal of places" (178). This "antisocial" treatment does not suggest that these women were not valued; rather, their value was not of the social variety. Cihuateteo were warriors who died on the battlefield, so their flesh possessed the sacred power of sacrifice, the dangerous charge of boundary-crossing. The burial party for a woman who died in childbirth "risked attack by warriors desperate to seize a fragment of the magically charged flesh—a lock of hair, a finger—to carry into battle" (178). By choosing

15. Cecelia Klein writes that Cihuateteo were represented in rituals by masked men who performed as "the shades of Nahua women who had died during childbirth": "Like today's Carnival transvestites, the Cihuateteo were regarded as 'mockers of the people.' It was feared that they would return to earth at crossroads, either at midnight or during eclipses, to inflict illness and deformities on the living, especially children" (207). Klein's interpretation of the Cihuateteo has a playful ominousness; their central features are performance, ambivalence, and transformation. Moraga's "Cihuatateo," however, seem more foreboding, not men playing women but women playing death. *The Hungry Woman* also makes the ritualization of creation and destruction an exclusively female act (since Moraga's Cihuatateo are women).

Cihuateteo as the pillars of her play, Moraga charges *The Hungry Woman* with the sacredness of boundary-crossing. This backdrop values female "malevolence" (especially toward children) as a signal of the intersection between the realms of life and death, social and sacred, human and divine. The fact that Cihuateteo are victims of their children's birth also complicates women's mythic culpability.[16]

This play also invokes the myth of the Aztec moon goddess, Coyolxauhqui, who was chopped to pieces at the hands of her brother, the sun/war god Huitzilopochtli (Moraga, *The Hungry Woman* 56); see Plate 3b. In Moraga's telling, Coyolxauhqui had planned to kill her pregnant mother (Coatlicue), to stop the birth of Huitzilopochtli, "rather than submit to a world where War would become God" (*The Last Generation* 73). After Huitzilopochtli dismembers his sister, he throws the pieces up into the sky, where she remains as the moon—an image of dispersal and recovery, waning and waxing.[17] Anthropologist Rosemary Joyce's

16. Women's culpability is at the center of Euripides's *Medea*. Medea kills her two sons "to hurt" her husband, who has taken another wife (Euripides 796). (Moraga's Medea has the additional justification of being forced to choose between her son and her female lover.) Euripides's Medea acknowledges that killing her own children is "the most unholy crime" (773), but it seems to be the only avenue to express her vengeance and her agency: "Let no one think me weak, of no account / Submissive. I am made of different stuff: / Good to my friends, but grievous to my enemies / Such people win the greatest glory" (785–88). Unlike warriors who have agency in battle, or Jason who chooses a different wife, Medea's only sphere of power seems to be mothering. Euripides writes Medea as apparently destined to suffer because of her lack of power and her sex, "a hapless woman's fate" (1225), almost absolving her of responsibility for her crimes, despite the lines above that describe her violence as self-assertion. The chorus, too, seems to describe the crime as a feature of her sex, lamenting: "Woman's bed, full of suffering, / What troubles you have caused mankind" (1270–71). These lines follow a retelling of how Zeus's wife, Ino, killed her sons, making the act seem more sexually universal than particular to Medea. The Medea story corresponds to the Aztec view of childbirth as being intertwined with death (through the ambivalence of Coatlicue as well as the central mythification of death in childbirth). Both Medeas, Moraga's and Euripides's, echo this conflation of life and death—when Moraga describes birth as death and death as birth, and when Euripides's Medea describes the moment of killing her sons as an origin, "where life's misery begins" (1220). Yet Moraga's Medea, though constrained by the homophobia of Aztlán, eludes much of the tragedy she echoes.

17. Carmen Aguilera argues that Coyolxauhqui represented the Milky Way, not the moon, and suggests that the Aztec moon god was male, Tecciztecatl,

interpretation of the myth provides additional qualities that could under-gird lesbian feminism: since Coyolxauhqui combined her female-sexed body (often depicted with visible vulva and breasts) with gendered male warrior actions, her myth and image posed a danger to the Aztec empire through "the threat of nonconformity" (Joyce 166). Coyolxauhqui makes brief appearances in both *Waiting in the Wings* and *The Hungry Woman*, indicating Moraga's investment in the power of this myth to change our thinking about women's bodies. In a 1991 essay, "en busca de la fuerza feminina," Moraga provides a graphic, almost sensual linguistic portrait of Coyolxauhqui's mutilation: "breast splits from chest splits from hip splits from thigh from knee from arm and foot" (Moraga, *The Last Generation* 73). She claims this image as her own, as the communal Mexican woman's wound, which the author "picks up" with "the frag-ments of . . . dismembered womanhood" (74). When Moraga reenacts dismemberment in her writing—in both "the real" of the hospital as well as the "myths" she retells—she emphasizes the fluidity of lunar em-bodiment that Coyolxauhqui represents, the fertile landscape created from her bloodshed, and an alternate story in which dismembered god-desses defeat patriarchal militarism and death.

The Hungry Woman encompasses the multiple identities and commu-nities that meet in Moraga's recent writings. The motherhood narrative runs parallel to the narrative of lesbian love in a homophobic society. Indeed, Medea's lover is named Luna, which means moon in Spanish and, thus, Coyolxauhqui in the Aztec framework—making her, symboli-cally, both daughter and lover to Medea (whose identity is collapsed into Coatlicue, mother of both moon and sun). When Medea sacrifices Luna for the son she can only retain in the guise of heterosexuality, we can also see Coatlicue sacrificing Coyolxauhqui for Huitzilopochtli. The play ends with a series of sacrifices and births—Medea birthing Luna, Medea killing Chac-Mool, Medea birthing herself, Chac-Mool potentially kill-ing Medea—but the final image is that of the moon waxing, which I read as Coyolxauhqui/Luna victorious, and Chac-Mool returning to comfort his mother as she slips off into sleep/death. This incoherent narrative chronology reflects the impermanence of life and death or the

---

made feminine in erroneous Spanish translation (Aguilera 53–54). I discuss Co-yolxauhqui as the moon here because that is still the dominant trend in Latin American Studies and, most importantly, because Moraga adopts her as a moon goddess.

intersection between the two.[18] And the incoherence of the character identities in the final birth/death sequences reflects the permeability of identity—and the intersection of cultural traditions and time periods—that Moraga experiences in the clinic.

The play thus queers patriarchal and heterosexist myths of motherhood, as Moraga's experiences in *Waiting* mandated. It adopts the Aztec myth but rejects the militaristic ending in which Huitzilopochtli triumphs over Coyolxauhqui. It adopts the Mexican myth of La Llorona but rejects its ending with the death of her children. Finally, it adopts and rejects the contemporary "myth" of lesbians needing to sacrifice their sexuality in order to be mothers. It also dismisses linear narratives of conception and destruction by refusing to abide by their logic. "Medea and Luna kept the faith, / fasted by the phases of the moon / but did not pierce their flesh / for they bled regularly between their legs / and did not die" (Moraga, *The Hungry Woman* 97). Yet it is impossible to claim a simply happy resolution for *The Hungry Woman*, since it is unclear in the end if Medea is dying or sleeping, if Chac-Mool is dead or alive, and if Luna and Medea will be reunited or permanently split. By making her ending so ambiguous, Moraga maintains the pain and destruction built within motherhood while refusing to grant finality to death; we remain instead at the sacred intersection of life and death, romance and tragedy.

In *Illness and Culture in the Postmodern Age*, pain theorist David Morris talks about how suffering gets narrativized in familiar genres, and tragedy is certainly one of those. Moraga's rerouting of Medea's suffering removes this icon from Aristotelian conceptions of tragedy. Instead, *The Hungry Woman* more closely resembles the postmodern narrative emplotting that Morris notes in the "guerilla" demonstrations of the AIDS Coalition to Unleash Power (ACT UP). Morris finds in the "guerilla theater" of ACT UP "an effort to insert a secular, censored, unruly text about suffering into" dominant institutions and narratives—the dogma of the Catholic Church, the liberal state, health care agencies, and pharmaceutical companies (Morris, *Illness and Culture* 214–15). The resulting cacophony of voices questions any single authority's claim to truth. Moraga likewise re-plots different narratives, including that of the suffering

18. First, while preparing herbs for an abortion, Medea gives birth to Luna, stillborn (Moraga, *The Hungry Woman* 87). Then, Medea feeds atole poisoned with powdered herbs to Chac-Mool (90–91). Luna later claims that Medea gave birth to herself (95). And Chac-Mool returns in the end to give his mother a drink full of powdered herbs (99).

mother and that of the healing public sacrifice, and the spectacles her play enacts on the stage demonstrate the performativity of pain while injecting difference into those performances. Morris concludes that "a postmodern perspective finds in narrative a compendium of diverse voices with a potential to readjust the 'human position' of suffering" (200). Moraga's "compendium," however, is not necessarily postmodern. Rather, the *mestiza* consciousness that her identity and her work embody itself explains this dissonance of narratives.[19] The intersection of cultural domains within *mestizaje* means that any linear narrative will be interrupted by a different narrative encoding its own cultural experiences of suffering. The icon of Medea's suffering is disrupted by the competing icons of Aztec sacrifice, as embodied by Chac-Mool and Coyolxauhqui, as well as La Llorona's Mexican/*mestiza* wailing. This juxtaposition reveals friction between culturally different kinds of suffering and prevents either from becoming the central tragic act.

Heart of the Earth provides another look at the link between creation and death. Using puppets modeled after Mayan glyphs, the play—like the *Popul Vuh*, itself—expands beyond Euro-American conceptions of embodiment. The Mayan *Popul Vuh* narrates numerous failed attempts in the initial creation of humanity. By retelling this creation story in her play, Moraga frames any "failures" associated with her own pre-term delivery in the context of indigenous world-building. The primeval grandparents face repeated disappointment in their first two attempts to fashion the human race—the first "mud-person" dissolves in water (Moraga, *The Hungry Woman* 133–34) and the second "wooden-man" is pounded to sawdust by the angry kitchen pots whom he has abused (137–38)—but they are ultimately satisfied with the creation of "corn people." One of the central motifs of the Mayan *Popul Vuh* is the regeneration of dismembered bodies. The youthful god Hunahpú repeatedly loses parts of his body (including his head), but he is always reassembled and restored to apparent health—an appealing myth for a mother whose son must have part of his intestine removed in surgery.

One difference between Moraga's "*Popul Vuh* Story" and the original is her emphasis on a mother's struggle to let her sons go. In order to link

19. Gloria Anzaldúa most famously theorizes *la conciencia de la mestiza* as "a tolerance for contradictions, a tolerance for ambiguity—She learns to juggle cultures. She has a plural personality, she operates in a pluralistic mode" (Anzaldúa, *Borderlands* 79). See Bost, *Mulattas and Mestizas*, for a discussion of the theoretical affinity and political/historical/cultural differences between postmodernism and *mestiza* consciousness.

the Maya with her own context, Moraga's *Popul Vuh* represents the first-generation divine twins as contemporary Chicano youths who play "fútbol" and whose mother wonders "where they pick up . . . barrio slang" like "¡Ay te watcho, jefita!" (112–13). The mother must allow her hijos to travel to the underworld to face the Lords of Death (whom Moraga names Patriarchal Pus and Blood Sausage).[20] Though the original twins are careless and lose their heads to the decapitating obsidian blade of Blood Sausage (120), this death is part of a larger process of sacrifice, and new twins are born from Hunahpu's saliva. This maternal letting go is repeated with the second-generation twins, who learn that "we can defeat death only by surrendering to it" (146). The second Hunahpu and his brother Ixbalanque race to the top of the pyramid and throw their bodies into a fire pit after commanding Tecolote (the owl) to grind up their dead bones and sprinkle them in the river (146–48). The play ends with fertility, and the sons are reborn "in the womb of [the] river," their ribs formed "from the sculpted sands beneath the water."

Moraga's revision of the *Popul Vuh* focuses primarily on the exploits of the divine twins, and she omits the second half of the Mayan narrative: how the corn people formed the Quiché Maya empire that was subsequently defeated by the Spaniards. There are logical reasons for this revisionist framing. Moraga's political purpose is not to honor an empire (as in the original text) but, rather, to counter Euro-American and patriarchal standards of family and healthy embodiment. Moraga's play ends with the creative command, "multiply and become numerous, occupy the north and the south" (153), without enacting the battles involved in this peopling. The *Popul Vuh*, itself, ends more violently. According to Albertina Saravia's Spanish-language transcription, "*nuestros primeros padres sujetaron a los pueblos* [our first parents subjugated the peoples/ tribes]" in a most tormenting fashion (*Popul Vuh* 138). The original narrative, too, ends with a prayer that the Quiché may increase and prosper, but only after we have learned of the formation of a warrior culture and the practice of placating the gods with blood (151). Moraga's revisions of indigenous legend still feature "blood" sacrifice (symbolically reinvented as tattooing, as giving birth, or as plowing the earth), but she frees these stories from the mandate that the survival of humanity must include

20. The "real" Mayan Lords of Xibalba (gods of the underworld) were believed to cause many illnesses in mankind. These gods bear names that translate to "Flying Noose," "Blood Chief," "Pus Maker," "Bile Maker," "Bone Staff," "Skull Staff," "Filth Maker," and "Wound Maker" (Orellana 42–43).

warfare. When she adopts a body in pain, it is a gesture of openness, acceptance of the personal effects of history's violence, and not about retribution. She revises the cultural tradition to imagine a future apart from imperialist or patriarchal control over bodies.

Moraga makes her *Popul Vuh* story playful. Amputation, bleeding, and burning are met with replies like "¡Ay, Carajo! Ouch!" The decapitated head of Hunahpu is still able to speak, and he later survives with a squash in place of his head until his real head is retrieved from the ball game in which it was kicked around (143–44). Absurdity provides critical distance between stage play and viewing audience as laughter disrupts perceptions of pain. The use of puppets augments this critical distance and renders suffering as a stylized and symbolic performance. David Morris explains that "pain is not a sensation but a perception dependent upon the mind's active ongoing power to make sense of experience" (Morris, *Illness and Culture* 118). In this sense, the framework of regeneration that "makes sense of" the twins' experience suggests that pain is healthy. As with the tattooing rituals enacted in *The Hungry Woman*, sensation is mediated by the awareness of the productivity of the sacrifice.

Heart of the Earth makes a joke out of Moraga's worst medical fears, in that the Chicano boys survive multiple amputations with humor and vitality intact, but their pain is not erased by the happy ending. When Ixmucane allows her boys to journey to "the land of the mirror people of pale and sickly reflection" to meet the obsidian blades of Patriarchal Pus and Blood Sausage (117), we can imagine Moraga letting Rafael Angel go into the operating room to meet the white doctors and their medical instruments. The Lords of Death, who allegorically represent the doctors, are described as "güeros" (whiteys), "with all the blood sucked out of 'em" (115)—a description whose informal diction deflates the white patriarchs' authority so that they are no more intimidating than Uncle Fester of the Addams family. The doctors alone do not have power over life and death. They will surgically alter the baby's body, but (as such premature babies often are) he will never be totally "healed," always on the brink of danger. This danger is key to Moraga's critical stance toward modern medicine, defying its insistence on anesthetizing pain and its preference for healed, mute, and static bodies.

The Politics of Sickness

The Aztecs and the Maya used public spectacles of pain—imperial ceremonies at the pyramids as well as choreographed victories on the ball court and the battlefield—to demonstrate their power over subject peoples. The bodies at the center of these ceremonies inspired communal terror as manifestations of the power of sacred forces and military might (forces that intersect for successful empires). (The other half of *mestizaje*, Catholic Spain, had its own sacred-imperial pain spectacles, but Moraga's anti-Conquest politics translate into an almost exclusive focus on indigenous Mexico.) It is not unproblematic that Moraga appropriates the corporeal perceptions of former empires. In the empire of postmodern Euro-America, however, where capitalist medicine dictates corporeal norms, these perceptions challenge the ideal of white bodies sealed off from pain, infection, and each other. In the contemporary context, Moraga's spectacles present a radical critique of sanitized Americanness. But do corporeal states shed their imperial origins when they are moved across national borders? When the critique of the dominant culture's numbness to pain is framed in terms of a formerly dominant culture's obsession with pain, what terms are left for critiquing the violence of domination?

In a March, 2004, public lecture, Moraga explained the progression from myth to political change: "myth is history is story that makes medicine." "Medicine" in this context refers to Native American rituals of world-making, but, given the clinical framework of so much of her recent work, one could extend this progression to include clinical practice, as well. In her talk, Moraga asserted her faith in the ability of metaphor to change consciousness and claimed Coyolxauhqui as the metaphor for twenty-first-century Chicana feminist politics. The mythical moon goddess is dismembered because she opposes the Aztec warrior culture (microcosmically embodied by her brother Huitzilopochtli), and Moraga reclaims her dismembered pieces as a critique of empire. She elevates the moment of lunar eclipse, when Coyolxauhqui blocks out her brother, as symbolic for overcoming warrior culture, for imagining history and myth otherwise. Moraga's emphasis on pain, like Coyolxauhqui's amputated body, moves us and unsettles our perceptions. It demands the creation of new medicine to care for bodies that are not whole.

Moraga explicitly expresses her interest in "unravel[ing] la mujer mexicana/chicana" in an interview with Mary Pat Brady and Juanita Heredia: "the work that I gravitate towards is a work that tries to tear it apart. Even then if all you see is the raw guts and it does not smell or look good, at least you are starting from somewhere. That is what moves me as a writer" ("Coming Home" 155). Tearing a body apart is painful, shocking, and thus an urgent call to action. Moraga reiterates that this disassembled Chicana is "incredibly painful to look at. It is not pretty how we have been distorted. . . . It is not nice. It is not a pretty picture" (155). The political message of this ugly picture depends upon the background, the frame, and the source of its distortion. In the context of Moraga's earlier writings, this unraveling represents a scathing critique of the cultural violence inflicted by racism, sexism, and homophobia: friction between her own body and dominant norms. But this interview was conducted in 1994, not long after Rafael Angel's birth and during the composition of the plays. In this context, pain and "raw guts" are more literal, uncannily normative.

Lisbeth Gant-Britton describes the "ruined bodies" in *The Hungry Woman* as a "metaphor of future corporeality" (Gant-Britton 270). Though its cultural references are ancient, the play is set in a dystopian future Aztlán, whose temporality evokes not just the potential outcome of today's social and political short-sightedness but also a demand that we use the lessons of the past to think politically about the future. Gant-Britton reads the ending of the play more pessimistically than I do, as the destructive endpoint of 1980s idealism regarding hybridity and technology. But she only looks from the present forward, not accounting for the ways in which the Aztec and Mayan cosmologies Moraga invokes frame the play's final "deaths" in the context of regeneration and render "raw guts" as part of divine illumination. Calling to mind the laughable images of Patriarchal Pus and Blood Sausage forces us to think differently about "ugly" unraveling bodies. The social system underlying the logic of sacrifice viewed human bodies as intertwined with each other, the gods, and the environment. Sacrifice was not about the individual being sacrificed (whose identity was often masked) but about communal needs and sacred beliefs. Despite the violence of this act, its radical difference from capitalist individualism makes it appealing. While historical fiction is fatalist, dooming its conclusion to what we know to be true of the past, Moraga unmoors her narrative from the past. Like science fiction, *The Hungry Woman* uses the open-ended possibilities of the future to twist bodies/ stories we recognize just enough for us to imagine them otherwise. It is in this light that she asks us to consider sacrifice as progressive or a *Popul Vuh* without war. As an imaginative historiographer, Moraga privileges potential over fact, trying on ugly truths from different pasts but transforming them with her own political vision in order to make new medicine.

Moraga's time in the clinic likely shifted her thinking about body politics. The body as revealed through sonograms, blood tests, and microscopes is a locus of constant fluctuations; it is also positioned as matter in need of care, vulnerable. Her plays incarnate a critique of current Euro-American body norms. "Medical consumerism" has turned bodies into sites for capitalist exploitation, manipulation, and standardization. (The language of health "management" reflects medical corporations' control over individuals' bodies.) Or, as David Morris quips, "Health (or an appearance of health) has become a prized commodity, as proudly displayed as a new SUV, while illness is an evil warded off with multivitamins and gym memberships" (Morris, "Narrative, Ethics, and Pain" 59–60). Given current levels of medical and pharmaceutical intervention in the United States, the unhealthy body represents a breakdown in defense for the medical engines; it is unruly, unstandardized, traitorous. Illness not only presents an affront to the capitalist medical system; it also reveals fractures in the myth of a healthy American society. Rather than submitting docilely to militaristic body mythology, the premature, bleeding, or wounded body points out the limits of the dominant medical system by inhabiting its outside. People on the margins, those without wealth, people of color, queer people, and any others who do not fit the dominant norms are less likely to receive adequate medical care, more likely to be "sick," and also more likely to be excluded from the national image. If the bodies of its people reflect the security and prosperity of the nation, making illness visible presents an affront to the sanitized, white, misogynist, commodity-invested self-image of the United States: "[B]ecause we do not fit *we are a threat*," Anzaldúa writes (Anzaldúa, "la prieta" 209, original emphasis). Moraga's most recent writings, like those of Anzaldúa and Castillo, focus on continual illness, vulnerability, and disequilibrium, rather than medicalized closure and mythic postoperative perfection. The picture is indeed "not pretty," according to dominant standards today, making all the more visible these writers' challenge to the ways in which we judge and defend bodies.

In the way of the Aztecs, Moraga makes sickness a public concern rather than closing it off as a shameful, personal matter. (We are all, after all, only temporarily healthy.) According to Linda Singer, in *Erotic Welfare: Sexual Theory and Politics in the Age of Epidemic*, in the wake of AIDS a "logic of contagion" suppresses our shared vulnerability, quarantining "at-risk" groups with cultural stigmas and drawing firm boundaries between people to prevent infection. "Communication has become communicability; access is now figured as an occasion for transmission and contagion" (Singer 28). Corporeal vulnerability, fluctuation, and suffering are radical to the ideals of Western modernity, bracketed from "safe" and "healthy" social interaction, and contained within the clinic or the lore of the ancients. Moraga's recent writings break down those brackets. What is most radical about *The Hungry Woman* and *Heart of the Earth* is their enactment of ancient lore in the contemporary world. And what is radical about *Waiting in the Wings* is not opposition to the dominant culture (which is precluded by Rafael Angel's dependence upon the doctors and machines in the ICN) but nondifferentiation between "healthy" and "sick." The narrative locates sickness everywhere: in Moraga's community of Chicana/o and gay/lesbian artists and writers, in her garden, and in her own presumably "healthy" self. Rafa's tenuous embodiment becomes the norm.

The intellectual field that has done the most to complicate our understanding of bodies is Disability Studies. Analysis of disability exposes the unpredictability of embodiment as well as the constructedness of medical norms. In their essay "Bodies Together: Touch, Ethics, and Disability," Janet Price and Margrit Shildrick note how people are led to reflect on their own vulnerable boundaries when they care for the vulnerable bodies of others:

> [W]hat was uncovered during that acute period of Janet's illness [multiple sclerosis] was that, through the mutuality and reversibility of touch, we are in a continual process of mutual reconstitution of our embodied selves. Moreover, the instability of the disabled body is but an extreme instance of the instability of all bodies. (Price and Shildrick, "Bodies Together" 72)

Needing caregivers, medications, or prostheses, or likewise caring for someone experiencing these crises of body and identity, reveals the permeability of the bodies we perceive as defining us. Sharing this permeability defies the taboo against public demonstration of bodily processes and defies the cultural logic that "separation rather than contact figures the adult self" (71). Moraga's plays and her narrative reconfigure the bounded ideal for bodies and for identities, and this instability infects all it touches—perhaps even audiences.

Disability Studies circulates outside the logic of contagion, resisting the fear of otherness that leads to quarantine. For instance, Nancy Mairs values the sensibility that comes from intimacy with people with disabilities and views the absence of such intimacy as a lack: "I don't think it's the normals' own fault that they lack disabilities to deepen and complicate their understanding of the world" (Mairs 72). Her narrative *Waist-High in the World* traces the shift in her relationships with others as MS makes her body increasingly dependent. As her legs and arms lose muscle control, she relies upon her husband, sister, and children to help her bathe, dress, and travel. In turn, her family's perception of what counts as "normal" and what labors one should be expected to perform alone is transformed (34–35). In soliciting care from others, disabled bodies challenge the American ideal of "self-reliance."[21]

Caregiving, like sacrifice, crosses boundaries between people and gives parts of oneself to others. Yet the ethics of care are clearly different from the politics of sacrifice. Sacrifice strengthens the power of the healer, the empire, or the martyr, but caregiving (as Price and Shildrick, Mairs, or Moraga represent it) is mutual and reciprocal, a meditation on shared permeability.[22] Though Rafael Angel's medical regimen is intertwined with the power structure, Moraga's writing about it defies hierarchy. Since the doctors, nurses, and mothers are all touched by each other in the process of caring for the baby, they ultimately recognize commonality and mutual concerns. Caregiving leads to intersubjective perceptions of self and other rather than solidifying the ego of the caregiver. According to Mairs, knowing that another body depends upon you for its maintenance disciplines "the part of the human psyche that transcends self-interest" (Mairs 78–79). If caregiving is reciprocal, then receiving care is also an active way to give care: "Permitting myself to be taken care of is, in fact, one of the ways I can take care of others" (83). This is clearly an idealistic vision, but it is one sustained by the logic of permeable bodies. Neither docile nor dominating, neither aggressive nor defensive, the communally embedded sick body challenges the individuated subject at the base of hierarchy and domination.

In *States of Injury* (1995), a text that has been celebrated by postmodernists but denounced in many recent defenses of identity politics,

---

21. Rosemarie Garland Thomson notes how Emerson's "naturalized man" and "American ideal" are "profoundly threatened by what Richard Selzer has called the 'mortal lessons' that disability represents": "The four interrelated ideological principles that inform this normate self might be characterized as self-government, self-determination, autonomy, and progress. . . . However, these four principles depend upon a body that is a stable, neutral instrument of the individual will. It is this fantasy that the disabled figure troubles" (Thomson, *Extraordinary Bodies* 42).

22. Thomson is less optimistic about romantic notions of an "ethics of care": "The controversial feminist ethic of care has also been criticized by feminist disability scholars for undermining symmetrical, reciprocal relations among disabled and nondisabled women as well as for suggesting that care is the sole responsibility of women" (Thomson, *Extraordinary Bodies* 26).

Wendy Brown analyzes the nature of identity politics that are organized around states of injury, like sexual oppression, racial discrimination, or exclusion based on disability.[23] Paradoxically, an identity that calls attention to suffering in order to demand an end to suffering "at the same time becomes invested in its own subjection," "predicated on and requiring its sustained rejection by a 'hostile external world'" (Brown 70). The same paradox could be noted in the injuries Moraga highlights in her critique of clinical norms. Yet, as I demonstrated above, her suffering is not "predicated on" opposition to a "hostile external" structure; baby, mother, and clinic infuse and reform each other. Indeed, suffering is where the boundaries between Chicana-dyke mother, new baby, and clinic break down. Identity politics based on injury are counterproductive, Brown argues, when they do not "subject to critique the sovereign subject of accountability that liberal individualism presupposes, nor the economy of inclusion and exclusion that liberal universalism establishes" (70). She proposes, at the end of her essay, "What if we sought to supplant the language of 'I am'—with its defensive closure on identity, its insistence on the fixity of position, its equation of social with moral positioning—with the language of 'I want this for us'?" (75). It is precisely this kind of being that Moraga explores: needy, open to others, never fully healed. Pain, illness, and corporeal transformation expand the structure of identity politics—reaching out to new groups with which one's needs become intertwined—as they expand the structure of bodies. They also challenge the individuated corporeality assumed in current biomedical studies and health-care policies.

Ironically, medical processes designed to enforce sterility and to defend bodies from otherness highlight the very contaminations they attempt to eradicate. (Similarly, for the Aztecs and the Maya, the public spectacles designed to display the empire's power simultaneously highlighted the vulnerability of individual humans to each other and to the gods.) Moraga's experience in the clinic provides a meditation on the

---

23. Critics of Wendy Brown's work include Susan Hekman, *Private Selves, Public Identities* (2004), and Tobin Siebers, "Disability Studies and the Future of Identity Politics" (2006). As Siebers notes, part of what makes scholars in Disability Studies oppose Brown's argument is her assumption that "injury" and "suffering" are undesirable and her implicit reinforcement of the stigma surrounding disabled embodiments (Siebers, "Disability Studies and the Future of Identity Politics" 27). I take up Siebers's criticism of Brown at greater length in Chapter 4.

dynamics of healing. She uncovers revolutionary potential from the meeting of those corporeal states the clinic would mend away with those clinical structures she would formerly have opposed. Feeling and community meet medical technology when bodies need healing. Trying on wounded embodiments opens up different ways of doing medicine. Moraga and her *familia* leave the clinic transformed, but they also leave a snarl in their wake: "the gash sewn back into a snarl / would last for years" (Moraga, *Loving in the War Years* 60).

4

MOVEMENT: ANA CASTILLO'S SHAPE-SHIFTING IDENTITIES

> Every week in group [therapy] I take out the paring knife, I peel away and peel away and I suspect that finally there will be nothing, like what my old yoga instructor told me happens when you are in pursuit of the meaning of life. Ultimately you find that existence is nothing, the void. But to achieve the void is everything, the very essence of existence.
>
> Castillo, *Peel My Love Like an Onion*

If we accept pain and illness as viable corporeal states, we must think more about how such bodies are able to move and to thrive in the world. In *So Far From God* (1993)—the Ana Castillo novel that might seem like the most obvious "fit" for this study because of its emphasis on pain, illness, and medicine—the sick and injured characters do not do this. Though three of the four sisters in this novel return after death through channeling and miraculous "ectoplasmic" apparitions, all four do die, and none is able to navigate through the material world in her wounded state. A better example of alternative embodiment can be found in Castillo's 1999 novel, *Peel My Love Like an Onion*, which turns directly to the matter of mobility with disability in the body of a "crippled" flamenco dancer.

The identity politics of Castillo's writing have shifted since the early 1990s, when she coined the term *Xicanisma* to describe contemporary Chicana feminism as a descendant of pre-Conquest, pre-Christian, and pre-patriarchal cultures. In *Massacre of the Dreamers* (1994), she traced the "strength and endurance" of Chicana feminism back to ancient Meso-american spirituality, taking the "X" from the Mexica tribe (whom the

Aztec people claimed as ancestors) and creating an opposition between the patriarchal and hierarchical cultures imposed by European conquest and a supposedly more peaceful and egalitarian indigenous worldview (Castillo, *Massacre of the Dreamers* 95). *So Far From God* carries this tension into contemporary New Mexico, posing female-centered spiritualities grounded in Native traditions (*curanderas*, mystics, and strong women who cook wicked red chile) against the implicit violence of patriarchal Christianity. Though the Chicana main characters resist the ways of the dominant culture, their organic, communal values are ultimately not strong enough to combat Catholic *penitente* fanaticism, U.S.-waged war in the Middle East, AIDS, or the environmental destruction caused by high-tech industry. Because of its clear Chicana feminist political critique, its ironic humor, and its participation in exotic myths of U.S. Southwestern culture, this novel has received disproportionate critical attention relative to the large body of Castillo's published work.[1] Its Southwestern orientation actually makes *So Far From God* anomalous in Castillo's career, and centering on this novel misses the ways in which Castillo's writing otherwise pushes the boundaries of Chicana feminism and resists neat packaging in terms of ethnic, regional, or sexual identities. While *So Far From God* depicts Chicana politics in binary terms—as a battle between the Native and the Christian, *Nuevomexicanos* and Anglo colonizers, female and male—*Peel My Love Like an Onion* (which is set in Castillo's cosmopolitan hometown, Chicago) is less clear about where the battle lines are drawn. I focus here on *Peel My Love* not just because it is more recent but because it defies any unitary interpretation of identity. Why did Castillo choose a disabled flamenco dancer as her heroine at this point in her career? One of my tasks in this chapter will be to tease out this counterintuitive turn from *Xicanisma* to identifications not historically associated with Chicana feminism.

Castillo's characterization of Carmen la Coja (Carmen the Cripple) enables a detailed exploration of the relationship between embodied disability, mobility, and identity. Carmen is a surprising heroine in Chicana literature, and *Peel My Love* offers a marked deviation from the poetics and politics of 1980s Chicana feminism. The novel is traditional in that it focuses in great depth on one character as it traces her physical and

1. As of September 2008, of the sixty-nine entries the MLA Bibliography located about Ana Castillo's work, nineteen were dedicated explicitly to *So Far From God*, five explicitly about her first novel, *The Mixquiahuala Letters* (1992), six about her novel *Sapogonia* (1990), and one about *Peel My Love Like an Onion*.

psychological development from early youth, when she suffered her first bout of poliomyelitis, to mid-life. Castillo disrupts conventional characterization not with code-switching, narrative intrusions, or overt Chicana feminist politics, as Gloria Anzaldúa, Cherríe Moraga, Sandra Cisneros, and even Castillo herself have been known to do. Instead, Castillo fragments her character's development in other ways. The chronology of the novel is radically ruptured—indeed, the text does not sustain any single narrative thread for more than a few pages—which makes it difficult to witness a continued process of psychological development or physical deterioration, as one might expect of a *bildungsroman* with a disabled heroine. Moreover, Carmen's story itself defies ideas of progression in its unevenness and unpredictability. Although dance enables her to develop her leg muscles and neurological control, her polio returns unexpectedly at various points throughout her life, true to the instability of much disability. Even secondary details—where and with whom Carmen is living, working, and loving—shift around to create an incoherent background. The combined effect of these narrative techniques unsettles the contours of identity just as much as Anzaldúa's Coatlicue states that I describe in Chapter 2, though *Peel My Love* deconstructs its heroine in a manner far subtler than Anzaldúa's works. The novel fails to present a clear model of *Xicanisma*: its heroine is not linked to a Chicana/o community, and she is doggedly dedicated to unfaithful men, concerned with superficial appearance, and too busy dancing for politics. She is variously described as self-absorbed, pathetic, shabby, and drunk. As I will demonstrate, the unpredictability of Carmen's identity and the emplotment of her disability transform our thinking about the relationship between identity and politics. Maybe it is because of this transformation that critics invested in Chicana/o Studies and Disability Studies have not, or at least not yet, celebrated this novel.

Underneath her glamorous costumes and heterosexually attractive exterior, Carmen's body is asymmetrical and unreliable. She compares her spine to "shattered stone," she sees her face as a "Picasso forgery," and she wonders if her pain medication will enable her to forget about her body for long enough to survive two hours on stage (Castillo, *Peel My Love* 52, 53, 173). Castillo likely alludes to Frida Kahlo's self-portrait *The Broken Column* (1944), which depicts the artist's spine, literally, as shattered stone (see Plate 4a). Kahlo herself suffered from childhood polio and was sometimes called "Frida la coja" and "Pata de palo" ("peg-leg") (Herrera, *Frida* 413). In her 1925 bus accident, she broke her spinal column, along with her foot and her pelvis (Fuentes 10–11). *The Broken*

Column represents one of Kahlo's clearest images of corporeal violation, with her naked body punctured from within and without. The back brace seems to hold her body together, but underneath she is slit down the center with a shattered Ionic column in the open gash. Though her eyes and mouth are steady, and her head is held straight and firm, exaggerated tears falling from eyes to lips express the stifled pain of a body so ruptured. The "Picasso forgery" to which Carmen compares herself might allude to one of Pablo Picasso's cubist renditions of his lover, Fernande Olivier (see Plate 4b). While in Horta de Ebro in 1909, Picasso experimented with Cubist portraiture in a series of sketches and sculptures of Fernande, who suffered from kidney infections, headaches, and depression during this period. Jeffrey Weiss's exhibition catalogue for *Picasso: The Cubist Portraits of Fernande Olivier* reveals the ways in which Fernande acted as an aesthetic and philosophical object for Picasso during his development of Cubism, and I would like to think that Fernande's pain and depression had at least some influence on Picasso's fragmented representation of her form. The dozens of Kahlo self-portraits and Picasso's dozens of portraits of Fernande reflect an aesthetic and philosophical obsession with how pain, injury, and illness modify identity. Since Castillo, herself, is a painter, it is not surprising that she draws upon models from portraiture to make physical suffering visible. Seeing "shattered stone" in print creates an effect far less visceral than seeing the familiar-looking form of Frida Kahlo torn open with the weight of her head resting on a shattered spine. But unlike the self-portraits of Kahlo or Picasso's portraits of Fernande, Castillo's novelistic form enables her to develop a wider variety of metaphors for describing pain as an experience—"broken hoof" (55), "little ice box" (152), peeling with a paring knife (190–91)—as well as to narrate a variety of situations in which her character learns to reconcile her disability with her needs for mobility. While the visual portraits remain static, with their pain frozen in time, Castillo's character moves through situation after situation in which her pain develops new meanings and in which she must develop new responses.

Castillo is one of the few critics to have written about Anzaldúa's pain. She suggested that Anzaldúa's "exceptional physical maladies" and "tremendous physical and emotional anguish" influenced her elaboration of the Coatlicue state, which Castillo interprets as a "desire for disembodiment that would free her from" illness (Castillo, *Massacre of the Dreamers* 172–73). Such a claim, according to my reading, misinterprets Anzaldúa's body politics, since it refuses to consider sustained physical pain as an avenue for expanding consciousness. One might then expect *Peel My Love*, like *So Far From God*, to reject pain or to use it only as a vehicle for critiquing the exploitative and destructive systems that inflict pain on Chicanas. Instead, Carmen's response to her pain suggests expansive ways of being that exceed the boundaries of her disability and of her working-class Latino neighborhood (providing literary examples of Anzaldúa's late theory of "new tribalism," which I discuss in my introduction).

Unlike Anzaldúa, who self-identifies as a body in pain, Castillo's fictional heroine tries to mobilize her body in such a way as to escape pain: "Ever since I began to experience all that pain that I had not felt in so long and never thought I would again because I was strong and young and could dance my way through it, I've been trying to figure out an escape from the little ice box that is my body's ongoing agony" (*Peel My Love* 152). Sealed, frozen, and inorganic, an ice box is not open to human development. Compared to an icebox of pain, achieving the "void," as Carmen seeks to do in the epigraph to this chapter, would be a relief, a means of distancing oneself from one's body in pain. Yet psychotherapy and yoga, the two methods Carmen uses to reach toward the "void," do not transcend psychological or physical pain as much as they reiterate them, by retelling stories of trauma and repeating painful postures, in order to experience their pain differently, to feel it as less damaging to the self. They isolate the self as an object whose histories and movements we can understand and whose contact with the outside world—painful or not—can provide self-knowledge. Psychotherapy and yoga lead Carmen to explore different ways of being herself. Her very identity as the dancer "Carmen la Coja" is founded on her disability and her body's straining against disability, but claiming "the cripple" as an identity shifts the term from imposed judgment to self-proclaimed source of meaning. "Carmen la Coja" is an identity developed at the intersection of inescapable physiological conditions and individual desires and movements.

Even if we can never transcend our bodies, we can alter our perceptions and our movements. In unraveling this link between mind and body, pain and movement, I have divided this chapter into three sections, first exploring the Mesoamerican cultural history that underlies Carmen's disabled mobility, focusing particularly on the god Tezcatlipoca and practices of shape-shifting. The second section reveals how identity, in *Peel My Love*, is ultimately structured by movement rather than being bound by the categories that dominate earlier Chicana feminist writing. Castillo suggests a way in which we can use mobility—rather than race, class, sex, or any other restrictive social frameworks—to expand identity politics. The final section of this chapter considers the implications of Carmen's movements for Disability Studies and Chicana feminism.

Shape-Shifting

I believe that Castillo's depiction of Carmen la Coja is meant to invoke an ancient Mesoamerican form of the sacred. In his study of Nahuatl corporeal ideology, Alfredo López Austin claims that "physical defects were considered signs identifying men as individuals with supernatural powers," since people who were chosen by the gods were often marked in some visible way (López Austin 360).[2] According to the Florentine Codex, some women with magical powers were marked as *mometzcopinque*, shape-shifters who were capable of "detaching the lower part of [their] legs to replace them with birds' feet and fly through the air" (360)—an embodiment reminiscent of Frida Kahlo as well as Carmen la Coja's own mystified "peg-leg."[3] In an argument that reclaims the

2. López Austin uses the cultural term "Nahuatl" rather than "Aztec," identifying the people by the language they spoke. There is some debate about the appropriateness of the term "Aztec" to describe the dominant culture of Central Mexico preceding the Conquest. According to Inga Clendinnen, "The word 'Aztec' has been used to mean a number of things, from the 'empire' which sprawled across much of modern Mexico, to the people of the magnificent lake city who were its masters" (Clendinnen, *Aztecs* 1). Clendinnen uses the ethnic term "Mexica" "to avoid the heavy freight that 'Aztec' has come to bear" (1). The fluidity of my terms thus reflects the contestation surrounding the term "Aztec."

3. In a 1953 journal entry, written as she learned from her doctors that her right leg would be amputated below the knee, Frida Kahlo writes "*Pies para qué los quiero si tengo alas pa' volar*" [Feet, why do I want them when I have wings to fly?] beneath a sketch that disassociates her feet from her body. In the drawing, two crossed feet are displayed on a pedestal, with the surrounding page covered in red watercolor blood. The right foot and ankle eclipse the other in this image, ending abruptly mid-calf with a profusion of veins (or perhaps thunderbolts?) emerging from the terminus. The ankle, itself, is fractured internally, as well (Kahlo 134). A later sketch, dated August 1953, tells the other half of this story, depicting a naked body with wings for arms and a dove where its head should be. Rather than focusing on the amputated leg—which appears only as a long cyclone in this image—the body is objectified, with the legs called supports ("*apoyos*") and the spinal column down the center repeating the image from *The Broken Column*. The text accompanying this image reads: "*Se equivocó la paloma. /*

Aztecs as humanitarians, counterpoising their reputation as bloody imperialists, Arturo Rocha celebrates what he views as the Aztecs' care and reverence for people we would regard today as "disabled": "*los individuos señalados por alguna descapacidad o deformidad corporal, o aquejados de males como la epilepsia, incluso los nacidos mellizos, inspiraban en aquella cultura singular respeto, por no decir temor, por el vínculo con lo divino que representaban* [individuals signaled by a disability or corporeal deformity, or suffering complaints like epilepsy, including those born twins, inspired in that culture singular respect, to say nothing of fear, for the bond with the divine that they represented]" (Rocha 20). A more common interpretation of Aztec body politics is that they regarded deviations from the corporeal norm as punishments by the gods for wrongdoings (Burkhart, *The Slippery Earth* 176; Aguirre Beltrán 43–47). Louise Burkhart interprets ancient Nahuatl sources as valuing bodies that are "straight," well-formed, and unblemished (Burkhart, *The Slippery Earth* 177). Yet she also acknowledges "the power of chaotic elements" and the association of one of the central deities, Tezcatlipoca, with "physically deformed persons" (177). Disorder and "deformity" undermine human control and would thus have signified the imbrication of the divine in the human. Since Tezcatlipoca, the god of providence, was associated with "dwarves and cripples" (176), physical disability was likely revered, or at least respectfully feared, for its association with his unpredictable and inescapable power. I hesitate to say that the Aztecs were more generous toward people with disabilities than other civilizations (a claim that would echo a long tradition of romanticizing the Aztecs as noble savages). Yet much of what we know about Aztec culture revolves around the instability of bodies. Self-inflicted wounds and fasting were sacred rituals designed to

---

Se equivocó [The dove was wrong / it was wrong]," suggesting that perhaps her earlier optimistic pretensions toward flight were false (141). An earlier 1953 sketch depicts Kahlo's winged body engulfed in what seems to be a burning forest with the captions, "*Te vas? No. ALAS ROTAS* [Are you going? No. Broken wings]" (124). The narrative entries in Kahlo's journal during this period also undermine the optimism of "feet, why do I want them?" On one page she writes, "*Mi estructura inconforme por inarmónica, por inadaptada. Yo creo que es mejor irme, irme, no escaparme* [My structure is uncomfortable for being inharmonious, for being not adapted. I think it is best for me to go, to go, not *to escape myself*]" (136, emphasis original). I use my own less graceful but more literal translations here, rather than those of Sarah Lowe, included in the Abrams publication of the journal, to foreground the feelings of discomfort and placelessness Kahlo records as she adapts herself to the idea of amputation (Kahlo 134).

denormalize identity, reminding humans of the tenuousness of their flesh and their vulnerability to the gods.[4] The bodies of warriors, lords, and priests were marked with scars, filed teeth, and plugs inserted through holes in their lips, noses, and ears, indicating that corporeal anomaly was associated with (but perhaps reserved for) sacred and royal status.

One of the ways in which Mesoamericans understood mystical transcendence was through shape-shifting (also called *nagualism* or *nahualism*): assuming the forms of other beings.[5] These shifts were achieved through departures from everyday perception, as in dreaming, dancing, masking, self-bleeding, and intoxication. The Aztecs were obsessed with order, hierarchy, and equilibrium on a daily basis, so all boundary crossings (including inebriation, contact with filth, or flesh piercing) were dangerous and reserved for sacred ritual because they potentially opened a path to the divine. Boundary crossing was the work of priests and magicians. Shape-shifting was one of the indigenous beliefs most feared by the Spanish invaders, and there is evidence that, after the Conquest, its practice became more widespread (crossing class boundaries and including *mestizos*) among those who refused submission to Spanish cultural and spiritual forms. Archeologist Daniel Brinton, writing in the nineteenth century, calls *nagualism* "a superstitious idolatry, full of monstrous insects, sodomites and detestable bestialities," "inspired by . . . detestations of the Spaniards and hatred of the Christian religion" (Brinton 29, 35). Brinton interprets *nagualism* as a "counteracting ceremony" to annul Christianity (35), a means of courting the devil (29), a source of "race-hatred" against the Spanish (38), and a sexual threat, too, embodied by serpent women and eagle women who enchanted and then massacred men in battle (41–45). Shape-shifting thus figures as a powerful means of deceiving potential conquerors and eluding conquest.

4. The Olmecs, other ancestors of the Aztecs, also regarded corporeal abnormalities as sacred. In his (often judgmental) popular history of Mexico, T. R. Fehrenbach describes the Olmecs as "Magicians," "obsessed with monsters in human form. Their figurines portray men with genital or glandular deformities, with pointed Mongoloid heads, with cleft skulls, and with animal mouths. They appear to have believed such persons holy. . . . The Magicians also practiced self-mutilation, possibly in emulation of some historic deformed births" (Fehrenbach 16).

5. Gloria Anzaldúa also claimed to be a shape-shifter: "I become the jaguar. I become the serpent, I become the eagle" (Anzaldúa, *Interviews* 284), embodying the mobility of sacred Aztec totems. A *nahual* or *nagual* is a spiritual projection of or companion to oneself.

According to López Austin, "Whoever could at will cross the frontiers of the invisible world, travel to places forbidden to other mortals, refuse or attract influences, receive divine fire in his body, or freely release animistic entities and act through them had acquired these powers" from the gods, from their birth sign, or from their own *tonal* (anima/spirit) (López Austin 360). Travel itself was sacred/dangerous as a boundary crossing. Among his catalogue of Aztec medical diagnoses, López Austin includes one disease that is particular to travelers: he describes *xoxalli* as a malignant force that would accumulate in the legs as skin tumors, hernias, or swelling (266). For the Aztecs, travel and shape-shifting were parallel disruptions in the rigid social framework, so from this perspective, Carmen's constant travels in *Peel My Love* might be a logical extension of her unpredictable disability. According to a Mesoamerican worldview, both kinds of movement would likely mark her as sacred—not "blessed" or "damned," as a Christian views sacred intervention in human life, but, rather, something more like transcendent, touched, or, perhaps, ecstatic (remembering that Aztecs ritually inflicted pain upon themselves, often while under the influence of hallucinogens, in order to touch the divine).

Tezcatlipoca is the primary god associated with shape-shifting. Originally a Toltec god whom the Aztecs later incorporated into their own pantheon when trying to solidify their imperial rule with ancient Toltec legitimacy, Tezcatlipoca was the god of providence, known to appear (especially on the roads and usually at night) in various guises bearing evil omens, and he was blamed for a multitude of illnesses.[6] In Michael

6. The Aztecs dominate most Mesoamerican cultural histories because they were the last Amerindian empire in Mexico, but the Aztecs idealized the Toltecs as the source of their cultural and spiritual traditions. In the preface to *My Father Was a Toltec*, Castillo tells readers to "look up the Toltecs on the Internet" to discover that "No Aztec worth his salt did not claim lineage to that noble civilization" (Castillo, *My Father Was a Toltec* xviii). Most of what we know about the Toltecs is filtered through the codices, stories, and admonitions left by the Aztecs. Though the Spaniards destroyed the Aztecs' temples and their dream books during the Conquest, the Aztecs were also the focus of Spanish research and missionary work documenting Mesoamerican life in the sixteenth century, leaving many published sources about Aztec beliefs, rituals, and aesthetics. While Chicanos of the 1960s celebrated Aztec culture in defiance of European conquest, Castillo establishes a different sort of relationship to a culture that predates the Conquest era. (Yet Castillo, herself, relies primarily on sources about the Aztecs, including Caso, Brundage, Coe, Fehrenbach, and Sahagún.) The Toltecs

Coe's account, there were initially four Tezcatlipocas to correspond to the four cardinal directions. The "real" Tezcatlipoca, the god of war and sorcery, giver and taker away of life and riches, was the "Black Tezcatlipoca" of the North. The White Tezcatlipoca of the West became Quetzalcoatl (later Tezcatlipoca's rival), the Blue Tezcatlipoca of the South became Huitzilopochtli (the war god descended from Coatlicue), and the Red Tezcatlipoca of the East became Xipe Totec, the "flayed god" whom the Aztecs celebrated by ritually flaying the skins of sacrifice victims (Coe 178–79). Luis Barjau identifies twelve different names for Tezcatlipoca in the Nahuatl and early Spanish codices.[7] These various names attribute opposing qualities to him, including making jokes and mourning, being the enemy and the creator. The idea of multiplicity and ambiguity, and the possibility of fragmentation into other coherent identities, is thus built within Tezcatlipoca (regardless of how many different names or incarnations one attributes to him). The primary Aztec festival in his honor, Tóxcatl, featured the year-long veneration of a young man chosen to act out the role of Tezcatlipoca. The Tezcatlipoca "actor" was given fine foods, women, and musical instruments, and was celebrated throughout Tenochtitlán until the end of the year, when he would willingly break his flutes and mount the steps of a pyramid to be sacrificed. Shortly thereafter, a new god actor would be chosen and feted. Barjau interprets this festival as an object lesson in dissolution and regeneration,

---

are blurrier in written history, but Castillo cites evidence that they were a people with woman warriors and "queens who ruled" (xviii). Her feminist impulse reaches back before the imposition of Aztec imperialism to "female indigenous energies" repressed by the Aztecs long before the Spaniards arrived (*Massacre of the Dreamers* 146). This is an idealistic gesture, romanticizing the Mexican past to legitimize contemporary politics as much as Castillo's Chicano predecessors did. Castillo's gesture is not more true to history, but it is a reminder that Chicana/os' claim to Aztec identity is not the product of direct inheritance but rather of particular political claims. Castillo's view of the Mexican past is contingent upon her own "Chicana feminist caveat" (*My Father Was a Toltec* xviii), mediated by the unbounded connections of the World Wide Web, and likely subject to subsequent revisions.

7. The twelve names of Tezcatlipoca are Tezcat (smoking mirror), Titlachuan (he whose slaves we are), Iáutl (enemy), Moyocoya (creator), Nezahaulpilli (knight/horseman of mourning and fasting), Monenequi (whimsical tyrant), Teyocoyani (he who invents the people), Teimatini (providence), Moquequeloa (he jokes), Tzoncozqui (with yellow hair), Telpochtli (youth), and Tlamazincatl (he who lives in Tlamaltzinco, site of his grand temple) (Barjau 13–14).

reminding the people that all wealth and happiness turn to pain and death, following the cycle that ultimately governs all planetary life (Barjau 33, 102–3). According to legends in Nahuatl, Tezcatlipoca was responsible for the downfall of the Toltecs, tricking and distracting their rulers in the guises of a green chile vendor, an old man with debilitating potions, and the leader of a puppet dance. Even after the Toltecs stoned him to death, they "were unable to rid themselves of his now festering, rotted body" (Coe 133). He reappeared again and again to travelers as he made his way South out of Tula and down to Tenochtitlán to become lord of the Aztecs' providence. (See Figure 1.)

I suggest that Castillo invokes Tezcatlipoca as a symbolic principle much as Anzaldúa and Moraga ground their politics upon interpretations of the Aztec goddesses Coatlicue and Coyolxauhqui. Yet Castillo mentions Tezcatlipoca only three times in her published work, once in *Sapogonia* and once each in two poems I discuss below, and she provides no discussion about the significance of this god.[8] There is no elaborated "Tezcatlipoca state," but the god does bear an uncanny resemblance to and relevance for Carmen la Coja. Also known as Lord of the Smoking Mirror, he was sometimes depicted with a sacrificed leg and a smoking mirror emerging from his stump (Rocha 152; Caso 29). The smokiness of his mirror suggests that he revealed to people their own images clouded with malevolence, veiled by other forms, and/or blurred by

Figure 1. Tezcatlipoca.

8. *Sapogonia*'s antihero, artist, wanderer, and ladies' man, Máximo, is compared to Tezcatlipoca, "personification of the night wind," when he arrives unexpectedly on the doorstep of his sometimes lover Pastora (Castillo, *Sapogonia* 224).

indeterminacy.[9] Carmen la Coja, like the one-legged Tezcatlipoca, is a trickster figure, poised at the crossroads and shifting forms strategically to accommodate particular situations.[10] Indeed, Tezcatlipoca was associated with dance, and, Carmen, too, has a mirror, a gift from her parents for her twenty-fifth birthday. This makeup mirror (the kind that "a star" should have) is meant to freeze her image in the form of success, reflecting back her "real beauty," not the "broken hoof" cut off below its reflection. Yet it is in the magnifying side of this two-sided, duplicitous mirror that Carmen ultimately sees her face as a "Picasso forgery" (Castillo, *Peel My Love* 52, 55). Carmen's sacred power is her ability to project a dancing "star" image on top of the reality of her disabled body. As with Tezcatlipoca, Carmen's identity is not based on one incarnation but is rather dispersed among different performances and different perceptions.

As with Anzaldúa's work, the key to understanding Castillo's "major" works sometimes lies in often-ignored "minor" ones. Tezcatlipoca is never actually named within the novel *Peel My Love Like an Onion*, but he is mentioned in a short poem by the same title. "Peel My Love Like an Onion" was originally published in 1991 (in *Berkeley Poetry Review*), revised and republished in 1999 as the epigraph to *Peel My Love*, and, in 2000, collected in *I Ask the Impossible*, suggesting that Castillo had been thinking about shape-shifting and onions as models for identity for a while.[11] The poem begins:

9. Barjau interprets his mirror as a sign that "*la divinidad es un complejo formado entre ella y sus fieles, in forma del espejo y la imagen, el hombre y su conciencia de sí* [the divine is a complex formed between the god and his followers, in form of the mirror and the image, the man and his self-consciousness]" (Barjau 15). In this way, Tezcatlipoca and his mirror break down individuation, showing how identities are established through mutual perception and interdependence between humans and the divine.

10. Tezcatlipoca's "trickster" function in Mesoamerican tradition is parallel to the role of Esu-Elegbara as trickster in African traditions. As Henry Louis Gates Jr. describes him: "Esu is the guardian of the crossroads, master of style and of stylus, phallic god of generation and fecundity, master of that elusive, mystical barrier that separates the divine world from the profane" (Gates 6). Tezcatlipoca, too, is associated with sexuality. Seducing women was one of his methods of trickery, and he is depicted in some stories with "an unusually large penis" (Tompkins 80–81). And Esu is also "said to limp as he walks precisely because of his mediating function: his legs are of different lengths because he keeps one anchored in the realm of the gods while the other rests in this, our human world" (Gates 6).

11. In *Massacre*, Castillo translates her hometown, Chicago, as "Place of Wild Onions" (Castillo, *Massacre of the Dreamers* 7).

Peel my love like an onion,
one transparent layer following the next,
a Buddhist infinity of desire.
I breathe your skin
and a vapor of memory arises,
tears my orifices raw
with the many smells of you.

(Castillo, Peel My Love *epigraph)*

Like Tezcatlipoca, onions are composed of different layers that give way
to each other, their transparency signaling this multiplicity. Also like Tezcatlipoca, onions have no true "core." Their layers are their bodies—a
model for identity that Castillo takes up in her depictions of Carmen's
shape-shifting flamenco. In the poem, peeling away the layers "tears my
orifices raw," as psychotherapy and yoga peel away at a body's pain (in
the epigraph to this chapter). Stripping the self does not lead to annihilation but, rather, "a Buddhist infinity of desire" unfurls with each layer,
suggesting a process without end. The last seven lines reveal that the
"you" who is peeling the layers is not simply a lover but Tezcatlipoca,
himself, defined in Castillo's footnote in *I Ask The Impossible* as the
"Night Sky God" and "the god of providence" (*I Ask The Impossible*
88). (Cryptically, the novel contains no such explanatory footnote, and
this one line of the epigraph is its only mention of the god's name.) This
poem thus depicts one of those sacred boundary states where gods appear
to humans. As with Aztec sacrifice rituals, the flayed "skin" of the poem's
speaker represents this crossing of boundaries and the vulnerability/di-
vinity of the human self.

Since the lover in this poem is Tezcatlipoca, it is possible that the
unnamed speaker is Xochiquetzal, the goddess of flowers he once se-
duced, according to some interpretations of Aztec legend.[12] Xochiquetzal

12. Hernando Ruiz de Alarcón notes that the name Xochiquetzal is sometimes used to refer to "wife," in general (Ruiz de Alarcón 31), making it difficult
to know the particular details of this goddess's "history." Two of the sources
Castillo cites in her bibliography for *Massacre*—Alfonso Caso's *The Aztecs: People
of the Sun* (1958) and Burr Cartwright Brundage's *The Fifth Sun: Aztec Gods,
Aztec World* (1979)—both tell the story of Tezcatlipoca seducing Xochiquetzal.
I believe that Caso was the direct source for this poem, since he identifies Tezcatlipoca in the same terms as Castillo's footnote, as both God of the Night Sky and
God of Providence, and one of the few details Caso provides in his brief introduction to Tezcatlipoca is that he carried off Xochiquetzal saying, "I shall have
her, not tomorrow nor the next day nor the next, but right now, at this moment,

also rules love, sex, magic, the arts, and changes, making her an appealing goddess for Castillo.[13] Both Tezcatlipoca and Xochiquetzal are shape-shifters, gods of indeterminacy and fluidity, which is consistent with the poem's depiction of the lovers merging and subsequently changing form:

> When you leave, Tezcatlipoca,
> it is I who have evaporated you perhaps,
> horned creature to whom
> I have given wings, come back. Rest again, in my
> thin arms, limb with limb
> like gnarled branches entwined in a sleep
> of a thousand years.
>
> *(Castillo,* Peel My Love *epigraph)*

Contact blends the two bodies, leaving them "entwined," "limb with limb." Their bodies shift, interact, and mutate without threatening identity. (I initially wrote "coherence" but realized that such a term is not relevant in this schema.) In my epigraph to this chapter (taken from the novel *Peel My Love*), peeling away layers of selfhood ultimately uncovers a void. Yet the poem "Peel My Love" finds no such void. The onion

---

for I, in person, am he who ordains and commands it so" (Caso 29). Caso's account of this seduction is immediately followed by the amputation of Tezcatlipoca's foot, suggesting that Castillo would know the god as one-legged. The name Xochiquetzal was also used in sacred occasions to represent women's role as keepers and regulators of sexuality. (People who engaged in excessive sexual indulgence were said to be punished by her (Clendinnen, *Aztecs* 164).) During the festival Tóxcatl—when a youth chosen to represent Tezcatlipoca for a year acted out the god's capricious whims and voluntarily sacrificed himself at a time of his own choosing—Xochiquetzal was the name given to the four "wives" handed over for the pleasure of the Tezcatlipoca actor (105).

13. Castillo invokes Xochiquetzal directly though cryptically in her short story "La Miss Rose." In a paragraph that seems like a digression from the story, Xochiquetzal, St. Anne, and Erzulie are credited with the (multicultural) creation of the sunset: the three goddesses are having a "wienie roast" when "the coals tipped over and set the sky on fire" (Castillo, *Loverboys* 185). "La Miss Rose," published in 1996, also has a heroine named Carmen, who moves from the desert to Chicago with a friend named "Stormy" and the one-eyed Miss Rose, and who wears "cross-trainers" like Carmen in *Peel My Love*. One of Castillo's literary trademarks is cross-referencing her other works, and this repeated convergence of themes—Xochiquetzal, disability, cross-trainers, and Chicago—suggests a definite link, for Castillo, between mobility, disability, the cosmopolitan city, and Mesoamerican creativity and shape-shifting.

metaphor in the poem shifts identity away from the "core" to the layers, themselves: a slippery and many-faced form in which one layer slides into the next.

The speaker of "Peel My Love" could also be Coatlicue, the goddess of fertility and destruction who also sometimes appears as a female counterpart to Tezcatlipoca.[14] Castillo's first published reference to Tezcatlipoca is in a Spanish-language poem, "Lamento de Coatlicue," in which Tezcatlipoca appears, intimately, to a first-person Coatlicue.[15]

> *Cierro los ojos* [I close my eyes]
> *y estás aquí* [and you are here]
> *convertido en noche* [converted into/at night]
> *Tezcatlipoca,*
> *hijo malcriado* [unruly boy/ill-bred son].
> *(Castillo,* My Father Was a Toltec *30)*

After Tezcatlipoca comes to Coatlicue, cadavers emerge to surround her (*"vienen / los cadaveres / a rodearme"*). For the Aztecs, cadavers, particularly those of sacrifice victims, were revered as sacred relics of the meeting of the human and the divine. Pieces of dead bodies were manipulated, paraded through city streets, shared with the populace, and displayed on skull racks, at temples, and sometimes even in private homes. Inga Clendinnen interprets this intimacy with dead flesh as an emblem of humans' forced acceptance of "the decay and dissolution of the self" as part of life's cycles (Clendinnen, *Aztecs* 96). This poem also seems to initiate something like Anzaldúa's Coatlicue state, in which allowing the body to dissolve enables continual life-making. The informal second person in *"Lamento de Coatlicue,"* as with the speaker's reference to him as an *"hijo malcriado,"* establishes intimacy with Tezcatlipoca, providence, and, perhaps, death. The first two and final two lines of the ten-line poem emphasize the speaker's closed eyes: a gesture of submission, trust, and/or fear. Her individual agency is irrelevant in the boundary states of love and death—and in intimacy with the god known as "He Whose Slaves We Are" (Clendinnen, *Aztecs* 147).

14. Castillo pairs Tezcatlipoca with Coatlicue, at least implicitly, in *Sapogonia*: Max (who is once compared to Tezcatlipoca) thinks of his lover Pastora as Coatlicue "incarnated" (Castillo, *Sapogonia* 144).

15. The lament form was common in Aztec poetry, which was not personal or narrative in content but collective, formulaic, self-consciously aesthetic, and generally intended to reveal resemblances between this world and the gods (Clendinnen, *Aztecs* 218–19).

In both poems, the presence of Tezcatlipoca tugs at the outer tissues of the speaker's identity, challenging individual stability and integrity. Ancient Mesoamerican understandings of identity can shed light on Castillo's onion metaphor. In his study of mysticism in Mesoamerica, Ptolemy Tompkins describes how Aztec priests attempting to induce shapeshifting or otherworldly communication would often smear their bodies with "a thick paste composed of blood, soot, tobacco, crushed scorpions, spiders, and rattlesnakes and a mixture of hallucinogenic plants" (Tompkins 111). By adding this extra layer of "skin" to their bodies, the priests relinquished their everyday identities and went naked into the wilderness to experience mystical states beyond their individual bodies' boundaries. The sacred substance of this "paste" fuses the life force of blood with the death force of soot; it invites ecstatic hallucination; and it invokes the regenerative power of the snake that lives by shedding its skin and rattles. The shed skin of snakes—like the peeled ear of corn and the flayed skin of sacrifice victims—was a particularly important symbol of sacred life cycles. All three symbols provide a glimpse of the simultaneity of creation and dissolution, and the key to these symbols' power is the ability to see through the "dead" outer layer to the new life (edible corn kernels, seeds for the next crop, the heart pumping blood) inside. The onion, too, could provide this glimpse of regeneration, particularly if one regards its layers as "transparent," as the poem "Peel My Love Like an Onion" does. The real meaning of the layers lies in the possibility of continued shedding, as the central feature of shape-shifting identities is the boundary-crossing itself. In many human sacrifice rituals, particularly those in honor of Xipe Totec, priests ritually dressed in the flayed skin of the dead. They did not, thereby, become the sacrifice victim; nor did they remain themselves. The individual identities of sacrificer and sacrificed would be eclipsed, transformed by the powerful touching of the two skins, the meeting of life and death, and the visible duality of this embodiment. Numerous Toltec and Aztec codices and sculptures reflect this shape-shifting duality by exposing the live body under the flayed skin.

In my interpretation, ancient Mesoamericans understood identity as contextual, expandable, and irreducible to one body. Postmodernism, Disability Studies, Eco-Feminism, and other schools of thought have reached similar conclusions by way of continental philosophy, but the Mesoamerican and Chicana sources I privilege here enable us to see "real" fluid embodiments relative to the cultures and time periods in which they emerge. One philosophical source that has especially influenced my interpretation of Tezcatlipoca and Carmen la Coja is the phenomenology of Maurice Merleau-Ponty. Linda Martín Alcoff, too, bases her simultaneous critique and reclamation of identity on Merleau-Ponty's "realist" argument that "lived experience is open-ended, multilayered, fragmented, and shifting not because of the play of language, but because of the nature of embodied, temporal existence" (Alcoff 109–10). I find in Merleau-Ponty an accurate accounting of the multilayered and shifting reality of embodied identity. His philosophy of "being in the world" views all embodiment as an "interweaving" between bodies and their environments: "overlapping and fission, identity and difference" shape bodies in dialogue with others and with the world around them (Merleau-Ponty, *The Visible and the Invisible* 142). Bodies become themselves at the points where they meet something else. As a body moves and its surrounding context shifts, so does the "identity" of the flesh that meets the world. Movement itself initiates a departure from stasis and activates the situation (or the "being") of identity. In *Phenomenology of Perception*, Merleau-Ponty suggests that "the spatiality of our body is brought into being" by action (*Phenomenology* 102). Given this insight, we can see how shape-shifting bodies form and reform identity by crossing boundaries, creating new interfaces, new points of differentiation, and new sources of definition. For Merleau-Ponty, we understand being through analysis of movement (102), which is where my chapter turns now.

Carmen's identity exceeds the boundaries of disability as her body moves beyond the expected postures for a woman with a leg brace. Neither nostalgic nor inclined to transcendental martyrdom, Carmen rejects Frida Kahlo's romantic claim, "What do I need feet for when I have wings?" (Castillo, *Peel My Love* 185; Kahlo 134). Carmen's identity is all about her feet, the one that is "bald and featherless, a limp dead heron fallen from its nest" (Castillo, *Peel My Love* 12–13) earning her the name "*la Coja*," and the other with its extraordinary muscles propelling her body across the stage. Her reputation is based upon the difference between her legs: she is legendary because she is "the cripple" who dances. The content of her identity is asymmetry and surprise, both of which are experienced in motion rather than stasis. Her childhood shame for the discordance of her "crippled-girl style" dance step—"PAS-nothing" rather than the symmetrical "PAS-PAS!" of traditional flamenco (16, 18)—is replaced by an appreciation for the *poderosa* (powerful) sound of her own rhythm: "the soft one-two step since one leg is shorter than the other," each "good" step followed by "one without a sound, like a feather dropping" (68, 73). Carmen dances on the "very fine line . . . between very pathetic and excruciatingly sublime" (119), dismissing her girlhood longing for a matched pair of legs and the naive belief that "two things identical and equal to each other were the essence of symmetry and the sublime" (13). Flamenco provides a choreography of individual exploration and seduction. The focal point of flamenco is movement of the hands, arms, and torso, so Carmen is able to seduce audiences with the illusion of mastery by moving her upper body, while her legs limp unevenly beneath her long skirts.[16] Her body is not just split from left to right; it is also split horizontally, from top to bottom. Yet her legs are never invisible, since her transparent stage name highlights the "disabled" layer (un)hidden under her skirts.

Flamenco critic Antonio Parra views the style of flamenco as an expression of the pain, exile, and forced wanderings of the gypsy diaspora:

> The tragedy in flamenco is not only a rendition of personal anguish, or of the gypsies' persecution, or the hunger and despair of the poor and downtrodden. . . . There is a third stage for humanity, which returns us to "living" rather than "belonging." It is a stage that is between the confusing, the painful, the finite, and space without time. It is where we seek the gifts and grace, and it is where we find forms of flamenco. (Parra A1)

Though Parra's description is romantic and floats above material and cultural context, this idealism reflects his point that flamenco is an expression of being unmoored from a homeland. Flamenco dancers chart their own materiality with movement rather than "belonging" to one place. One of the few articles published thus far on *Peel My Love* regards flamenco as a "utopian" identity. Silvia Lorente-Murphy concludes that *"La vida de Carmen, como el baile y el canto flamencos, son imprevisibles, se van moldeando de acuerdo con las circunstancias, se van improvisando* [Carmen's life, like flamenco dance and song, are unforeseeable, they mold themselves according to circumstances, they improvise]" (Lorente-Murphy 131). Unlike more strictly choreographed dances, Carmen's flamenco experiments with potential embodiments and finds ways to move with and through pain and "disability." Since flamenco is associated with an exiled and nomadic community, Lorente-Murphy interprets it as *"la expression del sufrimiento, del rechazo, de la lucha de un pueblo por sus derechos y finalmente del triunfo de gente con coraje y que valora el simple hecho de estar*

---

16. Silvia Lorente-Murphy points out that Carmen la Coja is most likely a reference to the flamenco legend Enrique el Cojo (1912–1985), who was disabled from the waist down and whose torso and arm movements eclipsed the relative immobility of his feet (Lorente-Murphy 129).

vivos pese a todo [the expression of suffering, of rejection, of a people's fight for their rights and finally of the triumph of a strong/brave people who value the simple fact of being alive in the face of it all]" (Lorente-Murphy 131). The movements of flamenco allow for the abject (the exiled, the disabled) to be triumphant. And if flamenco is to express the suffering of its dancers, as Lorente-Murphy suggests it must, its aesthetic must be dual, alternately signaling suffering and triumph.

Throughout the novel, Carmen's movements shift as her body changes shape. Castillo carefully dissects these movements, from Carmen's asymmetrical dance steps to her power walks in Nike cross-trainers, studying the supports that underlie mobility. The fluidity of Carmen's identity is not just a feature of her disabled body but also of contextual supports: assistance from instructors and prosthetic devices, access to painkillers, divergent cultural perceptions. Her being is filtered through networks of power. Taking up with gypsy (or, as Carmen's "gypsy" friends call it, *calorra*) culture is for Carmen an avenue for mobility and income. The muscle development that comes from regular flamenco practice enables her to go for a while without crutches or leg brace, and the income from public performance enables her to buy better health insurance and better housing. Her health and her success depend upon each other: she is most physically sound when she is the most financially successful, and she is the most financially successful when she is physically sound. In circular fashion, without dance she cannot dance. Flamenco literally lifts her out of her demanding and dysfunctional working-class Chicano family, with whom she is forced to live when not dancing, through the mobility it enacts and the monetary earnings it provides. Renting an apartment of her own, like finding her own place on stage, enables her to be an individual "free" from the obligations and stasis of her race, class, and community. When she is physically able to move on stage, Carmen is also able to move on a larger scale, traveling internationally to perform, so her dancing identity knows no physical boundaries. She becomes a gypsy. *Calorra* culture is defined by placelessness rather than singular racial genealogy or geographic location, so Carmen is (paradoxically) able to find home(s) and belonging in exile. The mystique (appeal and terror) of perpetual exclusion and migration contributes to the popularity of flamenco and enables eccentrics like Carmen to make a transnational career out of it, invited and celebrated by audiences around the world.[17]

17. One of the heroines of Castillo's first novel, *The Mixquiahuala Letters,* has a gypsy grandmother who sang spine-tingling lullabies. In this novel, "gypsies

Like the priest who covers his body in magical paste to change forms in sacred ritual, the flowing skirts and clapping hands of flamenco project Carmen's body outward into abstract space and imagination (her own and the audience's). What she admires most about dance is its velocity, the ways in which it blurs the boundaries of a body and stages a dynamic illusion out of flesh, blood, and bone. For the Aztecs, too, dance was a way of eclipsing the human body. According to Inga Clendinnen, the stylized movements, elaborate costumes, and shifting rhythms produced "a shifting in awareness and of the boundaries of the self. And only then, as the self evaporated and the choreographed excitements multiplied and the sensations came flooding in, did the god draw near" (Clendinnen, *Aztecs* 258–59). Castillo sometimes represents the dancing of Carmen's idols as an alchemical transformation. Her lover Manolo's body spins itself to "crackling embers" (Castillo, *Peel My Love* 135), and María Benítez's "long arms all over the place" make her like the goddess Kali (186), but Carmen's body ultimately must "follow the law of gravity" (135). While dancing she is glamorous, able to use her hands, her confidence, and her *duende* to cover for what her legs cannot do. The context of flamenco cloaks the other shapes of her disabled body. But sometimes her polio takes over and she can't perform. At these times, she is no longer a dancing gypsy but a pathetic, impoverished Chicana. Her body changes. She starts going bald: "the more I worry about having no income, the more I lose my hair" (116).[18] And this body has access to only minimum-wage work. "Feet that used to dance in heeled shoes, that ached with pleasure from doing what they did so well" become "just feet" that develop burning pain from running around behind a pizza counter (8). Her skin is saturated with the smell of artificial popcorn

---

are an oppressed dark people who nevertheless live celebrating death through life," and Alicia's parents "never wanted anything to do with that mongrel race, the lost tribe, and fought in America for American ideals and the American way of life" (Castillo, *The Mixquiahuala Letters* 31). This cross-reference suggests that Castillo had already been thinking about gypsy culture as a model of oppression, dispossession, and opposition to American assimilation.

18. In an odd image of cyclicality and regeneration, Carmen's hair starts to grow back. When she runs her fingers over her scalp, after telling Vicky that she's losing her long hair, she discovers, "I *am* growing in a whole new crop of hair and it does feel a little creepy but nice too. It's about an inch high all around, like newly mowed grass" (Castillo, *Peel My Love* 116). Describing her hair as a crop that she is growing further suggests a comparison to the cyclicality of life's seasons.

butter when she works at a movie theater (155). She is almost deported by the INS while sewing in a sweatshop (126–27). Poverty, rendered even more inescapable by racism, sexism, and prejudice against disability, condemns her to a series of humiliating embodiments, bodies with which no one would expect her to dance. Her body takes in her contexts, and she, in turn, is taken for a dancer, a popcorn vendor, or an "illegal" immigrant, depending upon where she is. And those who take her to be so are not mistaken, for her identity shifts with her bodily matter.

Shape-shifting changes the form of a body without abandoning the body. Carmen understands this fluctuation in terms of yoga, dance, and polio, all of which provide different models of shape-shifting as an organic experience. Indeed, the metaphors for shape-shifting multiply and shift shapes throughout the novel. Toward the end of the novel, on Carmen's fortieth birthday, we get a new metaphor:

> Like a lotus that has grown out of the mud underneath water and blossoms when it reaches light and a new life unfolds. I am a big lotus blossom, lovely and impermanent as everything else. In our own skin we can be reincarnated. You don't have to have a baby, reproduce yourself for a new and improved you. You don't have to die first. You don't have to die at all. (197)

The lotus blossom is moored in mud, but each day it opens anew. As with the duality the Aztecs saw in an ear of corn, the lotus blossom opens and closes, not dying but reincarnating itself ("reproduc[ing] yourself" without dying or giving birth to another). One of the novel's trickiest aspects is its exposure of Carmen's multiple layers, multiple metaphors, and multiple embodiments. Rather than forming her heroine into a singular, coherent "character," Castillo unfurls layer upon layer to keep Carmen's identity in motion. This unfurling continues beyond the boundaries of her own skin and beyond the mud of organic origins. Readers recognize her by her narrative voice, but each chapter places her in new and often unexpected locations.

The novel includes several scenes in which Carmen's identity is publicly misrecognized, as if one layer were more "real" than another. Some audiences cannot see (or cannot believe) two layers at once. At the beauty parlor where Carmen works for a while as a shampoo girl, the clients barely humor her illusions; for them, she must overcome her "handicap" and dance before them to be believable as a dancer (117–19). One scene at the end of the novel reverses this dynamic, posing Carmen's "disabled" body as dubious, eclipsed by her dazzling outer layers.

Though her polio has returned at this point in the novel, her flamenco career has shifted in her body as she turns from dancing to singing. Signing CDs in New York, a successful World Music star, Carmen is living "a fantasy come true." Though initially "nobody, starting with me, could believe that I was really officially a singer," the success of the CD, radio play, and the presence of fans at the signing make her so, with "Dorothy's ruby slippers skipping down the Yellow Brick Road" (187). Her disability is utterly remote from this—highly contextual—colorized stardom when one fan asks, "Why are you called Carmen la Coja?" (186). When Carmen replies that she *is* "crippled," the fan is "offended": "You shouldn't say that about yourself!" (187), as if being crippled is offensive in itself. Carmen pushes the boundaries of "polite" silence about identity and difference by lifting her dress to provide the fan a "peek" of her "bum leg" (188). This encounter reveals two important things: First, shape-shifting exists across time and is difficult to see at any single moment. Even when the "real" leg is revealed to her in a private striptease, the fan cannot accept Carmen's disability because it conflicts with her limited perception of the vocalist signing CDs. Readers laugh at this misrecognition because, by this point in the novel, we have learned to accept a multiplicity of identities as "Carmen la Coja." But, in reality, public perception has difficulty with shape-shifting and multi-layered identity. It is not that Carmen is no longer crippled, but this aspect of her identity (this "support") is no longer the most visible layer.

This encounter also reveals another crucial tension. Carmen attributes the fan's confusion to a "cultural misunderstanding" and tries to explain her disability as a cultural phenomenon: "In my culture, people get called by their most evident characteristics. I really am a *coja!*" (188). Carmen realizes that it is not clear "what culture I'm talking about" (188). "Chicana," "Mexican," and "Latina" are not mentioned at all in this scene, though "*coja*" is articulated in Spanish. In the music store, her CD is categorized multiply as "Latin and International," "World," "Pop/Reggae," and "even under Musicals" (188), since, like "gypsy," Carmen's public identity crosses cultural boundaries. The laughable list of "cultures" applied to Carmen's CD demonstrates how identity exceeds cultural scripts. Turning from the political ideal of *Xicanisma* to a disabled "gypsy" dancer shifts the parameters of what counts as identity from the relatively fixed categories of race, sex, and national culture to the unpredictable movements of disability. As a transcultural "culture," disability crosses between races, sexes, and cultures. Culture is meant to draw boundaries around a coherent set of shared, scripted, and histori-cally reiterated practices; it is by nature opposed to instability and unpre-dictability. Disability and *calorra* make visible the straining of internal heterogeneity and mobility against the static labels of culture. By the end of the novel, Carmen's attempt to uncloak an "identity" can only be taken as a parody.

Identity and Trans-Culture

In *The Rejected Body*, feminist disability scholar Susan Wendell values illness and disability "as either sources of knowledge or valuable ways of being," forcing the nondisabled (or the "normate") to think differently about their own ways of life and their expectations for others' bodies (Wendell 64). People with visible disabilities thus have a potential politi-cal impact, as "constant reminders of the inability of science and medi-cine to protect everyone from illness, disability, and death" (63). Seeing disability paired with poverty or minority racial status could present an implicit critique of the (implicitly racist) capitalist medical system. When Carmen's flamenco obfuscates her disability, she might thus seem like a political failure. Wendell writes: "Some people with disabilities, the 'dis-abled heroes,' symbolize heroic control against all odds, and their public images comfort non-disabled people by reaffirming the possibility of overcoming the body" (64). By obscuring their disabilities, these "he-roes" dull their political impact. Tobin Siebers also discusses how the political content of disability often depends upon its visibility to others:

> Those who pass improve their own life, but they fail to change the existing system of social privilege and economic distribution. They may win greater acceptance and wealth but only by pretending to be someone they are not and supporting the continued oppression of the group to which they do belong. (Siebers, "Disability and Masquerade" 19)

If Carmen were a "disabled hero," striving to transcend her disability, then one might argue that Castillo chose disability as a subject simply to highlight her heroine's individual strength rather than to critique the culture of ableism. Yet Carmen's dancing is not a negation of disability, and she does not choose one identification over the other. The dancer is *la coja*. Wendell's argument poses disability as a unique culture separated from "normal" by visible difference. Castillo, instead, locates difference within a single character whose identity appears to be sometimes *enabled* and sometimes disabled. She does not "pretend to be someone she is not," because there is not just one thing that she *is*. Carmen's physical fluctuation and mobility offer commentary on managing difference, and her story demands recognition for bodies that are not just different from others—as monolithic identities—but for bodies that, in themselves, are not recognizable as stable or categorizable entities. Carmen's body exceeds individuation and self-sameness in the same way that her identity exceeds the bounds of conventional identity politics. Siebers's critique of passing emerges in a discussion of how people sometimes need to perform invisible or variable disabilities to be recognized as disabled. When a deaf woman is spoken to as if she could hear, or when Siebers, who also suffers from post-polio syndrome, is denied early boarding on airplanes when he is not using his leg brace or crutches (1), they are not "passing"; their misrecognition is a symptom of the incommensurability of corporeal variety with our limited categories of identity. Terms like "passing" and "overcoming" assume a single, stable, and visible identity to overcome, something that shape-shifters do not possess.

Elizabeth Grosz provides a way to think about the multiple alterities within any individual:

> Bodies themselves, in their materialities, are never self-present, given things, immediate, certain self-evidences because embodiment, corporeality, insist on alterity, both that alterity they carry within themselves (the heart of the psyche lies in the body; the body's principles of functioning are psychological and cultural) and that alterity that gives them their own concreteness and specificity (the alterities constituting race, sex, sexualities, ethnic and cultural specificities). Alterity is the very possibility and process of embodiment: it conditions but is also a product of the pliability or plasticity of bodies which makes them other than themselves, other than their "nature," their functions and identities. (Grosz, *Volatile Bodies* 209)

Such a conception of identity makes it difficult to locate sameness and belonging. How do we figure the "shared alterity" of a group when each of its members is "plastic" by "nature"? Carmen, herself, embodies her "others," a flamenco legend, a "deer with a broken hoof," a "medicated cripple in a flannel nightgown," a handicapped Mexican garment-worker, a gypsy enchantress, and a singer famous for her performances on jazz radio, gospel radio, and World Music radio (Castillo, *Peel My Love* 55, 93, 127, 138, 188–92). She does not assume that any one of these selves will last, and she is self-reflexively aware of the plasticity of her body. This internal alterity makes it difficult to establish a line between Carmen and other, disabled and not.

Carmen's internal divisions lead to a "crisis" that reframes the contours of identity:

> Mexicans, superstitious as we may be, churchgoers or not, don't customarily place any faith in psychologists. But I had and I would again. Anyway, I'm not really Mexican, I told myself. I looked around like someone was talking over my shoulder. These were the kinds of strange thoughts I was coming up with every day. A major identity crisis. Not just because I'm forty but because I'm forty and falling apart. (Castillo, *Peel My Love* 160)

The physical reality of Carmen's "falling apart" is mirrored by her distance from the identity marker "Mexican" and the self-dislocation whereby she hears her own thoughts as a voice over her shoulder. Her body is fragmented, her cultural identification is fragmented, and her psyche is fragmented. In addition to not holding together internally, her exterior boundaries also seem incoherent. She is unable to detach herself from her overbearing and dependent mother, and her heterogeneous community of friends is made up of people whose personal boundaries are likewise threatened: nomads, cripples, a drug addict, an AIDS victim, and a transvestite prostitute who is brutally murdered. Picasso's 1909 Fernande portraits capture this dissolution of both internal and external boundaries. Fernande's face, breasts, and legs are broken internally into cubist angles, while her body's exterior blends into a background of similar shapes, colors, and angles. The fragmentation of cubism itself makes the central figure nearly indistinguishable from that which surrounds it. Picasso breaks these boundaries to manifest a Modernist view of representation as well as, perhaps, Fernande's sickness during their stay at Horta de Ebro (Weiss 39). But for Castillo, the pain and the fragmentation reflect something bigger than a single identity or an aesthetic sensibility.

When Carmen goes to a therapist to discuss her "identity crisis," Castillo takes us out of the realm of psychoanalysis: "No plush couch to lie down on, no nicely dressed guy in tweed with an Austrian accent and monocle taking notes like you see on TV. Just this: a paper mess everywhere. A hundred forms to fill out each time to make sure he gets reimbursed by the city for seeing me" (Castillo, *Peel My Love* 161). The investigation of Carmen's unconscious is apparently out of the question, since she claims not to dream anymore. A recalcitrant subject, she presents nothing for her therapist to analyze but a mess of paperwork and a challenge to the viability of social services. Her identity is incoherent to the frameworks of the free clinic. Or perhaps the patients who must utilize the free clinic are incoherent to the frameworks of psychoanalysis (in Castillo's view, at least). This is one of the few points in the novel where Castillo's politics emerge with some clarity. She argues that no analytical framework can adequately "heal" the impoverished and disabled flamenco dancer because she deviates too much from the universal "mind" or "body" of most medical and psychological approaches. Carmen's shape-shifting disability more visibly separates her from the norm than race or sex do. The latter have been contained by rhetorical, psychological, and sociopolitical frameworks, but Carmen's episodically returning polio and her gypsy performances mystify clinicians.[19]

In an interview with Bryce Milligan (1999, the same year that *Peel My Love* was published), Castillo describes the shift of her political focus from *Xicanisma* to global disenfranchisement in a manner that recalls Fernande's cubist shape. In the 1990s, she began to realize that:

> Her realistic allies are . . . other women who come from this background, who are not necessarily of Latina background, quote unquote, or even Mexican background, but are now joined together by their economic position in the world. So what I determined in writing *Massacre of the Dreamers* is that who concerns me is the *maquila* [factory worker] in Juarez, and the *maquila* in Southeast Asia, and in Los Angeles, and in New York, and in Chicago. She can be of Mexican or Asian or Indian background or whatever. So this is the new way, I feel, to look at this identity in the world at this point in time. (Castillo, "An Interview" 23)

Even as "Latina" is marked as a bordered identity ("quote unquote"), it is linked to other identities beyond race and nation through a shared

19. The therapist ultimately turns Carmen away to a support group for people with post-polio syndrome because "misery loves company" (Castillo, *Peel My Love* 161), meaning that he believes there is more likely to be mutual understanding within a group of polio sufferers. This incident asks us to think about what makes identity and what forms the basis for commonality. And here, too, the question of how to get there comes up and is answered by Vicky, who agrees to drive her unless she goes blind ("Vicky's always been a little paranoid that way") (162).

relationship to labor. "*Maquila*" is a manufactured identity that recurs in multiple geographic locations. In the context of global capitalism, identity loses its borders to "or whatever." This orientation focuses not on bodies, places, or races but on activities (labor, dance, mobility) and needs (like social services, insurance, or transportation).

The two constants throughout the story of Carmen's shape-shifting body are the swamping of identity categories and the near-constant presence of cabs, trains, planes, and other modes of transportation.[20] I think that these two themes are conceptually intertwined. As a member of a working-class, one-car Chicano family, and as an individual "woman with a brace," Carmen relies upon public transport. The connection between personal mobility and public mobility is established immediately in the novel, which opens with Carmen "power-walking" through her Chicago neighborhood, a device that enables Castillo to create a vision of her heroine as being physically empowered as well as to provide a glimpse of the cultural and national boundaries Carmen crosses (both within her cosmopolitan urban home and without). The power-walking scene is interrupted with a memory of international travel in the Frankfort airport (her "last gig" as her "polio inflicted condition is suddenly worsening") and followed by a scene in which Carmen is taking the train to work at a pizza counter in the Chicago airport (when she can no longer travel, herself, but is surrounded by "people who are going away someplace, career people with business accounts" "moving moving," and "me meanwhile tossing little frozen pizzas into a hot oven . . . eight days a week") (*Peel My Love* 3–4, 7). For Carmen, race, class, and polio intersect to shift her personal and public mobility when she is thrust from gypsy dancing and air travel to dependence upon busses, trains, and stagnant fast food jobs.

The power-walking scene also provides the occasion for political reflection on the materials and labor that underlie mobility:

20. Studying Carmen's personal mobility alongside the various means of mass transit that appear throughout the novel highlights the ways in which her body's movements are mediated by technology and urban geography as much as the subway is. Though the female characters of *So Far From God* are, to quote Deborah Madsen, "subjected to the torture of high-tech medical treatment" (Madsen 100), instituting a binary opposition between Chicanas and the tools of the dominant culture, *Peel My Love* reflects a more complicated relationship between identity and technology. Castillo unravels Carmen's public persona to reveal the medications, braces, and busses that support her mobility, forming identity at the shifting intersections among "nature," technology, and place.

You put on your new cross-trainers assembled in a foreign land by women and children at slave wages so you try not to think of what you paid for them, and begin to walk the streets of your city at sunset. You say your city the way some Americans say this is their country. You never feel right saying that—*my country.* For some reason looking Mexican means you can't be American. . . . But you can say this is my city because Chicago is big and small enough to be your city, to be anybody's city who wants it, anybody at all. (3)

Carmen's shoes (and perhaps her leg brace, her CD, and her bottles of medicine) were likely assembled by underpaid women in an overseas sweatshop established by a multinational corporation: the product of an economy that links and exploits across national boundaries. Global capitalism places Carmen in a transnational community of women of color: "this face of mine may very well be related to the one who assembled these bright white cross-trainers somewhere, very foreign, obscurely foreign" (6). Indeed, when she can't dance, Carmen, herself, ends up working with "illegal" immigrants in a sweatshop for three days until her friend Vicky calls in the INS. Carmen shares economic and racial marginality with these women, based on her status as not fully "American," but compared to them she is privileged, mobile, "first world," even when she, too, is working in a sweatshop. Chicago and *calorra* enhance this difference because they provide the means of Carmen's movement.

In an essay called "Mobility Disability," Celeste Langan insists that we should rethink the boundaries of social classification, especially terms like "physically disabled," which essentialize and segregate individuals based on bodily attributes. Instead, her term "(auto)mobility disability" focuses on social policies and social constructions that restrict mobility for all marginalized groups, including the poor, the "disabled," and people of color. Following the trend in Disability Studies to break down presumed oppositions between disability and the norm, Langan argues that we all begin life, from infancy, equally immobile and dependent (Langan 482). For all of us equally, public transportation is "the extension of those conditions that allow the potential for mobility to develop" in individuals (482). In the context of late capitalism, transportation commodities and technologies extend conditions of mobility beyond the natural body based on access to capital, meaning that poverty erects barriers that are perhaps more insurmountable than disability. She proposes a new ethics of "just transportation" as a way to extend mobility for all. Rather than replicating class hierarchies within the disabled—allowing greater access to those who can afford automated wheelchairs and specially equipped vans—free mass transit would separate access from both class and embodiment so that neither poverty nor physical difference would restrict an individual's mobility. As an ideal framed by movement, "just transport" is literally "trans" cultural.

Langan's framework places Carmen and the makers of her shoes in the same category. Since Carmen shares skin color and poverty with these women, that which enables Carmen to be both consumer and laborer for multinational corporations must be more than class and race. It is a question of access, which depends upon local economies and social services rather than corporeal traits. Carmen's mobility depends on health care and public transportation, political needs she shares with others across the gerrymandered boundaries of contemporary "identity." Perhaps we could consider Castillo's depiction of gypsies in Chicago as groundwork for a new type of identity politics based on movement. Movement is by nature a crossing of boundaries, whether they be immediate corporeal states or international borders. It is possibility and change rather than stasis.

Carmen, unlike the heroines of Castillo's other novels—especially unlike the small-town Nuevomexicanas in So Far From God—is estranged from her family and alienated from a Chicana/o community. In fact, Peel My Love implicitly mocks Chicana/os' attempts to "find themselves" in Aztlán: after Manolo leaves Carmen, Castillo dedicates one paragraph to narrating how Carmen took her savings from all of the nightclub gigs and spent two years in the desert with "Spanish Catholic artistas" to try her hand as a potter. This retreat fails for Carmen, whose alienation within this (likely New Mexican) location is reflected in the lack of narrative space dedicated to it as well as in the heroine's conclusion, "What did I know of the desert or clay? What did I know of the music of silences? I only knew dance, the sound of my heels on the hard wooden platform" (Castillo, Peel My Love 5).[21] Pottery is rooted in place, in dirt. It expresses a vision or a need by reforming clay, like building houses made of earth and "sweeping . . . dust off the patio" (5), as Carmen does for months until she realizes that her identity is not defined by land or ethnicity but by dance. Her belonging in Chicago is based on the city's

21. This scene is likely a self-reflexive reference to Castillo's own time in New Mexico, while she was working on So Far From God, so far from her Chicago home.

largeness, its openness to "anybody at all" (3), and her ability to move around within it on stages, busses, subways, and cross-trainers.

The cultural world Carmen does choose to associate herself with, the Chicago gypsy community, is nomadic. Though Anzaldúa includes "Gypsy" in her long list of "identity boxes" that are "no longer enough" for planetary "new tribalism" (Anzaldúa, "now let us shift" 561), Castillo uses *calorra* culture as a "box-less" culture or, rather, a transculture. Carmen's gypsy friends are racially diverse international travelers, and her public identity is in "World Music" (a category that, in its literal interpretation, is so all-inclusive that it does not function as a cultural category). Manolo has five passports, challenging what it means to have a passport: "That's how I get around," he says, "and wherever I'm going next I'll just get there. But none of that means who I am" (Castillo, *Peel My Love* 84). Just as flamenco moves the body, gypsy identity is by definition uprooted and oriented toward possible travel. Since Carmen is a shape-shifter at the corporeal level, her identifications at the communal level are world-traveling. In her oft-cited 1987 essay "Playfulness, 'World'-Travelling, and Loving Perception," María Lugones embraces travel as a feminist political framework, "a skillful, creative, rich, enriching, and, given certain circumstances, . . . a loving way of being and living" (Lugones 390). According to Lugones, when travel is enacted without arrogance, with a willingness to take on the perspectives of others, and with "openness to self-construction or reconstruction and to construction of or reconstruction of the 'worlds' we inhabit playfully," then it becomes conducive toward loving across cultures (401). Afro-Caribbean critic Carole Boyce Davies is critical of this sort of approach, which celebrates travel as free movement and elides the enforced, desperate, and restricted migration that is a common experience for women of color (Davies 23, 36).[22] Yet it is precisely this freed movement that Castillo imagines—in nearly utopian fashion—for her dancing gypsies. Their

---

22. Linda Martín Alcoff provides a similar critique of Rosi Braidotti's theory of nomadic subjectivity: "Braidotti's imagery evokes for me the figure of the person who resists commitment and obligations, one who tries to avoid responsibility by having only 'transitory' attachments." Alcoff continues: "the nomad self is bounded to no community and in actuality represents an *absence* of identity rather than a multiply entangled and engaged identity" (Alcoff 277). I wonder if this critique applies to Carmen la Coja? Rather than posing a lack of identity, I have suggested that her identity is tied to motion, which would make it multiply entangled and engaged in multiple cultural sites. Yet there is a way in which her life with the *calorras* is an escape from her family, from her family's poverty, and

travel is radically outside dominant culture patterns and enforcements. Though Manolo's people were originally exiled from Serbia, his own travels to Chicago, to San Francisco, and to Spain are chosen routes. And though he makes money from dancing in these locations, he travels and dances for pleasure, too. This nomadic travel is different from the usual spatial conceptions used to describe Chicana/o politics—Aztlán, border-lands, even diaspora—which are defined in relation to national belong-ing.[23] Carmen's dancing and fluctuating identity enables her to move outside the system more than the makers of her cross-trainers. As in Lugones's ideal, she is constantly self-reconstructing, reorienting her body to new contexts. Rather than having been rehabilitated to a norm or a socially recognized category of marginalization (after all, she isn't "really" a gypsy either), Carmen cannot be pinned down.

Is it problematic that Carmen appropriates gypsy culture to find a "home" for her disability? Or is it a problem that Castillo appropriates disability to find a body for her fluid identity aspirations? In an earlier essay, "A Countryless Woman," Castillo responded to Adrienne Rich's ideas about the politics of location: "As a mestiza, a resident of a declin-ing world power, a countryless woman, I have the same hope as Rich who, on behalf of her country aims to be *accountable*, *flexible*, and learn

---

from her obligation to care for her sick mother. Though Carmen does develop political commitments, they are never specifically Chicana/o. In any case, Alcoff ultimately contradicts her own critique, to some degree, when she celebrates Anzaldúa's theory of border-crossing for providing a "positive . . . though ex-hausting" identity based on negotiation, mediation, translation, and travel (279). Indeed, Alcoff, herself half "white" and half Latina, claims to move between locations "as events or other people's responses propel me" and concludes that "peace has come for me by no longer seeking some permanent home onshore" (284). What this contradiction reveals is the mobility of real identities when compared to the posed fixity of group categories. I would argue that this mobil-ity is particularly significant for Mexican Americans, whose identities straddle racial, national, and cultural divides. The terms "Chicana/o," "Latina/o," and "Hispanic" all refer to a "group" that is heterogeneous in terms of genetics, skin color, class, language, and national affiliation.

23. As Mary Pat Brady has observed, Chicana/o literary attempts to "dou-ble-cross" the border—"to trick the extensive machinery of containment, of discipline, and of exploitation that has historically made the border a proving ground not simply for citizenship but for humanness as well"—"nevertheless continue to do battle with the system itself," are "never completely outside of the border system," "even as they imagine the route outside" (Brady, *Extinct Lands* 53, 81).

new ways to gather together earnest peoples of the world without the defenses of nationalism" (Castillo, *Massacre of the Dreamers* 24, my emphasis). In this response, Castillo's racial/cultural mixture and her sense of U.S. nationalism's (self-)destruction lead her to identify herself as "countryless." Yet a woman who identifies with a single tribal affiliation in a "third world" country defending itself against neo-colonialist infiltrations from the "first world" would certainly be more reluctant to let go of "the defenses of nationalism." Likewise, and for good reason, many disability activists are reluctant to let go of "disability" as a defensive term. (Disability activists might also resist the romanticization of mobility in *Peel My Love*.) The proposition to keep identity fluid is consistent with the political vision I drew out from Anzaldúa's work, but the context in which Castillo develops this position reveals the "politics of location" that underlie such an idealistic proposition. The makers of Carmen's cross-trainers have been forced to be flexible and to learn new ways in order to survive, while Castillo's proposed flexibility is a resistant response to U.S. politics of domination. And what of the "cripples" who can't dance? What "A Countryless Woman" offers, most importantly, is also a politics of "accountability," which I assume would recognize and compensate for unequal exercises of power. This accountability would require a tricky balancing game, condemning racism, sexism, ableism, classism, or homophobia but letting go of the identities against which these judgments are leveled.

The tension between nationalist identification and unbounded travel has been one of the primary subjects of Castillo's work, from her 1986 epistolary travel novel, *The Mixquiahuala Letters*, to today.[24] *So Far From*

24. Castillo's poems follow the author's personal migrations from Chicago to Germany to California to New Mexico to Florida and back to Chicago. Her most recent poetry collection, *I Ask the Impossible* (2000), locates each poem in a particular city and year but questions, in its introduction, what the continual relocation of "not only people but also nations" says about "that sense of commitment, loyalty to a specific community that so marked cultures in prior centuries" (xvii). "We relocate . . . not to plant roots," she writes. We are always ready to "pick up the stakes and move again," shifting our identities to new locations. Even places themselves are not stable: "Countries like Yugoslavia, Tibet, and the Soviet Union, for example, have been disassembled or absorbed" (xvii). Against this backdrop of rootlessness, Castillo's work has frequently tried to ground itself in a particular nation. Yet each of these nationalist gestures is threatened by internal incoherence or outside intrusions—whether it be to the Chicago neighborhood where her father's "Toltec" gang reigned (*My Father*

God comes the closest to cultural nationalism of all of Castillo's works, and its heroines are in fact rooted in the *nuevomexicano* desert that Carmen la Coja does not feel at home in.[25] As in *Peel My Love, So Far From God* uses bodies to provide a concrete image of its social politics, symbolically depicting the violation of community "health" through painful illnesses suffered by the individual members of the community whose boundaries are threatened. All four of Sofi's daughters' bodies are attacked by outside forces: cancer, AIDS, war, rape, and environmental pollution from multinational corporations. Fe (faith) develops cancer from her work at a weapons-manufacturing plant, inspiring defensive politics to protect the vulnerable bodies of global capitalism's Chicana victims. After the "torture" of medical treatments that "scraped" cancerous moles from Fe's legs, arms, chest, and back, her body is physically

---

Was a Toltec xvii), to which Castillo returned later in life, or to the fictionalized nation of Sapogonia, which she describes as "a distinct place in the Americas where all mestizos reside, regardless of nationality, individual racial composition, or legal residential status—or, perhaps, because of all of these" (*Sapogonia* 1). The hometown Chicago neighborhood was displaced by the University of Illinois at Chicago's new campus (*My Father Was a Toltec* xvii), and "the Sapogón pueblo finds itself continuously divided and reunited with the certainty of the Northern winds that sweep across its continents to leave evershifting results" (*Sapogonia* 2). The "border outline" that defines Sapogonia is itself a product of the "slavery, genocide, immigration, and civil uprisings" that have "besieged" its people (1). It is a nation shaped by national unrest and transnational movement.

25. *So Far From God* contains numerous proto-nationalist gestures. The mother of four daughters, Sofia idealistically declares herself to be "La Mayor" of the town of Tome, creating "Los Ganados y Lana Cooperative," by which the community becomes self-sufficient based on the raising of sheep and the production of wool products. The purpose of this communal organization is insular: to resist the gradual erosion of the longtime Tome residents' landholdings. Sofia's comadre mourns that "my familia once had three hundred acres to farm and now all I got left of my father's hard work—and his father's and his father's—is casi nada." (*So Far From God* 139). This claim establishes her relationship to the land as a product of multi-generational family labor, in opposition to "los gringos coming here," buying land, and raising foreign commodities like peacocks: "Now, I ask you, what can you do with peacocks? Do these New Yorkers eat them, like in fancy restaurants or something?" (139). The opposition between productive local labor and outside infiltration is clear in such passages. The communities Sofi represents are the "Native and hispano families," those who suffer most from corporate exploitation and uranium mining (242), and her own (perhaps only semi-facetious) multinational organization, the Mothers of

reduced, converted from flesh to scars, leaving her unable even to walk (186–87). What enables Carmen, then, whose body is similarly reduced and withered by polio, not only to walk but to dance and to travel? I believe that Castillo's newest work reflects a shift in her political grounding. Since her early works tried to define a nation, community, or neighborhood to be home for Chicana/os, the bodies in these works are similarly oriented toward stability. In contrast, *Peel My Love* abandons this search for a *Xicanista* nation, and its bodies do not require solid grounding or defended boundaries. As the daughter of transplanted renters who no longer share the same home, Carmen feels no nostalgia about roots. Without an emphasis on stable identity, culture, or homeland, political movements would have to be more mobile.

Post-Identity Politics

Unlike the rest of Castillo's work, *Peel My Love* seems not to be about Chicana feminist politics. Castillo might have chosen to weave together concerns from Chicana/o Studies with those of Disability Studies, which would make a productive political and theoretical marriage, but there is no overt engagement with the political or theoretical content of either of those movements. Indeed, there is no clear political message. The "culture" of the novel, on the surface at least, is transcultural rather than identity-based, contemporary rather than historically rooted, and seemingly inauthentic: Carmen talks about the Chicago Bulls, performs at the yuppie Spanish-themed restaurant Olé Olé, dis-identifies with Mexico, and "power-walks" in mass-produced cross-trainers. Just as "the Toltecs," in *My Father Was a Toltec*, refers to a twentieth-century Chicago gang, culture is detached from its historical and geographic origins in Carmen la Coja's Chicago. Castillo compares her father's Chicago Mexicanness to Mayor Daley's Chicago Irishness (*My Father Was a Toltec* xvii), showing how original cultures are transformed in transcultural contexts. Chicago Toltecs are culturally hybrid and geographically displaced. And as a gang, "Toltec" becomes a self-declared filiation among neighbors (an "imagined community") rather than racial inheritance or nationality. If gangs look homogeneous, it is because their individual members choose to eclipse individuality with a performance of filiation.

This shift in how we understand culture and individuality shifts how we understand identity politics. Wendy Brown, whose work is often

---

Martyrs and Saints. Pain and suffering mark the outlines of these cultural communities.

cited as emblematic of the postmodernist critique of identity politics, writes that one of the ways in which "identity politics may . . . be read [is] as a reaction to postmodernity's cross-cultural meldings and appropriations, as well as its boundless commodification of cultural practices and icons" (Brown 35). Identity politics gained new momentum in reaction against the best and the worst of postmodernism, investing in race, ethnicity, and sexuality just as those identifications were being commodified, eroded, or decentered.[26] We can see this understanding at work in *So Far From God*, where Chicana and feminist identity politics intersect with a rejection of "postmodern" industry and "postmodern" disease. We can also see how this investment in identity was, in turn, romanticized and commodified by "postmodern" readers and publishers. Ellen McCracken notes how *So Far From God* was promoted by Penguin as an "ethnic commodity," "an optic similar to Orientalism that attempts to manage and even produce the U.S. Latina Other" (McCracken 320). McCracken argues that *So Far From God* strains against this packaging as an appetizing comestible, rupturing its "saleable multiculturalist imagery" with "representations of social antagonisms" (327). Yet, the political confrontations and antagonisms in *So Far From God* fall into predictable places—Chicana versus Anglo; community versus multinational industry; New Mexico's beautiful natural environment versus chemically induced disease; and female-centered family versus corrupt father, priests, and male lovers—reinforcing the otherness of Chicanas and the clear line separating them from postmodernity. These false binaries perpetuate misogynist and racist mythologies about Mexican women's attachment to old-fashioned and exotic traditions (like *So Far From God*'s lessons in traditional New Mexican cooking) as well as untamed nature to be conquered. *Peel My Love* demythifies Chicana identity by situating it in a cosmopolitan urban context, by eroding the binaries installed in *So Far From God*, and by devoting meticulous attention to "Amá's" dirty and unhealthy kitchen, microwaved food, and meals in front of the TV (Castillo, *Peel My Love* 12, 103, 105–7).[27] In Brown's interpretation, postmodernism can unmoor dangerous romantic notions about identities:

26. The "realist" movement associated with Satya Mohanty, Paula Moya, and Linda Martín Alcoff, which I discuss in my introduction, exemplifies this trend.

27. Frederick Luis Aldama similarly argues that Castillo's use of "polymorphously ethnosexual Chicago metropolitan space" in *Peel My Love* allows her to disengage her heroine from the stereotype of "brown woman as exotic" more radically than *So Far From God*'s "own play with exotic rhetoric usually used to contain the Latina as ethnic-object specimen" (Aldama 104).

The postmodern exposure of the imposed and created rather than discovered character of all knowledges—of the power-suffused, struggle-produced quality of all truths, including reigning political and scientific ones—simultaneously exposes the groundlessness of discovered norms or visions. It also reveals the exclusionary and regulatory function of these norms. (Brown 47–48)

Understanding the "exotic" Chicana as an icon isolated from a backdrop of heterogeneous ways of being Chicana—and created amidst political struggles in which "orientalizing" or "othering" Chicanas supports the reigning (white, male, industrial) regimes of power—undermines its claim to nature and reveals, instead, its "exclusionary and regulatory function."

The primary problem with identity politics is their focus on singular ways of being, which invariably installs norms and ideals. Identity politics are based on "settled practices and identifications" (49) that isolate identity from larger contexts and networks of power. As Brown suggests, "Drawing upon the historically eclipsed meaning of disrupted and fragmented narratives of ethnicity, race, gender, sexuality, region, continent, or nation, identity politics permits a sense of situation—and often a sense of filiation or community—without requiring profound comprehension of the world in which one is situated. Identity politics permits positioning without temporal or spatial mapping" (35).

Nostalgia for belonging creates an "excessively local" understanding of the individual, and identity politics assume "clean, sharply bounded, disembodied, [and] permanent" understandings of identity. What Brown advocates, instead, is a political position that is "heterogeneous, roving, relatively noninstitutionalized, and democratic to the point of exhaustion" (49–50). This would be a movement politics rather than an identity politics—a very apt framework for understanding Castillo's Carmen la Coja, whose identity unfurls itself in multiple directions. Examining her movements literally takes us across maps, crossing the race- and class-based demarcations around Chicago neighborhoods, confronting barriers to mobility faced by people with disabilities, and witnessing the moving encounters between cultures, classes, and causes in international airports. Critics of Brown tend to focus on her claim that those engaged in identity politics are invested in their own "subjection" and their own "injuries," and Tobin Siebers worries that her approach focuses too much on "the intellectual and emotional resources of the individual and not on political action by people working in groups" (Siebers, "Disability Studies and the Future of Identity Politics" 16). This is a fair criticism, and

Brown's analysis does rely heavily on the terms of individual psychology. But this criticism overlooks the outward orientation of Brown's "roving" alternative to identity politics as well as her proposal that we orient politics from a "vision about the common ('what I want for us') rather than from identity ('who I am')" (Brown 51). Indeed, in my interpretation, Brown's vision provides exactly what Siebers is asking for: "What would it mean to define political identity not on self-interest but on common interests?" (Siebers, "Disability Studies and the Future of Identity Politics" 16). Brown's vision for politics beyond identity is defined not by the individual or the individual's search for others like her but by spaces where different subjects meet in their roving. Carmen la Coja's movement through the world is what leads her to encounter shared concerns with flamenco dancers and sweatshop laborers. Movement encounters difference and crosses barriers, while identity politics seek sameness and protect the boundaries around identities.

Does moving ground jettison the idea of identity? "Gypsy" and "disabled" are identities without borders. Both refer to a heterogeneous range of embodiments that are ex-centric to normative ways of being and belonging. Their movements are, by definition, in friction with fixed identities. Perhaps this can be "the beginning of an entirely new way of thinking about identity categories" (Davis 5). Like Celeste Langan, Lennard Davis argues that we are all, to some degree, disabled: "all groups, based on physical traits or markings, are selected for disablement by a larger system of regulation and signification" (29). Rather than focusing on particular corporeal markings, like femaleness, blackness, or deafness, as that which determines "ablement," focusing on impairment in general encompasses the various ways in which mobility is limited by social structures. If we understand all corporeal agency as in need of outside assistance—medications, prostheses, vehicles, or even ladders and tools—we can debunk the mythic autonomous subject and shift the political focus to access, not bodies or identities. Rather than seeking inclusion for marginalized identities or assuming neutral, universal *rights*, politics would be oriented toward embodied *needs*. Unlike rights or identities, needs and wants refer to the world around them and are embedded in particular bodies' cultural contexts. This is not to romanticize exile or disability as "better" or more progressive identities, but they offer powerful lessons about how identity and politics might be detached from corporeal boundaries. Siebers warns us not to frame disability as "a friend to humanity," "a secret resource for political change," or an "advantage." The material details of Carmen's narrative remind us that neither disability nor exile is "a well of delight for the individual" (Siebers, "Disability in Theory" 145–46), but telling stories like Carmen's, or like Siebers's, shifts our focus from bodies' lacks and identities' boundaries to the material contexts that inhibit or enable movement. Indeed, Siebers suggests that Disability Studies' focus on bodies' movements through the environment "might effect a sea change by asking that the inclusion-exclusion binary be reconceived in terms of accessibility and inaccessibility" (Siebers, "Disability Studies and the Future of Identity Politics" 26). This sea change suggests that social significance is determined not by the distinctions between bodies but by the spaces that enable or limit movement for any body.

Since individuals contain multiple, different layers of embodiment, and various, sometimes conflicting political desires, stable identity is an insufficient ground for politics. Shape-shifting, however, accommodates movement and acknowledges the many different forms that any individual assumes. Though one could never be certain what guise Tezcatlipoca might appear in, his presence was indeed recognized in various shapes throughout Toltec and Aztec history, and he was credited with a variety of good and evil works. Shape-shifting is simultaneously fluid and materially embodied. And it, better than identity, presents an accurate way to understand how we experience ourselves as belonging to multiple, different identity groups, feeling different on different days, acting differently in different contexts, and changing through time, yet still the same person. No single political agenda emerges clearly from *Peel My Love Like an Onion*, but a variety of intersecting need-based critiques emerge from particular moments in Carmen's trajectory: a demand for better low-cost mental health care emerges from her depression, a demand to end the exploitation of economically disadvantaged workers emerges from her time in the garment industry, and a demand for accessible public transportation emerges from her painful commutes on crutches. None of these needs assumes a particular identity, but they are common to particular situations, like Brown's proposed "what I want for us."

It is, of course, difficult to imagine how fluid political wants translate into political platforms or legislated satisfaction. How do we get what we want when our wants constantly change form? Perhaps Castillo falls into the same trap as many critics of identity politics, romanticizing alternate identifications—like hybridity, performativity, or nomadism—as a way out of existing political traps without describing how these alternate forms might function politically. Indeed, we never really see how shape-shifting could be viable beyond the remarkable successes of one "crippled" flamenco dancer. Carmen's success seems purely individual, based on the particular convergence of eccentricities that form her "being in the world." One could argue that Castillo employs disability and *calorra* like a freak show, twisting bodies into positions that are radically other and posing marginality itself as a potentially lucrative position, but it would be offensive to people with disabilities or exiled peoples to assume that they could or should capitalize on their "injuries" (and perform them on stage) like Carmen la Coja does.

Carmen's disability is her "ticket" for many social programs. As a child, she was sent, with a scholarship, to "the School for the Handicapped," where the unitary label "handicapped" betrayed the diversity of blind, deaf, and mentally disabled children who were grouped together because of their "treasonous bodies" (Castillo, *Peel My Love* 14, 17). (As in the free clinic, many of these identities were illegible to the school administration, including Alberto from Puerto Rico, whom the teachers thought "deaf and dumb" because he didn't speak English [15].) After first trying flamenco in Physical Rehabilitation class, Carmen began to take dance instruction seriously, staying after school for private lessons, even though "this meant that I had to miss the free school bus and take public transportation but it was worth it" (18). Although her dance lessons are a product of social services and "rehabilitation," Carmen is not "rehabilitated." She is still disabled, and, as an aspiring dancer, pathetic, dehumanized even: "this poor creature . . . ¡Pobrecita!" (17). Her mother "thought it was a great waste of time, a crippled girl wanting to be a dancer," but believed that at least it kept her "off the streets, from becoming a vagrant, a wayward adolescent, a girl gang leader perhaps" (17). We know, however, that her mother was wrong, and Carmen's dancing career does make her somewhat "vagrant" and "wayward."

Once a "rich old guy" paid for the "crippled" kids to take a field trip to Riverview Amusement Park, where Carmen and her friends became fascinated by the freak shows: Fat Lady, Half-Man, Lobster Boy "with claws for hands" (176). These identities signify "freakishness" because the bodies they refer to are excessive or insufficient relative to the norm. One day Carmen and a few of her classmates, "like Jerry Lewis's muscular dystrophy kids," begged for bus money to return to the amusement park in order to free the Lobster Boy and to enroll him in their "special" school (176). The line between "freak" and student originates in the medicalization of bodies and the implementation of public services to regulate them. Freaks are a throwback to the era in which bodies were seen as mystical. They were put on display to bear witness to a realm beyond nature: perverse, irretrievably and damnably other. Jerry Lewis's

kids, in contrast, are medically understood, naturally ill, potentially curable, and politically situated, soliciting money to include more children
into the fold of cared-for subjects. Carmen and her friends see the socially
constituted nature of the boundary between circus freaks and school-
children, and their efforts to bring a supposed Lobster Boy to their school
blur this differentiation between "others" and social subjects.

Rather than dutifully playing the role of a "Jerry Lewis kid," Carmen
deviates from the path down which social services directed her. She remains alone, independent, making her money at night (when she can)
with a career that doesn't count as "real work" in the eyes of her family,
drinking to excess, and "us[ing] up all [her] good motor units that have
been compensating for the defunct ones," leaving no muscle reserve to
rehabilitate (109–10). Rather than nursing her disability, she dances with
it and consumes her own body. Posing as a flamenco dancer rather than
a Jerry Lewis kid leaves Carmen, in the eyes of the medical professionals,
uncurable—assuming that the cure lies in rehab, "booster shots," and
fund-drives for "the handicapped" rather than flamenco (110). Her public identity is based on continual ex-centricity and misrecognition as her
shape-shifting body defies (or at least only temporarily inhabits) familiar
frameworks, even the boundaries established for the term "disabled."
This ex-centricity earns her fame, but does it have a political impact?
Can it change the world?

In some ways, Carmen's story resonates on the Horatio Alger theme:
a poor, "handicapped" girl is "saved" by a teacher who makes her believe that she can dance, and when post-polio syndrome prohibits dancing, she is "saved" yet again by a musician with a recording contract
who helps her to discover her singing talent. But this "rags-to-riches"
scenario is consistently pulled back to earth with very material reminders
of pain, poverty, and illness. When she is not on stage, "the real world"
does not regard her disability as lucrative. The political institutions represented in the novel, like the free clinic or the INS, (mis)recognize Carmen as a "needy," disabled, and perhaps undocumented, woman of
color. Castillo shows us how deviance is reviled unless it is converted into
spectacle. When given the choice between rehabilitation and spectacle,
Carmen chose spectacle. Yet viewers' pleasure in (and payment for) spectacle is derived from the stigma of the freak, so Carmen's choice potentially reinscribes this stigma. The novel does not show us what sort of
impact a woman with a brace might have if she had chosen more realistic
(or simply less abject) political avenues. Carmen's shape-shifting eccen-
tricity is a relic of ancient sensibilities that have been purged from modern individualism. Modern political institutions do not know how to

handle shape-shifters, and few contemporary societies regard boundary-crossing as sacred (or even legal). Of course, novels need not provide realistic political visions. *Peel My Love* is an imaginative fiction that imagines how stigmatized identities might be viewed otherwise. It also, at least implicitly, critiques our political system for its fixing of individuals into bounded social positions. Yet it doesn't imagine how a disabled Chicana might get by in Chicago without being a freak.

Postmodernist feminist Rosi Braidotti studies the progression from the "fantastic dimension" of monstrosity to the "more rationalist construction of the body-machine" in modern medical discourse as emblematic of the ways in which "Western" thought has approached difference in order to exclude it (Braidotti 83–84). The otherness of difference is nullified when it is understood and classified as an illness to be cured. Freaks, in contrast, exceed this rational logic and defy "Western" containments of difference. They remain challengingly other. Braidotti cites them as figures for the abject, the liminal, the mixed, or the ambivalent (77–78) because they defy the distinctions upon which the stigmatization of difference rests. This liminality and ambivalence are opposed by modern medicine, which views monstrosity as an illness to be eliminated according to a normalizing "health care" regimen. "Freaks" like shape-shifters are excluded from healthy modern societies because they exceed stable and predictable subject positions. As Elizabeth Grosz suggests, "they imperil the very definitions we rely on to classify humans, identities, and sexes" (Grosz, "Intolerable Ambiguity" 57). The freak who will not be "cured" or "regulated" is relegated to the realms of fantasy, history, or their capitalist byproduct, entertainment. In contemporary Chicago, the stage is the most likely place for an "uncured" freak like Carmen to become legendary rather than pathetic. (Studies that compare daytime talk shows, rock stars, and science fiction to freak shows suggest that we have not "evolved" much beyond the roadside freak shows so popular in the Victorian era.[28]) Many disability scholars have reconsidered the power behind terms like "freak" and "cripple," not just for the shock value of reclaiming the epithet (as with "queer" and "nigga"), but for the particular content and history of these terms.[29] Rosemarie Garland

28. See Rosemarie Garland Thomson's edited collection, *Freakery*.

29. Elizabeth Grosz, for instance, prefers "freak" to its euphemistic substitutes because "it makes clear that there are very real and concrete political effects for those thus labeled, and a clear political reaction is implied by those who use it as a mode of self-definition" (Grosz, "Intolerable Ambiguity" 56).

Thomson, one of the most important critics in disability literary studies, suggests that the term "freak" might still be redolent of its premodern legacy of "revelation" and "awe" (Thomson, *Freakery* 3). "Freaks" have been sought after, feared, and systematically eliminated—all different responses to radical otherness—because they point out the insufficiency of our normative identity categories. They demand that we think about bodies beyond what we normally think of as identity, and they require us to accept unpredictable deviation as a viable human condition.

Ancient Mesoamerica, as I interpret it, presents social norms that do not privilege bounded and stable identities and that recognize the blending and transforming of bodies as a sacred ideal. If shape-shifting is valued, then disability and freakery can no longer function as the absolute "other" to health. Alluding to ancient Mesoamerica helps Castillo to maintain shape-shifting as a viable and instructive way of being. We can thus read *Peel My Love* as an appeal to a premodern understanding of identity, free from the rigid racial and sexual classifications instituted by the biological and psychological sciences and supported by identity politics. But to make her challenge to these classifications applicable to the contemporary world, Castillo foregrounds contemporary terms rather than fantastical figures like Coatlicue, Coyolxauhqui, or Tezcatlipoca. It is difficult to translate *"La herencia de Coatlicue"* or Coyolxauhqui's dismemberment into the contemporary political realm, but making Carmen a disabled gypsy diva rather than a more literal rendering of Tezcatlipoca translates shape-shifting into (and beyond) the language of modern identities.

Since these corporeal boundary states are relegated to the status of "freak" in the contemporary United States, depicting Carmen as a dancing "cripple" provides a glimpse of how ex-centricity is devalued by identity regulation today. Modern society accepts that disabled bodies often change unpredictably and sometimes require people to incorporate prostheses or to allow caregivers to trespass their personal boundaries, but it also regards these dependencies as anomalous, pathetic, and tragic. With Carmen la Coja (celebrated, empowered, sexy, and glamorous), Castillo inverts modern perceptions of bodies that are impaired. Making Carmen freakish, rather than participating in identity politics, allows Castillo to demonstrate how bodies move in friction with existing sociopolitical categories. Unless the world changes, to the extent that identity is perceived differently, ex-centricity is not allowed in the socio-political structure. Castillo's disengagement with familiar political forms (like "Chicana") thus fuels a much larger critique of modern assumptions about bodies and identities.

CONCLUSION
RETHINKING BODY POLITICS: MAYA GONZÁLEZ AND DIANE GAMBOA

A mi, las alas me sobran. Que las corten y a volar!! [I have more than enough wings. Let them be cut off and take flight!!][1]

Frida Kahlo, *Diary*

*T*he epigraph from Frida Kahlo separates mobility from corporeality when she suggests that she does not need wings to fly. Kahlo's injuries and surgeries led her to see past her body as the horizon of her being. In fact, she disavows disability in this statement, which comes at the end of a 1953 entry in her diary titled "Puntos de apoyo" (points of support), written just before the amputation of her leg:

Puntos do Apoyo

En mi figura completa solo hay *uno*, y quiero dos.
Para tener yo los dos me tienen que cortar *uno*.
Es el *uno* que no tengo el que tengo que tener
Para poder caminar
El otro será ya muerto!
A mi, las alas me sobran.
Que las corten y a volar !!

(Kahlo, The Diary of Frida Kahlo *139, original emphasis)*

1. This is my translation of the diary entry. Sara Lowe translates these sentences quite differently: "I have many, / wings. / Cut them off / and to hell with it!!" (Kahlo 276). I agree with the suggestion of "to hell with it" in "*a volar,*" but the reference to flight is crucial.

The syntax of this poem reflects the apparent incoherence of its author's body. The first line, "in my complete figure there is only one, and I want two," suggests that her body is both complete and incomplete with just one leg. The second line reinforces this sense of corporeal contradiction by saying that "in order for me to have two they have to cut off one"—a statement that defies either mathematics or human anatomy. The third line translates, roughly, to "it is the one that I don't have that I have to have," with the juxtaposition of "no tengo" (I don't have) with "tengo" (I have) embodying the friction between the body she has and the body she imagines. (The "tener" at the end of this line is also separated by a line break and an apparent sentence break, or at least a capital "P" at the beginning of the next line, "Para poder caminar" [in order to walk], separating the having from the walking.) What it means to have and not have at once takes shape in the line, "el otro será ya muerto" (the other will already be dead) and the knowledge that, even before the amputation, her gangrenous leg had ceased to function "normally." To have legs is not necessarily to walk, so perhaps mobility does not require legs. The logic of the entire piece defies the "normal" rules of corporeal functioning, reducing the body to medicalized "supports" and unnamed "ones," objects for doctors to cut off that seem to bear little relevance to the artist's mobility and identity.

Hayden Herrera contends that the amputation of Kahlo's leg offended her "aesthetic sensibility" and her "sense of integrity" (Herrera, *Frida* 417). Yet looking at the frequency with which Kahlo's self-portraits incorporate other animals into her body, link her body with trees or mechanical objects, and depict her body in painful contortions—all the while retaining the same steady and direct gaze—leads me to believe that Kahlo's sense of integrity and corporeal aesthetics exceeded the bounds of the ideal, independent, symmetrical body for decades before the amputation. I begin my conclusion with Frida Kahlo because her words, her life, and the visual images she created prefigure the body politics of contemporary Disability Studies: expanding our understanding of what counts as viable embodiment and what material supports are needed for mobility. This expansion carries over to identity, too, as Kahlo's self-perception as a complete woman who is able to fly differs from the doctors' understanding of her as a "cripple." (Kahlo's self-portraits as a man, as an animal, and as an Indian also exceed her identity as a half-Hungarian Mexican woman.)

Again, contemporary Chicana feminism echoes Kahlo. Gloria Anzaldúa explains in her last published essay: "Neither the physical self nor the physical body is the totality of a person. . . . [W]e're going to leave the rigidity of this concrete reality and expand it. I'm very hopeful" (Anzaldúa, "now let us shift" 285). As with Kahlo's "a volar!!" this hope assumes agency beyond the limitations of an individual body—an assumption that challenges the subjects and objectives assumed in Biomedical Studies as well as the public policies, stigmas, and exclusions supported by these studies. While the link between mobility and corporeality is very literal in the case of Kahlo's amputated leg, Anzaldúa's diabetes presents a more complex linkage. Diabetes can indeed lead to amputation, but it did not in the case of Anzaldúa. Instead, it altered her attentiveness, her energy level, her diet, and, perhaps most significantly, her way of relating to her own body. Perceiving one's body as constitutionally subject to chemical fluctuations, potentially deadly imbalances, and constant medical care forces one's sense of self to remain permeable. Designating "person" as something more than "the physical body," as Anzaldúa proposes in my quote above, suggests that identity might also include prostheses, caregivers, beliefs, and hopes. Pain and illness would not annihilate a person defined in this way but, rather, emphasize how s/he moves beyond the boundaries of his/her own tissue. This changed perception should expand the parameters of our ethical obligations from the biomedically constrained body to communities, contexts, and their (sometimes conflicting) cultural and spiritual projections. The medical gaze, as well as the political gaze, must take in more than the bounded body and consider other means of flight.

The previous chapter developed the idea of shape-shifting politics, but is shape-shifting a purely imagined ideal? Are Kahlo's wings invisible to everyone other than herself? Perhaps not. Biologist Lynda Birke, whose approach to science is embedded in feminist social theory, shifts the biomedical gaze from the isolated organism to external interactions, decentering "the body" in the process. Bodies exchange cells with their environments without losing coherence, and the passage of blood, food, and air reveals bodies to be intertwined with the space around them, absorbing some elements and expelling others. This awareness is not new for medicine, but (as in politics) such fluidity is usually suppressed in favor of delineating a fixed subject. In an argument that recalls Simone de Beauvoir, Birke instead views health as a dynamic process of "becoming" and open-ended future "possibilities," embracing fluctuation and exchange between corporeal tissues and the outside world as that which keeps bodies from being frozen in static (and, truly, unhealthy) "immanence" (Birke, *Feminism and the Biological Body* 151). Kahlo's self-portraits imaginatively show us what a rejection of corporeal "immanence" might look like by adding wings, animals, flames, and external blood vessels to link her body to different environments; at the same time, even when it bears a deer's body or a dove in place of her head, this body is consistent enough to be recognized as the same one in all of Kahlo's self-portraits. The body does not dissipate simply because it is changeable. Similarly, *Peel My Love Like an Onion* demonstrates that it is not just bodies but identities that lie at the moving intersection of permeable tissues, changing contexts, and other people. Yet, whether she is a gypsy dancer, a crippled patient, or an undocumented immigrant, Carmen is still recognizable as the same "I" throughout the novel. Perhaps health and identity can thrive without fixed borders.

What do the permeable and migratory politics of illness have to do with "Chicana feminism," as such? Is the new corporeal vulnerability in the latest works of Anzaldúa, Cherríe Moraga, and Ana Castillo a logical extension of the trajectory of Chicana feminism, or is it a rupture in this trajectory produced by coincidental shifts in the three authors' perceptions? I am not interested in claiming a common origin for the disabled bodies in their recent works, nor do I want to assume a biographical lineage for literary and political movement. My interest here is not cause but effect: How do the lessons learned from pain, illness, and disability extend Chicana feminist body politics? I propose that, though the permeable subject I've been analyzing throughout *Encarnación* incorporates needs and movements beyond the boundaries of Chicana identity, it speaks to the stated aims of Chicana feminism better than the corporeal nationalism of identity politics does.[2] Even as it overflows the denotation of "Chicana feminism," its connotation is deeply Chicana and feminist.

In her analysis of Chicana feminist art, Laura E. Pérez implicitly suggests that identity politics are the key to ending Chicanas' marginalization: "If gender and ethnic identity politics are passé, as some theorists

2. In "The Possibility of Women's Studies," Robyn Wiegman likewise argues that feminism benefits from the critique of identity politics. Wiegman embraces Wendy Brown's conclusion that "there might be 'no there there'" in Women's Studies, suggesting that a "non-identitical feminism," a feminist approach that did not assume a common identity, "women," at its foundation, "will not be efficient" and "will not have the clarity of productive order" (Wiegman 57). Yet, most productively, "it will not seek to guarantee that feminist struggle culminates in a future that we already know from the vantage point of our present" (57). Assuming a shared identitarian foundation overlooks the complexities of subject formation that feminism must address in order to think its way out of the status quo.

would have it, are we to assume that their [Chicana artists'] work has met with dominant cultural, mainstream, or feminist critical, if not economic, success?" (L. Pérez, "Writing on the Social Body" 52). If Anzaldúa, Moraga, and Castillo seem to have moved past identity politics, it is not because Chicanas have achieved "mainstream success." In response to critiques like Pérez's, I would suggest that the political urgency has not changed as much as what we mean by "identity." There is still most definitely a need for Chicana feminist movement, but this movement has changed shape. Rather than solidifying a Chicana identity with which to combat "mainstream" identity or mobilizing to achieve "success" in the terms of the dominant culture—two political approaches that conflict with each other in terms of method as well as aim—the writers and artists I analyze here depict bodies whose blurred boundaries swamp the competitive mechanizations of identity politics as well as the universalizing mechanizations of modern liberalism. More challenging than identity politics, these writers' and artists' conceptions of the world focus on the intersections between particular bodies, cultural contexts, and political needs.

This open-bordered approach to identity and politics is consistent with impulses of early Chicana feminism. As Chela Sandoval reminds us in a recent "Roundtable on the State of Chicano Studies," "Chicano/a (like the label feminist, Marxist, capitalist, socialist, and so on) is a *political* term" (Davalos et al. 149, original emphasis). The unifying ground of the term "Chicano/a" is political movement, not just identity. (The number of Mexican Americans who reject the label "Chicano" or "Chicana" is evidence of this fact.) "Chicano/a" is a political affiliation of people who are heterogeneous in terms of color, class, gender, sexuality, region, and generational distance from Mexico. It follows that the boundaries around Chicana feminism should be permeable. The Chicana feminism of Anzaldúa, Moraga, and Castillo, in particular, had its origins in building bridges between marginalized identities. It is significant that their first major publications were transcultural edited collections, not single-authored or exclusively Chicana statements. Their careers began by embracing difference. Anzaldúa and Moraga coedited the first edition of *This Bridge Called My Back* (1981) two years before Moraga's *Loving in the War Years* and six years before Anzaldúa's *Borderlands*, and Castillo joined Moraga for the Spanish-language edition, *Esta puente mi espalda* (1988) between Castillo's first and second novels and five years before her single-authored collection, *Massacre of the Dreamers*. Moraga suggested in her foreword to the second edition of *Bridge* that, if it were conceived

197

in 1983 rather than 1979, "it would speak much more directly now to the relations between women and men of color, both gay and heterosexual," and "it would be much more international in perspective." This more expansive perspective, though, is merely an extension of the political "heart" of the earlier vision: "Although the heart of *Bridge* remains the same, the impetus to forge links with women of color from every region grows more and more urgent" (Anzaldúa and Moraga, *This Bridge Called My Back*). Anzaldúa came closer to that ideal in her 1990 edition, *Making Face, Making Soul/Haciendo Caras: Creative and Critical Perspectives by Feminists of Color*, and again in her 2002 edition with AnaLouise Keating, *This Bridge We Call Home: Radical Visions for Transformation*, a collection that includes male and white authors. This history reflects an increasing detachment from identity politics, but the identity in these writers' politics has always had open borders.

The *mestiza* consciousness of Anzaldúa's 1987 *Borderlands* stretches between cultural/racial/sexual perspectives, "breaking down the unitary aspect of each new paradigm," kneading, joining, *moliendo, mixteando, amasando, haciendo tortillas de masa* (grinding, mixing, forming dough, making corn tortillas) (Anzaldúa, *Borderlands* 79–81).[3] Similarly, the metaphor of welding in Moraga's 1981 poem "The Welder," "understand[s] the capacity of heat / to change the shape of things" (Moraga, "The Welder" 220). This is a feminism that from the start has shifted shapes, stretched to assume new forms, and fused different elements. The new *mestiza* is willing "to make herself *vulnerable* to foreign ways of thinking. She *surrenders all notions of safety*, of the familiar. Deconstruct, construct. She becomes a *nahual*, able to transform herself into a tree, a coyote, into another person" (Anzaldúa, *Borderlands* 82–83, emphasis added). She is "suited to work / within the realm of sparks / *out of control*" (Moraga, *This Bridge Called My Back* 220, emphasis added). Though Anzaldúa's metaphors are more organic than Moraga's image of industrial labor, they both envision a feminism whose processes of synthesis, bridging, and coalition-building change the shape of familiar identity forms. This shifting is painful and risky, "out of control," letting go of the ego-reinforcing support of identity politics.

3. The centrality of *mestizaje* in early Chicana feminist writings—from Anzaldúa, Moraga, and Castillo to the critics who write about them like Alarcón and Yarbro-Bejarano—is itself evidence of the permeability built within Chicana feminism. See my discussion of the political significance of mixed identities in *Mulattas and Mestizas*.

It hurts to take embodiment beyond the "safe" borders of entrenched identities. Returning to *The Body in Pain*, Elaine Scarry sees pain as a force of negation and annihilation, and certainly her claim that pain is "world-destroying" is more obvious than any affirmation of pain's creative powers (Scarry 29). Scarry opposes pain to imagination, suggesting that pain contracts and negates, while imagination is expansive and explores alternative realities (168–69). Anzaldúa's, Moraga's, and Castillo's responses to physical pain have defied this binary opposition, imaginatively testing different modes of embodiment and the uses of stigmatized feelings. Anzaldúa's Coatlicue states, Moraga's bloody puppets (from *Heart of the Earth*), and Castillo's shape-shifting dancer exemplify this imaginative use of pain. Not celebrated or rejected, the pain and destruction in these writings are, literally, expansive, leading to the creation of new forms of being, following Catholic and Aztec traditions of re-genesis and cyclicality. These writers' lives and work have consistently overflowed the limits of normative identities, and these painful transgressions strengthen the oppositional power of their politics by shaking up the system.

Of course, it is much easier to describe these painful transmutations in writing than it is to imagine them with actual bodies. To trace how these theoretical ideals operate at a corporeal level, I conclude with a brief return to the visual arts. This is not to suggest that painting, sculpture, or photography are closer to "the real" than narrative or verse, but these media are more literally about the shape of things, interactions between forms and colors, and actual boundaries (frames, perimeters, intersections). I focus here on painting since, unlike sculpture, background is a part of its work: a particular context (even if it is blank) painted around and behind its subject. And unlike photography, painted portraits always make us aware that their bodies are creations of the artist, deliberate meditations on how to form a body, never a captured "reality." As with the self-portraits of Frida Kahlo that I analyze in Chapter 1, the paintings of Maya González and Diane Gamboa center on (recognizably or allusively) female bodies and denaturalize them with provocative ornamentation and surreal environments.[4] González's and Gamboa's use of

---

4. Many of González's and Gamboa's figures that I analyze are transgendered or trans-human, but all invoke "the female"—usually with female-looking breasts—and "the feminine"—with clothing (bustiers, jewelry, or handbags) and body postures (reclining sideways on a sofa, posed like the Madonna and child, or spreading legs as for a centerfold).

portraiture dissects the long-standing tradition of trying to represent the human form, questioning the ways in which portrait artists bind the bodies they paint with their choices of color, placement, and the demarcation between subject and background. González and Gamboa play around with these choices rather than turning to abstract or nonrepresentational modes. They invoke, but shift the shape of, conventional identity, representing corporeal fluidity and permeability with realistic bodies. Their works are still recognizably Chicana and feminist, filtering visual critiques of racism, misogyny, and homophobia through the lenses of Aztec culture, Catholicism, and Chicana/o counterculture. But rather than reifying any of these identifications in a clear form, the portraits I analyze make visible matter that is often cut out of—because it complicates—identity politics: the conflicting cultural traditions, corporeal excesses, racial or gendered ambivalence, and spiritual abstractions that underlie our experiences of identity.

I choose to conclude with these two artists for several reasons. One anonymous reader of *Encarnación* suggested that neither González nor Gamboa are "major enough to warrant a final analysis," which gets to my point precisely. I mean this conclusion to be more forward-looking than conclusive, opening out into the future of Chicana body politics, so I end with emergent rather than "canonized" artists. Unlike Kahlo, whose monumental image is my point of departure, González and Gamboa have not (or not yet, at least) become symbols of a movement or a nation. Instead, they represent departures from the bounded forms of identity politics and portraiture, and they offer potential future directions for aesthetic and political development. As they try out new aesthetic and political configurations, both artists blur the boundaries of the human figure, and I look forward to seeing the as-yet-unimagined upheavals that their future works will imagine.

The tradition of Chicano portraiture from which González's and Gamboa's contemporary works depart centered on the affirmation of identity. As with the singular "*Yo soy*" of Corky Gonzáles's 1967 *movimiento* poem "Soy Joaquín" (which I analyzed in Chapter 1), much early Chicana/o art focused on singular images and revolutionary icons (like the Virgin of Guadalupe, Emiliano Zapata, Frida Kahlo, or the pachuco).[5] To solidify the identity of the emerging Chicano movement,

5. The CARA exhibit includes examples of all of these figures: Rupert García's silkscreen *Emiliano Zapata* (1969), Yreina Cervántez's *Homenaje a Frida Kahlo* (1978), José Montoya's *Pachuco: A Historical Update* (1978), Carlos Fres-

paintings and posters affirmed that identity in clear terms, sometimes with iconic images floating alone in blank backgrounds. These images limit a viewer's focus to the bounded body of the (ideal or supposedly "typical") Chicano subject. Many examples can be found in the 1990 CARA exhibition (*Chicano Art: Resistance and Affirmation, 1965–1985*), a retrospective "visual history of the goals and struggles of el Movimiento" (Gaspar de Alba 8). Daniel De Siga's 1976 *Campesino* depicts a lone farm-worker, whose individual face is blocked by his large straw hat, stooped over a barren field against the backdrop of a completely empty sky. Harry Gamboa's 1979 *Zero Visibility* is a black-and-white photograph of a Chicano, dressed in a black suit with a black shirt and black sunglasses, pressed into the corner of a small room whose walls are blank white. Another nameless exemplar of Chicana/o typology can be found in César Martínez's 1985 *La Fulana* (*The Other Woman*): a black-haired woman, with a halter top revealing much curvaceous flesh, posed against a monochromatic green backdrop. All of these figures are clearly bounded and highly visible as distinct types: farmworker, urban Chicano, loose woman. All three are nameless, nonspecific, and isolated. Even Amado Peña's famous silkscreen *Mestizo* (1974), which captures the racial multiplicity of Chicana/os, fuses three differently shaded profiles into one head, creating oneness out of dissonance. Though the images by González and Gamboa that I analyze below are also portraits, even when they include only one human figure they are anything but singular.

Much recent analysis of Chicana feminist art has focused on representations of domestic spaces—like Amalia Mesa-Bains's home altars and bedrooms—or portraiture—like Yolanda López's and Ester Hernández's empty dresses or their reworkings of Virgin of Guadalupe iconography. Mesa-Bains argues that the primary locus of power relations for Chicanas is the domestic space:

> In this ordering of space, both public and private, only spatial ambi-
> guities and metaphors can function to shake the foundational patri-
> archy through challenging works in art. The Chicana strategies of
> domesticana that emerge from the spaces of femininity, such as the
> bedroom, the kitchen, and the yard, retake the gaze, the centrality
> for its own meaning and begin to reposition the Chicana through
> the reworking of feminine space. (Mesa-Bains 306)

---

quez's *Zoot Suit en los Rockies* (1984), and Ester Hernández and Yolanda López's feminist revisions of the portrait of the Virgin of Guadalupe.

Laura E. Pérez, in contrast, focuses on dress and body ornamentation as the site where cultural and gendered meaning is inscribed and resisted: "From pigment to physical build to comportment, the presentation and reception of the body is, following Butler, part of the performance that reinscribes or interrupts social roles attributed as normal to racialized and gendered bodies" (L. Pérez, "Writing on the Social Body" 30–31). González and Gamboa fuse these two spatial levels, painting bodies that move within, replicate, or intersect with their backgrounds. Like Kahlo, they often depict a central body whose gaze challenges viewers to stare at the same time that it seems to stare back, creating an intersubjective relationship. And, also like Kahlo, these bodies are surrounded by painted backdrops that, whether they be lush or starkly bare, are implicitly cultural and political. In many of the works I analyze, the distinction between figure and background blurs to reflect the ways in which they shape each other.

As portraiture helps us to understand bodies in new ways, it also objectifies bodies at some level. In her analysis of the CARA exhibit, Alicia Gaspar de Alba worries about the focus on the body in the works selected for the "Feminist Visions" section. The predominance of portraiture in the works displayed there—by López, Hernández, and others—and these works' focus on issues like pregnancy, sexuality, and the virgin/whore dichotomy potentially reinforce the limited gender identities associated with Chicanas. Though the artists might have been "decolonizing the female body by transforming it into an active speaking subject rather than a passive object of display and male gratification," the curators' decision to group all of the female artists in one room whose focus is the female body potentially replicates the misogynist assumption that all women have to say is about their own bodies (Gaspar de Alba 132–33). Gaspar de Alba also laments the male artists' "appropriation" of domestic spaces like the home altar and the curators' decision to privilege male perspectives on domesticity and spirituality (145). Ultimately, in her argument, CARA reinforces the idea that their bodies are the only meaningful subjects for women. The more recent portraits of González and Gamboa that I analyze here (from the late 1990s and early 2000s) more clearly break down the essentialist stereotypes and the body-centrism that Gaspar de Alba critiques.

Maya González has been exhibiting her paintings since the 1990s. Her most widely circulated works are illustrations for children's books, most frequently those of the award-winning writer Francisco X. Alarcón. While the genre of children's literature facilitates the playful break from realism in her illustrations, González's paintings are equally imaginative and surreal. The reference source *Contemporary Chicana and Chicano Art* describes how González draws new parameters for the female figure:

> González finds new ways of talking about Chicanisma by respecting the self, engaging the historical, and recognizing that the implications of both have consequences that are universal. In many ways, the women in González's paintings struggle with the core problem of the post-modern condition: how to exist in a specific and meaningful way in a world that defies both qualities. (Keller et al., *Contemporary Chicana and Chicano Art* 2:6)

Though I would dispute the idea that postmodernism represses meaning, this characterization captures the ways in which González's representations of Chicana bodies radiate outward beyond their racial and sexual particularity. She describes herself as a bridge: "A bridge of two cultures, two creative traditions, as well as two states of being: physical and spiritual" (qtd. in Keller et al., *Contemporary Chicana and Chicano Art* 2:6). This crossing is not just Chicana/o *mestizaje*; it is trans-corporeal, synthesizing body and spirit, matter and belief. In her online "Artist's Statement," she describes her paintings as a reflection of "a very deep personal/spiritual landscape," using the metaphor of haunting to describe this crossing between body and spirit, past and present: "My images most often begin as haunts within my mind. . . . These haunts are generally related to something going on in my inner life. . . . Sometimes these haunts are from other times, even other dimensions" ("Maya González's Artist's Statement").

González's works depict bodies shaped by pre-Columbian history, Catholic iconography, and their present environment. *Death Enthroned* (2002) depicts a realistically shaped female figure sitting naked and open-legged on a "throne" (see Plate 5). Gary Keller compares the positioning of the figure to the Madonna of Renaissance religious painting (Keller et al., *Chicano Art* 68). At the same time, the positioning also invokes the pornographic centerfold.[6] The figure's skin is painted in a manner suggestive of Native American ritual performance, its colorization on González's canvas making visible the fact that bodies are always colorized

6. This seated figure recalls an earlier work of González's, which is also likely a Madonna reference. *Pommegranate* (1994), which is featured on the cover of Carla Trujillo's edited volume *Living Chicana Theory*, depicts a dark-skinned, dark-haired, dark-eyed woman sitting on a blue chair with her legs spread and

through cultural perceptions. Yet this uncanny image layers different cultural perceptions so that it exceeds any single interpretation. It is familiar, but familiar to so many different things that it cannot be identified with any single filiation. The head—inhuman, un-female—resembles the death skull of Aztec codices, and the figure's skin color is also seemingly inhuman: white (actual white, not the tan color associated with "white" identity) and covered in splotches (or pox?) of yellow that resemble fruits.[7] The spotted skin invokes the jaguar, a shape-shifter for the Aztecs and an appropriate model for this painting's trans-human excesses. The patterns inscribed on the central body—the arch over the eyebrow, the rows of square teeth, and the half-red eye—are echoed throughout the painting—on the carpet, on the upholstery of the chair, in the crowned eye held in the figure's right hand—suggesting that the body is marked by or is overflowing into its surroundings. The portrait does not contain the body within its boundaries; nor does it make clear what viewers should be seeing when they look at it.

Another one of González's best-known paintings, *The Love That Stains* (2000), overlays the images of two nearly identical dark-haired women—one with dark skin and eyes opened, the other with white skin and eyes closed—holding onto each other (see Plate 6).[8] A hummingbird

---

her body open to viewers. She is wearing black thigh-high stockings and a black lace button-up bustier, revealing cleavage between her voluptuous breasts, a line of skin down her front between the buttons, and slits of skin between her stockings and black panties. In her right hand, she holds a skeleton by the neck, and in the left, a pomegranate, cut open to reveal its seeded red interior (which resembles female genitalia as well as the sacred heart of Catholic iconography). Rather than having her Madonna crush the serpent—a sacred animal in pre-Columbian iconography, associated with fertility and the goddess Coatlicue—this figure's high-heeled black shoe steps on the skeleton's right hand, suggesting that this fertility has defeated death. Perhaps *Death Enthroned* was conceived as an opposing counterpart to *Pommegranate*.

7. This pocked figure also recalls one of González's children's book illustrations: her depiction of "The Hungry Goddess" in Mary-Joan Gerson's *Fiesta Femenina* (2001) has the goddess's body covered first with mouths and then with eyes of the same shape as the sores on the skin of *Death Enthroned* (Gerson 14–15), suggesting an alternate Aztec source for this figure. (Cherríe Moraga's play, *The Hungry Woman*, refers to this same Aztec legend of the devouring woman.)

8. This painting is an obvious reworking of Frida Kahlo's *The Two Fridas* (1939), a double-self-portrait of the artist dressed in white European dress on the left and brightly colored indigenous dress on the right (see Plate 1a). Both figures

(a sacred Aztec figure associated with both the war god Huitzilopochtli and the creativity goddess Xochiquetzal) buzzes at the ear of the white figure, and the dark figure wears her heart on the outside of her dress, with blood spilling down her front (invoking both Aztec heart excision as well as the bleeding heart of Catholic iconography). This painting suggests that, like pre-Columbian gods and goddesses or like the many-named Catholic Virgin, the woman has multiple aspects or different incarnations that intertwine not just different cultural frameworks but different identities. Or, perhaps, it suggests that dark and light bodies are inextricable from each other, though the dark one bleeds with eyes open while the white one remains closed—a critique of racism, perhaps, or of the Europeanizing tendency to ignore the indigenous components of Latin American *mestizaje* (represented by the white figure's blindness to the hummingbird). This duality could also be less literal, with the white figure representing the "haunt" (to use González's term) of the past that inflects the living/colored body's experience in the present. As with *Death Enthroned*, the central body/bodies blend with their backdrop: the solid red background of *The Love That Stains* suggests that either the dark woman's bleeding heart has spread to saturate the world around her or that her bleeding comes from her surroundings. González herself describes this image as a vision of overflowing love that cannot be contained (qtd. in Keller et al., *Chicano Art* 87).

González's *Switching Rabbits* (2002), a portrait that has received less critical attention, blends a woman's body more fully with its environment (see Plate 7). The backdrop is a horizon, where the green sea below meets a black sky above, and a golden setting sun rests in the middle. All of the bodies in the painting, three or four animals and the woman at the center, are split in half by the horizon's borderline, and each half takes on the qualities of its context. The woman is green below, where her body touches the water, and the parts of her body that rise above the sea assume the gold color of the sun that frames them. A boat around her

---

wear their hearts outside their dresses, with blood spilling down the front of the white figure. An artery between the two hearts connects the two women, though they bleed in the cultural cleavage between indigenous Mexico and Spain. Laura E. Pérez argues that González's image is more positive about duality than Kahlo's: "rather than conveying *The Two Fridas*'s painful sense of being torn psychologically, the duality of the physical and spiritual sense is conveyed as a resource of strength, as the ghostly spirit embraces and comforts the living self" in *The Love that Stains* (L. Pérez, *Chicana Art* 292).

middle, half-green and half-gold, seems to hold the body suspended on the horizon. She holds a rabbit in her hand underwater, and a red spout flows out of the top of her head and feeds into another rabbit, which is hanging suspended in the air, perhaps recalling the snakes emerging from Coatlicue's head.[9] A border-crossing animal, half green and half red, half fish and half rabbit, rises up out of the water next to the woman. Where its mouth touches her head it takes on the brown of her hair, as its fin takes on the green of her leg underwater, suggesting that their individual identities are transparent, that they commingle passionately, or that one ingests the other and changes its form. The ambiguous verb "switching" in the title suggests that the figures in the painting are changing, moving, shifting, or taking the place of each other. The female body seems propped up by the animals and not threatened by this shape-shifting. Her thrown-back head and closed eyes could suggest pleasure or passivity. Though the woman and animals are realistically drawn, their juxtaposition reflects indeterminacy: the figures are all half-breeds who reflect their surroundings and blend into each other. Indeed, the only boundary line that is clear is the central horizon—the world in which bodies are figured—while the lines between human and animal, body and sea, and body and sun are eclipsed by the colors and shapes that the figures share across boundaries: one can hardly tell where the green arm leaves off and the green sea begins. Perhaps the best term for describing González's work is "defamiliarization." She takes recognizable figures but makes them uncanny, incomprehensible, leading viewers to question what they thought they knew about bodies and identities.

The provocative work of Los Angeles–based artist Diane Gamboa likewise defamiliarizes bodies and identities. From her performance art and paper fashions of the 1980s to her contemporary work with tattoos, her art is principally about body ornamentation, display, and excess. Several art critics have noted how her "Urban Royalty" and "Pin Up" series push beyond conventional boundaries of the human figure.[10] In a review

9. The ambiguity (and amphibiousness) of the bodies in this painting initially led me to see the underwater rabbit as a crab, until the artist pointed out to me that it was meant to be a rabbit. Long ears then became visible to me on all of the figures, so perhaps they are all "switching" (or switching into or out of) rabbits.

10. The portraits in Gamboa's "Pin Up" and "Urban Royalty" series could be described as a hybrid between the group portrait and the individual portrait. Even when individuals are alone, they are accompanied by "backgrounds" that are as dynamic as the foreground figure. In this way, even some of the solo

of a 2004 show, Suvan Geer describes her human figures as "some of the most arresting personalities, and dangerously stretched psyches around" (Geer). Tere Romo likewise emphasizes the ways in which Gamboa's works "explode from the canvas and push the boundaries of Chicano art":

> She populates her artistic world with an array of distorted human figures depicted in flat, garish colors and with sharp features and body tattoos. These portraits of couples, family life and individuals in everyday scenes are rendered in a shocking, exaggerated style, to the point that they become less human and more like the surrounding inanimate props. (Romo 27)

In works like *Little Gold Man* (1990) and *Pinch Me* (1997), for instance, the angular, tattooed, and heavily made-up figures are nearly identical to the garish and oversized tables, lamps, and vases that surround them (see Plate 8 and Figure 2). The people are no more central than the furniture, as the décor is personified and the people are objectified. Framed portraits and sculptures placed throughout these works self-reflexively point out the conversion of human identity into decoration. Yet the figures in *Little Gold Man* are framed in such a way that the boundaries of the painting cut off portions of their heads and bodies, suggesting that the identities in Gamboa's portraits exceed their objectifying frames— literally and metaphorically. The central figure in *Pinch Me* is excessively gendered, with a chiseled jaw and muscular arms and legs, stylized makeup reminiscent of transgendered performance, and tattoos drawing attention to female breasts and crotch. The figure, dressed only in panties, is "garmented" with numerous tattoos, bracelets, rings, giant earrings, high-healed shoes, and an evening bag. The effect seems to parody sexual objectification by going "over the top," exceeding the "frame" of any sex or gender, repelling and attracting the gaze (or the pinch, as it were) at the same time.

Pérez notes how ornamentation and interior spaces act as "emotional prostheses" for the figures in Gamboa's work, so that "the distinction between human and object surfaces is blurred" (L. Pérez, "Writing on the Social Body" 46). Indeed, the people seem to be wearing the furniture and décor around them as much as their scant clothing, jewelry, and

---

portraits seem as numerously peopled as her painting *Little Gold Man*, a group portrait crowded with fantastical figures that could be either animate or inanimate, including the eponymous "little gold man" who emerges from the head of a red devil.

Figure 2. Diane Gamboa, *Pinch Me* (1997). © Diane Gamboa.

tattoos: a "distortion of the ego" that Gamboa suggests is "a method of surviving the adverse conditions of the urban environment" (qtd. in L. Pérez, "Writing on the Social Body" 49). This quote poses the ego as a shape-shifting agent that interacts with its environment. But in Gamboa's art, it is not just egos and identities that stretch: it is bodies themselves. The processes by which bodies strain against their own boundaries are captured in an ink-on-vellum work called *Ceremonies Are Held* (2004) (see Figure 3). All of the objects in this drawing are attached to the central female subject, who is engaged in what appear to be masochistic pain rituals. Unlike the agency in Gamboa's assertion above, masochism acts by being an object. The passive voice in the title of this work, and the absence of body in the title, emphasize instead the agency of the ceremonial processes that define/form the figure. The blank space around the figure seems to deprive it of a backdrop, but the chains, tassels, and straps that adorn her body resemble pieces of furniture from Gamboa's other works, making the body itself the decorated room, a place where foreground and background merge. And, as in *Pinch Me*, the incorporation of objects associated with sadomasochism and depictions of contorted faces remind us of the corporeal sensation that is produced by the meeting of figure and ground.

All of these representations trouble the boundaries of identity. Gamboa's human figures are excessively gendered, and they seem not to be familiarly racialized. There are vague allusions to race and culture, but these allusions confuse rather than resolve identity. The paintings depict

Figure 3. Diane Gamboa, *Ceremonies Are Held* (2004). © Diane Gamboa.

eerily white-, blue-, and purple-skinned figures with green and red hair. Often the figures are naked, except for jewelry that is often Aztec-style and headpieces that often include fruit (reminiscent of Carmen Miranda, perhaps), vaguely echoing Latin American cultures through dispersed fetishes and exotic stereotypes. One figure in *Little Gold Man* might be wearing a purple and blue zoot suit; the crucifix on another's necklace might invoke Catholicism or gang culture. The "culture," if there is one in Gamboa's work, is hybrid, transgendered, punk, sadomasochistic, countercultural—defined by transgression and "otherness." Like *calorra* and disability in *Peel My Love Like an Onion*, these identifications cross between conventional cultural categories. In this light, her choice to use either surreal, flamboyant color or no color whatsoever (in her ink-on-vellum drawings) suggests a deliberate avoidance of familiarly racialized corporeality.

In contrast, González's portraits, with the exception of the white and spotted *Death Enthroned*, revolve around brown-skinned figures; indeed, they could be self-portraits. But they are not isolated figures. They are excessive like Gamboa's, but their excesses are inscribed differently. González's bodies are realistically drawn, invoking "the real" of Latina embodiment, but they also incorporate other beings. They invoke familiar images of objectified women, both centerfolds and Madonnas, but give these figures supernatural, spiritual, and superhuman qualities. By putting body parts in the wrong places or linking bodies to each other, they challenge our expectations for what a body should be and how a body should act. In this sense, they resemble Coatlicue and Coyolxauhqui as much as centerfolds and Madonnas. They also recall Frida Kahlo's self-portraits in their inter-corporeal fusions and their rejection of corporeal immanence.

Pain is a central feature of these portraits. González's figures are diseased, bleeding, and being consumed. The figures in Gamboa's work proudly display their tattoos (traces of past pain) as they ask to be pinched (inviting future pain), involving viewers in interactive pain practices. Even those figures not directly associated with pain ritual appear to be in pain, with contorted facial expressions, heads out of round, and heavy jewelry. Significantly, the pain practices represented here emerge from Aztec culture as well as contemporary U.S. pain cultures, not collapsing the two as much as denaturalizing the present by recalling the most feared and uncanny aspects of past cultures. In *Ceremonies Are Held*, the figure's necklace, earrings, and headpiece resemble Aztec adornments, while the knife tattooed on the inside of her arm and the tasseled pasties on her breasts reflect twentieth-century masculine and feminine erotic fashions. These figures repel viewers as they attract them, assuming some power over their own bodies and over their viewers by overflowing customary boundaries. They make us uncomfortable.

This discomfort should have an impact on our thinking about bodies and identities. Discomfort signals a threat to the system, a challenge to that which we perceive as "normal" corporeal stasis. Psychoanalyst Thomas Szasz, in his 1957 study *Pain and Pleasure*, describes pain as "a signal warning the ego of a certain (dangerous) state of affairs concerning the body" (Szasz 54). According to David Morris, "To be in pain is to be in a state of crisis. It is a state in which we experience far more than physical discomfort. Pain has not simply interrupted our normal feeling of health. It has opened a huge fault or fissure in our world" (Morris, *The Culture of Pain* 31). Crisis is often productive of new ways of thinking and new types of relationships. When the ego perceives a new relationship between body and context (to paraphrase the psychoanalytic characterization of pain), or when our perception of the world has been challenged (to paraphrase Morris), we are forced to think, to investigate, to develop new models. Pain sometimes provides "access to vision so alien from our normal consciousness that it can only be called prophetic, utopian, or revolutionary" (126). Modern medicine, however, has defined pain as a purely scientific matter, enclosed within the bodies of malfunctioning "patients." We have been taught to view pain as a matter of nerves to be numbed and ill to be eradicated. Bodies must be returned to an original state of "health," cutting off any productive potential involved in pain. Pain opens up questions; modern medicine closes them, fears the otherness of illness, and institutes normative embodiments. But pain is not just about bodies; it is about the contexts in which they are situated. Assuming that pain is no more than a signal of broken tissue overlooks the material world in which pain is produced and, therefore, often fails to eliminate its cause. Isolating bodies from their contexts also ignores power dynamics, cultural specificity, gender, affect, and social contexts in which pain might carry affirmative meaning (sadomasochism or the discourse of saints and martyrs, for instance).

González's and Gamboa's representations of bodies in pain restore spiritual, affective, and revolutionary dimensions to our thinking about bodies. They resist the objectifying power dynamics of medicine, portraiture, or identity politics, all of which isolate bodies for evaluation and assume that they must fit within certain frameworks. Instead, these bodies incorporate haunts of the past, spiritual beliefs, material surroundings, and each other. They bleed, they infect, they invite sex, and they invite pain. They demonstrate crises of the ego. This excess, in itself, is political. Yet, in failing to embody clear racial or sexual identities, they derail assumptions that Chicana feminist art must reflect Chicana feminist identity politics (which are, presumably, best represented by Chicana bodies). Though they invoke and critique the ways in which racism, misogyny, and homophobia distort Chicana identity (lopping off the tops of heads or splitting bodies in two), González and Gamboa ultimately redraw the boundaries of Chicana feminism. The political matter of their work, I would argue, is shifted from individual identities to the complicated intersections between bodies and environments. The upheavals and transformations of the figures they paint supersede the fixity/familiarity of identity and draw our attention to material processes in new ways. As when pain or illness shift our focus from identity politics to matters of tissues, feelings, and health care, these figures' corporeal crises force us to look closely rather than letting us identify them at a distance. They provoke a visual crisis, and they provide access to "alien" and "utopian" vision (to paraphrase Morris again). They force us to imagine how bodies could be otherwise, outside the normative frames of sociopolitical identity. Moreover, and most importantly, these figures are shaped by the "faults and fissures" of their backdrops, and their resistance can be seen not in the celebration or defense of an identity but in the ways in which they overflow their frames—an excess that implicitly critiques the limiting social formations that frame us (or the "central organizing principles of a society," to recall my discussion of Paula Moya in the introduction). The content of this sort of Chicana feminism is heterogeneous, permeable, and contingent.

Moraga worried about the shape-shifting dialogue between body and context in *The Last Generation* (1993):

> We light-skinned breeds are like chameleons, those lagartijas with the capacity to change the color of their skins. We change not for lack of conviction, but lack of definitive shade and shape. My lovers have always been the environment that defined my color. . . . For that reason, I got to be choosy 'bout who I hang with. Everybody so contagious, I pick up their gesture, their joke, their jive. (Moraga, *The Last Generation* 116–17)

It is important that these transformations are a result of "lack of definitive shade and shape" rather than lack of conviction. Moraga separates body, identity, and politics. One's body need not clearly signify an identity in order to be politically significant. Though our bodies certainly mediate our needs and expressions, they are not the sole origin of our identities or our politics. Moraga's light skin renders her identity amorphous, contextual, and border-crossing, but her Chicana feminist politics remain solid, even when she becomes Rican, Spanish, Cuban, Italian, Jewish, ladina, or extranjera, depending on whom she "hang[s] with" (116).[11] This *mestiza* identity has the ability to shift shapes to adapt to particular desires, communities, and contexts, like the figure in González's *Switching Rabbits* who becomes a fish in the water.[12] Presumably, it also has the ability to adopt additional political vectors, once it understands the needs of Ricans or sea creatures. Yet, as with Gamboa's *Ceremonies Are Held*, the body in this description is neither an independent agent nor a passive object in its interactions with the environment. Body and environment mediate each other. We can try to be choosy about whom we "hang with," and we can try to choose which qualities our bodies will pick up from the association, but sometimes our work, our bodies, or the world require us to move in unexpected ways. Where will our politics go then? And where our identities?

Since corporeal experience is shaped by environments, bodies alone are not the source of meaning. Their political situation, their political needs, and their political movements are about placement, not isolated identity—a lesson made clear by Disability Studies' focus on how environments restrict mobility. What I find in these painful and unsettling Chicana feminist portraits—both the visual and the literary—is a call to shift our focus from the makeup of identity to reciprocal relationships between bodies and their surroundings. These portraits show how bodies are physically and psychologically shaped, politically interpellated, and (im)mobilized by material environments. In turn, the health, needs, and movements of these bodies radiate outward into the world and beings

11. Moraga describes these shifts as aspects of her love life, which is, as we know from her earlier work, an important source of political meaning. Love, for Moraga, is about identification, longing, and political alliance. See, for instance, "Amar en Los Años de Guerra," "La Dulce Culpa," and "Loving in the War Years," all collected in *Loving in the War Years*.

12. The amphibious woman in *Switching Rabbits* recalls the drowning figure in Moraga's poem, "You Call it, *Amputation*." This poem, from *Loving in the War Years*, seems to lack the affirmed chameleon-ness of her later work, since the amputated body has difficulty adapting itself to water, "swimming in side stroke, / pumping twice as hard / for the lack / of body, pushing / through your words / which hold no water / for me" (Moraga, *Loving in the War Years* 82).

around them. For this reason, our understanding of identity must look beyond the body. The origins of suffering, violence, political mobilization, and desire must be found in contextual analysis of the interactions between bodies and environments. Since there is no single or constant locus of identification, our analyses must adapt to different cultural frameworks, shifting feelings, and matter that is fluid. In short, our thinking about bodies, identities, and politics must keep moving.

BIBLIOGRAPHY

Aguilera, Carmen. *Coyolxauhqui: The Mexica Milky Way*. Lancaster, Calif.: Laby-rinthos, 2001.

Aguirre Beltrán, Gonzalo. *Medicina y Magia: El proceso de aculteración en la estructura colonial*. Mexico City: Instituto Nacional Idigenista, 1963.

Alarcón, Norma. "Anzaldúa's *Frontera*: Inscribing Gynetics." In Arredando et al., *Chicana Feminisms*, 354–69.

———. "Chicana Feminism: In the Tracks of 'The' Native Woman." In *Living Chicana Theory*, edited by Carla Trujillo. Berkeley, Calif.: Third Woman, 1998. 371–82.

———. "Conjugating Subjects: The Heteroglossia of Essence and Resistance." In Arteaga, *An Other Tongue*, 125–38.

———. "Traddutora, Traditora: A Paradigmatic Figure of Chicana Feminism." In Grewal and Kaplan, *Scattered Hegemonies*, 110–33.

Alcalá, Rita Cano. "A Chicana Hagiography for the Twenty-First Century: Ana Castillo's *Locas Santas*." In *Velvet Barrios: Popular Culture and Chicana/o Sexuality*, edited by Alicia Gaspar de Alba. New York: Palgrave, 2003. 3–15.

Alcoff, Linda Martín. *Visible Identities: Race, Gender, and the Self*. New York: Oxford University Press, 2006.

Alcoff, Linda Martín, Michael Hames-Garcia, Satya Mohanty, and Paula M. L. Moya, eds. *Identity Politics Reconsidered*. New York: Palgrave, 2006.

Aldama, Frederick Luis. *Brown on Brown: Chicano/a Representations of Gender, Sexuality, and Ethnicity*. Austin: University of Texas Press, 2005.

Anaya, Rudolfo. "Aztlán: A Homeland Without Boundaries." In Anaya and Lomelí, *Aztlán*, 230–41.

———. *Heart of Aztlán*. Albuquerque: University of New Mexico Press, 1976.

Anaya, Rudolfo, and Francisco Lomelí, eds. *Aztlán: Essays on the Chicano Home-land*. Albuquerque: University of New Mexico Press, 1989.

Anderson, Benedict. *Imagined Communities: Reflections on the Origin and Spread of Nationalism*. London: Verso, 1983.

BIBLIOGRAPHY

Anzaldúa, Gloria E. *Borderlands/La Frontera: The New Mestiza*. San Francisco: Aunt Lute, 1987.

———. "Coming Into Play: An Interview with Gloria Anzaldúa." *MELUS* 25.2 (2000): 3–45.

———. "Daughter of Coatlicue: An Interview with Gloria Anzaldúa." In Keating, *EntreMundos/Among Worlds*, 41–55.

———. "Foreword to the Second Edition." In Anzaldúa and Moraga, *This Bridge Called My Back*, iv–v.

———. *Interviews/Entrevistas*. Edited by AnaLouise Keating. New York: Routledge, 2000.

———. "la prieta." In Moraga and Anzaldúa, *This Bridge Called My Back*, 198–209.

———. "now let us shift . . . the path of conocimiento . . . inner work, public acts." In Anzaldúa and Keating, *This Bridge We Call Home*, 540–78.

———. "Re: you & disability studies." E-mail to AnaLouise Keating, 15 October 2003.

Anzaldúa, Gloria E., ed. *Making Face, Making Soul/Haciendo Caras: Creative and Critical Perspectives by Feminists of Color*. San Francisco: Aunt Lute, 1990.

Anzaldúa, Gloria E., and AnaLouise Keating, eds. *This Bridge We Call Home: Radical Visions for Transformation*. New York: Routledge, 2002.

Anzaldúa, Gloria E., and Cherríe Moraga, eds. *This Bridge Called My Back: Writings by Radical Women of Color*. New York: Kitchen Table, 1981.

Anzures y Bolaños, María del Carmen. *Le medicina tradicional en México: Proceso histórico, sincretismos y conflictos*. Mexico City: Universidad Nacional Autónoma, 1983.

Arredondo, Gabriela F., Aida Hurtado, Norma Klahn, and Olga Najera-Ramirez, eds. *Chicana Feminisms: A Critical Reader*. Durham, N.C.: Duke University Press, 2003.

Arrizón, Alicia. "Mythical Performativity: Relocating Aztlán in Chicana Feminist Cultural Productions." *Theatre Journal* 52.1 (2000): 23–49.

Arteaga, Alfred, ed. *An Other Tongue: Nation and Ethnicity in the Linguistic Borderlands*. Durham, N.C.: Duke University Press, 1994.

Barjau, Luis. *Tezcatlipoca: Elementos de una teología nahua*. Mexico City: UNAM, 1991.

Barnard, Ian. "Gloria Anzaldúa's Queer *Mestizaje*." *MELUS* 22.1 (1997): 35–53.

Bartholomae, David, ed. *Ways of Reading*. 4th ed. Boston: Bedford, 1996.

Berkley, K. J. "Vive la difference!" *Trends in Neurosciences* 15.9 (1992): 331–32.

Bhabha, Homi K. "Signs Taken for Wonders: Questions of Ambivalence and Authority Under a Tree Outside Delhi, May 1817." *Critical Inquiry* 12 (1985): 144–65.

Birke, Lynda. "The Broken Heart." In Price and Shildrick, *Vital Signs*, 197–223.

———. *Feminism and the Biological Body*. New Brunswick: Rutgers University Press, 2000.

BIBLIOGRAPHY

Blom, Gerdien. "Divine Individuals, Cultural Identities: Post-Identitarian Representations and Two Chicana/o Texts." *Thamyris* 4.2 (1997): 295–324.

The Book of Chilam Balam of Chumayel. Edited and translated by Ralph L. Roys. Norman: University of Oklahoma Press, 1967.

Bordo, Susan. "Feminism, Postmodernism, and Gender-Scepticism." In *Feminism/Postmodernism*, edited by Linda J. Nicholson. New York: Routledge, 1990. 133–56.

———. *Unbearable Weight: Feminism, Western Culture, and the Body.* Berkeley: University of California Press, 1993.

Bost, Suzanne. "From Race/Sex/Etc. to Glucose, Feeding Tube, and Mourning: The Shifting Matter of Chicana Feminism." In *Material Feminisms*, edited by Stacy Alaimo and Susan Hekman. Bloomington: Indiana University Press, 2007. 340–72.

———. *Mulattas and Mestizas: Representing Mixed Identities in the Americas, 1850–2000.* Athens: University of Georgia Press, 2003.

———. "Women and Chile at the Alamo: Feeding U.S. Colonial Mythology." *Nepantla: Views from South* 4.3 (November 2003): 493–522.

Brady, Mary Pat. *Extinct Lands, Temporal Geographies: Chicana Literature and the Urgency of Space.* Durham, N.C.: Duke University Press, 2002.

———. "The Fungibility of Borders." *Nepantla: Views from South* 1.1 (2000): 171–90.

Braidotti, Rosi. *Nomadic Subjects: Embodiment and Sexual Difference in Contemporary Feminist Theory.* New York: Columbia University Press, 1994.

Breuer, Josef, and Sigmund Freud. *Studies on Hysteria.* Edited and translated by James Strachey with Anna Freud. New York: Basic Books, 1957.

Brinton, Daniel G. *Nagualism: A Study in Native American Folk-lore and History.* Worcester, Mass.: Press of Chas. Hamilton, 1894.

Brown, Wendy. *States of Injury: Power and Freedom in Late Modernity.* Princeton: Princeton University Press, 1995.

Broyles-González, Yolanda. "Indianizing Catholicism: Chicana/India/Mexicana Indigenous Spiritual Practices in Our Image." In Cantú and Nájera-Ramírez, *Chicana Traditions*, 117–32.

Brundage, Burr Cartwright. *The Fifth Sun: Aztec Gods, Aztec World.* Austin: University of Texas Press, 1979.

Brunk, Terence, Suzanne Diamond, Priscilla Perkins, and Ken Smith, eds. *Literacies: Reading, Writing, Interpretation.* New York: Norton, 1997.

Burkhart, Louise M. "Gender in Nahuatl Texts of the Early Colonial Period." In Klein, *Gender in Pre-Hispanic America*, 87–107.

———. *The Slippery Earth: Nahua-Christian Moral Dialogue in Sixteenth-Century Mexico.* Tucson: University of Arizona Press, 1989.

Burns, Bill, Cathy Busby, and Kim Sawchuck, eds. *When Pain Strikes.* Minneapolis: University of Minnesota Press, 1999.

Butler, Judith. *Bodies That Matter: On the Discursive Limits of "Sex."* New York: Routledge, 1993.

BIBLIOGRAPHY

————. *Gender Trouble: Feminism and the Subversion of Identity.* New York: Routledge, 1990.

Cantú, Norma, and Olga Nájera-Ramírez, eds. *Chicana Traditions: Continuity and Change.* Urbana: University of Illinois Press, 2002.

Carrasco, Davíd. *City of Sacrifice: The Aztec Empire and the Role of Violence in Civilization.* Boston: Beacon, 1999.

Caso, Alfonso. *The Aztecs: People of the Sun.* Translated by Lowell Dunham. Norman: University of Oklahoma Press, 1958.

Castañeda, Antonia I. "Presidarias y Pobladoras: The Journey North and Life in Frontier California." In *Chicana Critical Issues*, edited by Norma Alarcón. Berkeley, Calif.: Third Woman, 1993.

Castillo, Ana. *The Guardians.* New York: Random House, 2007.

————. *I Ask the Impossible: Poems.* New York: Anchor, 2000.

————. "An Interview with Ana Castillo." *South Central Review* 16.1 (Spring 1999): 19–29.

————. *Loverboys: Stories.* New York: Norton, 1996.

————. *Massacre of the Dreamers: Essays on Xicanisma.* New York: Plume, 1994.

————. *The Mixquiahuala Letters.* New York: Anchor, 1992.

————. *My Father Was a Toltec and Selected Poems, 1973–1988.* New York: Anchor, 2004.

————. *Otro Canto.* Chicago: Alternativa Publications, 1977.

————. *Peel My Love Like an Onion.* New York: Anchor, 2000.

————. *Psst . . . I Have Something To Tell You, Mi Amor.* San Antonio, Tex.: Wings, 2005.

————. *Sapogonia: An Anti-Romance in 3/8 Meter.* New York: Anchor, 1990.

————. *So Far From God.* New York: Plume, 1994.

————. *Watercolor Women/Opaque Men.* Chicago: Curbstone, 2005.

Castillo, Ana, and Cherríe Moraga, eds. *Este Puente, Mi Espalda: Voces de mujeres tercermundistas en los estados unidos.* San Francisco: Ism, 1988.

Centenario de Sta. Teresa de Jesus en Méjico. Breve Reseña de las Solemnidades Religiosas y Literarias Celebradas en la Ciudad de Toluca el Dia 15 de Octubre de 1882. Mexico City: El Centinelo Español, 1882.

Chabram-Dernersesian, Angie. " 'Chicana! Rican? No, Chicana-Riqueña!' Refashioning the Transnational Connection." In *Multiculturalism: A Critical Reader*, edited by David Theo Goldberg. Malden, Mass.: Blackwell, 1994. 269–95.

————. "I Throw Punches for My Race, but I Don't Want to Be a Man: Writing Us—Chica/nos (Girl, Us)/Chicanas Into the Movement Script." In *Cultural Studies*, edited by Lawrence Grossberg, Cary Nelson, and Paula Treichler. New York: Routledge, 1992. 81–95.

Chávez González, Rodrigo A. *El mestizaje y su influencia social en América.* Guayaquil, Ecuador: Imprenta y Talleres Municipales, 1937.

Clendinnen, Inga. *Aztecs: An Interpretation.* Cambridge: Cambridge University Press, 1991.

————. *Tiger's Eye: A Memoir.* New York: Scribner, 2000.

BIBLIOGRAPHY

Coe, Michael D. *Mexico: From the Olmecs to the Aztecs*. London: Thames & Hudson, 1962.

Conboy, Katie, et al., eds. *Writing on the Body: Female Embodiment and Feminist Theory*. New York: Columbia University Press, 1997.

Cooey, Paula. *Religious Imagination and the Body: A Feminist Analysis*. New York: Oxford University Press, 1994.

Corker, Marian, and Tom Shakespeare, eds. *Disability/Postmodernity: Embodying Disability Theory*. London: Continuum, 2002.

Davalos, Karen Mary, Eric Avila, Rafael Pérez-Torres, and Chela Sandoval. "Roundtable on the State of Chicana/o Studies." *Aztlán* 27.2 (Fall 2002): 141–52.

Davies, Carole Boyce. *Black Women, Writing and Identity: Migrations of the Subject*. New York: Routledge, 1994.

Davis, Lennard J. *Bending Over Backwards: Disability, Dismodernism and Other Difficult Positions*. New York: New York University Press, 2002.

Davis-Undiano, Robert Con. "Mestizos critique the New World: Vasconcelos, Anzaldúa, and Anaya." *Literature Interpretation Theory* 11.2 (2000): 117–42.

de Beauvoir, Simone. *The Second Sex*. Translated by H. M. Parshley. New York: Knopf, 1953.

de Certeau, Michel. *The Writing of History*. 1975. New York: Columbia University Press, 1988.

de Lauretis, Teresa. "Sexual Indifference and Lesbian Representation." *Theatre Journal* 40 (1988): 155–77.

Eagleton, Mary, ed. *Feminist Literary Theory: A Reader*. Oxford: Blackwell, 1986.

Eire, Carlos M. N. *From Madrid to Purgatory: The Art and Craft of Dying in Sixteenth-Century Spain*. New York: Cambridge University Press, 1995.

"El Plan Espiritual de Aztlán." In Anaya and Lomelí, *Aztlán*, 1–5.

Eng, David L., and David Kazanjian, eds. *Loss: The Politics of Mourning*. Berkeley: University of California Press, 2003.

Espín, Oliva M. *Latina Realities: Essays on Healing, Migration, and Sexuality*. Boulder: Westview, 1997.

Euripides. *Medea*. Translated by John Harrison. Cambridge: Cambridge University Press, 1999.

Fanon, Frantz. *The Wretched of the Earth*. Translated by Constance Farrington. New York: Grove, 1963.

Fehrenbach, T. R. *Fire and Blood: A History of Mexico*. New York: Da Capo, 1995.

Fernandes, Leela. *Transforming Feminist Practice: Non-Violence, Social Justice, and the Possibilities of a Spiritualized Feminism*. San Francisco: Aunt Lute, 2003.

Fillingim, R. B., and T. J. Ness. "Sex-Related Hormonal Influences on Pain and Analgesic Responses." *Neuroscience and Biobehavioral Reviews* 24 (2000): 485–501.

Finkler, Kaja. *Women in Pain: Gender and Morbidity in Mexico*. Philadelphia: University of Pennsylvania Press, 1994.

BIBLIOGRAPHY

Flores y Troncoso, Francisco de Asis. *Historia de la medicina en México: desde la época de los indios hasta la presente.* Mexico City: Instituto Mexicano del Seguro Social, 1982.

Foucault, Michel. *The Birth of the Clinic: An Archeology of Medical Perception.* 1963. New York: Vintage, 1994.

Fuentes, Carlos. Introduction to *The Diary of Frida Kahlo: An Intimate Self-Portrait.* New York: Abrams, 1995.

Fusco, Coco. *The Bodies That Were Not Ours and Other Writings.* London: Routledge, 2001.

Gant-Britton, Lisbeth. "Mexican Women and Chicanas Enter Futuristic Fiction." In *Future Females, The Next Generation: New Voices and Velocities in Science Fiction Criticism,* edited by Marleen S. Barr. Lanham, Md.: Rowman & Littlefield, 2000. 261–76.

Gaspar de Alba, Alicia. *Chicano Art Inside/Outside the Master's House: Cultural Politics and the CARA Exhibition.* Austin: University of Texas Press, 1998.

Gates, Henry Louis, Jr. *The Signifying Monkey: A Theory of African-American Literary Criticism.* New York: Oxford University Press, 1988.

Geer, Suvan. "Diane Gamboa." *ArtScene.* http://artscenecal.com/ArticlesFile/Archive/Articles2004/Articles 0604/DGamboaA.html.

Gendrault, Karim Philippe. "On Physical Pain: A Review." *Psychoanalysis and Contemporary Thought* 24.1 (2001): 31–66.

Gerson, Mary-Loan. *Fiesta Femenina: Celebrating Women in Mexican Folktale.* Illustrated by Maya González. New York: Barefoot Books, 2001.

Goldberg, David Theo. *Racial Subjects: Writing on Race in America.* New York: Routledge, 1997.

Gómez-Peña, Guillermo. *Temple of Confessions: Mexican Beasts and Living Santos.* New York: Power House Books, 1996.

Gonzales, Patricia, and Roberto Rodriguez. "The Crossing of Gloria Anzaldúa." *uExpress.* www.uexpress.com.

Gonzáles, Rodolfo. *I Am Joaquín/Soy Joaquín.* 1967. Ashland, Va.: McGraw-Page Library, 1991.

González-Torres, Yolotl. *El sacrificio humano entre los mexicas.* Mexico City: Fondo de Cultura Económica, 1985.

Grewal, Inderpal. "Autobiographic Subjects and Diasporic Locations: *Meatless Days* and *Borderlands.*" In Grewal and Kaplan, *Scattered Hegemonies,* 231–54.

Grewal, Inderpal, and Caren Kaplan, eds. *Scattered Hegemonies: Postmodernity and Transnational Feminist Practices.* Minneapolis: University of Minnesota Press, 1994.

Grosz, Elizabeth. "Intolerable Ambiguity: Freaks as/at the Limit." In Thomson, *Freakery,* 55–66.

———. *Volatile Bodies: Toward a Corporeal Feminism.* Bloomington: Indiana University Press, 1994.

Hall, Lynda. "Lorde, Anzaldúa, and Tropicana Performatively Embody the Written Self." *Auto/biography Studies* 15.1 (Summer 2000): 96–122.

BIBLIOGRAPHY

———. "Writing Selves Home at the Crossroads: Anzaldúa and Chrystos (Re)Configure Lesbian Bodies." *Ariel* 30.2 (1999): 99–117.

Haraway, Donna J. *Simians, Cyborgs, and Women: The Reinvention of Nature.* New York: Routledge, 1991.

Hedrick, Tace. *Mestizo Modernism: Race, Nation, and Identity in Latin American Culture, 1900–1940.* New Brunswick, N.J.: Rutgers University Press, 2003.

Hekman, Susan J. *Private Selves, Public Identities: Reconsidering Identity Politics.* University Park: Pennsylvania State University Press, 2004.

Helland, Janice. "Aztec Imagery in Frida Kahlo's Paintings: Indigenity and Political Commitment." *Woman's Art Journal* 11.2 (Autumn 1990–Winter 1991): 8–13.

Hernández Sáenz, Luz María, and George M. Foster. "Curers and Their Cures in Colonial New Pain and Guatemala: The Spanish Component." In *Mesoamerican Healers*, edited by Brad Huber and Alan Sandstrom. Austin: University of Texas Press, 2001. 19–46.

Herrera, Hayden. *Frida: A Biography of Frida Kahlo.* New York: HarperCollins, 1983.

———. *Frida Kahlo: The Paintings.* New York: HarperCollins, 1991.

Hull, Gloria T., et al, eds. *All the Women Are White, All the Blacks Are Men, But Some of Us Are Brave.* Old Westbury, N.Y.: Feminist Press, 1982.

Ingstad, Benedicte, and Susan Reynolds Whyte, eds. *Disability and Culture.* Berkeley: University of California Press, 1995.

Irigaray, Luce. *This Sex Which Is Not One.* Translated by Catherine Porter. Ithaca, N.Y.: Cornell University Press, 1985.

Joyce, Rosemary. *Gender and Power in Prehispanic Mesoamerica.* Austin: University of Texas Press, 2000.

Kahlo, Frida. *The Diary of Frida Kahlo: An Intimate Self-Portrait.* New York: Abrams, 1995.

Kaplan, Caren, et al., eds. *Between Woman and Nation: Nationalisms, Transnational Feminisms, and the State.* Durham, N.C.: Duke University Press, 1999.

Kavanaugh, Kieran. "The Book of Her Life." Introduction to *The Collected Works of St. Teresa of Avila,* translated by Kieran Kavanaugh and Otilio Rodriguez. Washington, D.C.: Institute of Carmelite Studies, 1987.

Keating, AnaLouise. "Charting Pathways, Marking Thresholds. . . . A Warning, An Introduction." In Alzaldúa and Keating, *This Bridge We Call Home,* 6–20.

———. "(De)Centering the Margins? Identity Politics and Tactical (Re)Naming." In *Other Sisterhoods: Literary Theory and U.S. Women of Color,* edited by Sandra Kumamoto Stanley. Urbana: University of Illinois Press, 1998. 23–43.

———. "Honoring the Life and Words of Gloria E. Anzaldúa (1942–2004)." *American Studies Association Newsletter* 28.1 (March 2005): 1, 18.

———. "Shifting Perspectives: Spiritual Activism, Social Transformation, and the Politics of Spirit." In Keating, *EntreMundos/AmongWorlds,* 241–54.

Keating, AnaLouise, ed. *EntreMundos/Among Worlds: New Perspectives on Gloria E. Anzaldúa.* New York: Palgrave, 2005.

BIBLIOGRAPHY

Keller, Gary D., et al. *Chicano Art for Our Millennium: Collected Works from the Arizona State University Community.* Tempe, Ariz.: Bilingual Press, 2004.

————. *Contemporary Chicana and Chicano Art: Artists, Works, Culture, and Education.* Tempe, Ariz.: Bilingual Press, 2002.

Klein, Cecelia F, ed. *Gender in Pre-Hispanic America.* Washington, D.C.: Dumbarton Oaks, 2001.

Kolmar, Wendy, and Frances Bartowski, eds. *Feminist Theory: A Reader.* Mountain View, Calif.: Mayfield, 2000.

Kutzinski, Vera. *Sugar's Secrets: Race and the Erotics of Cuban Nationalism.* Charlottesville: University Press of Virginia, 1993.

Lagarriga Attias, Isabel. *Medicina Tradicional y Espiritismo: Los espiritualistas trinitarios marianos de Jalapa, Veracruz.* Mexico City: Sep/Setentas, 1975.

Langan, Celeste. "Mobility Disability." *Public Culture* 13.3 (2001): 459–84.

Leiker, James. *Racial Borders: Black Soldiers Along the Rio Grande.* College Station: Texas A&M University Press, 2002.

Lindauer, Margaret A. *Devouring Frida: The Art History and Popular Celebrity of Frida Kahlo.* Hanover, N.H.: Wesleyan University Press, 1999.

López Austin, Alfredo. *The Human Body and Ideology: Concepts of the Ancient Nahuas.* Translated by Thelma Ortiz de Montellano and Bernard Ortiz de Montellano. Salt Lake City: University of Utah Press, 1988.

Lorente-Murphy, Silvia. "El baile y canto flamencos como metáfora de la vida en *Peel My Love Like an Onion* de Ana Castillo." In *Literatura y otras artes en America Latina.* Iowa City: University of Iowa Press, 2004. 127–32.

Lowe, Sarah. *Frida Kahlo.* New York: Universe, 1991.

Lugones, María. "Playfulness, 'World'-Travelling, and Loving Perception." In Anzaldúa, *Making Face, Making Soul,* 390–402.

Lunsford, Andrea, and Lahoucine Ouzgane, eds. *Crossing Borderlands: Composition and Postcolonial Studies.* Pittsburgh: University of Pittsburgh Press, 2004.

Madsen, Deborah L. *Understanding Contemporary Chicana Literature.* Columbia: University of South Carolina Press, 2000.

Mairs, Nancy. *Waist-High in the World: A Life Among the Nondisabled.* Boston: Beacon, 1996.

Markman, Roberta H., and Peter T. Markman. *The Flayed God: The Mesoamerican Mythological Tradition.* San Francisco: Harper, 1992.

"Maya Gonzalez's Artist's Statement." *Maya Christina Gonzalez Chicana Woman Artist.* www.mayagonzalez.com/html/statemeant.html.

McCracken, Ellen. "Rupture, Occlusion and Repression: The Political Unconscious in the New Latina Narrative of Julia Álvarez and Ana Castillo." In *Confrontations et metissages,* edited by Yves-Charles Grandjeat and Christian Lerat. Bordeaux, France: Maison des Pays Iberiques, 1995. 319–28.

McMaster, Carrie. "Negotiating Paradoxical Spaces: Women, Disabilities, and the Experience of Nepantla." In Keating, *EntreMundos/Among Worlds,* 101–6.

BIBLIOGRAPHY

Meléndez, A. Gabriel, et al., eds. *The Multicultural Southwest: A Reader.* Tucson: University of Arizona Press, 2001.

Mendoza, Louis Gerard. *Historia: The Literary Making of Chicana and Chicano History.* College Station: Texas A&M University Press, 2001.

Merleau-Ponty, Maurice. *Phenomenology of Perception.* Translated by Colin Smith. London: Routledge, 1962.

———. *The Visible and the Invisible.* Edited by Claude Leforte. Translated by Alphonso Lingis. Evanston, Ill.: Northwestern University Press, 1968.

Mesa-Bains, Amalia. "*Domesticana:* The Sensibility of Chicana *Rasquachismo.*" In Arredondo et al., *Chicana Feminisms,* 298–315.

Meyer, Michael. C., and William L. Sherman. *The Course of Mexican History.* New York: Oxford University Press, 1995.

Mitchell, David, and Sharon Snyder. "Exploring Foundations: Languages of Disability, Identity, and Culture." *Disability Studies Quarterly* 17.4 (Fall 1997): 241–47.

Monaghan, John. "Physiology, Production, and Gendered Difference: The Evidence from Mixtec and Other Mesoamerican Societies." In Klein, *Gender in Pre-Hispanic America,* 285–304.

Moraga, Cherríe. *Cherríe Moraga Reads and Is Interviewed by Ana Castillo.* Videocassette. San Francisco: American Poetry Archive, 1988.

———. "Coming Home: Interview with Cherríe Moraga." *Mester* 22–23 (Fall–Spring 1993–1994): 149–64.

———. *Heroes and Saints and Other Plays.* Albuquerque: West End, 1994.

———. *The Hungry Woman and Heart of the Earth.* Albuquerque: West End, 2001.

———. "Indígena as Scribe: The W(R)ite to Remember." Public Lecture for the Society for the Study of Multiethnic Literatures. San Antonio, Tex., 11 March 2004.

———. "An Interview with Cherríe Moraga: Queer Reservations; or, Art, Identity, and Politics in the 1990s." In *Queer Frontiers: Millennial Geographies, Genders, and Generations,* edited by Joseph A. Boone, Debra Silverman, Cindy Sarver, and Karin Quimby. Madison: University of Wisconsin Press, 2000. 64–83.

———. *The Last Generation.* Boston: South End, 1993.

———. *Loving in the War Years: Lo que nunca pasó por sus labios.* Boston: South End, 1983.

———. Preface to Anzaldúa and Moraga, *This Bridge Called My Back,* xiii–xix.

———. *Waiting in the Wings: Portrait of a Queer Motherhood.* Ithaca, N.Y.: Firebrand, 1997.

———. *Watsonville: Some Place Not Here and Circle in the Dirt: El Pueblo de East Palo Alto.* Albuquerque: West End, 2002.

———. "The Welder." In Anzaldúa and Moraga, *This Bridge Called My Back,* 219–20.

BIBLIOGRAPHY

Morris, David B. *The Culture of Pain*. Berkeley: University of California Press, 1991.

————. *Illness and Culture in the Postmodern Age*. Berkeley: University of California Press, 1998.

————. "Narrative, Ethics, and Pain: Thinking *With* Stories." *Narrative* 9.1 (January 2001): 55–77.

————. "Postmodern Pain." In Siebers, *Heterotopia*, 150–73.

Moya, Paula. "Chicana Feminism and Postmodernist Theory." *Signs* 26.2 (2001): 441–83.

————. *Learning from Experience: Minority Identities, Multicultural Struggles*. Berkeley: University of California Press, 2002.

Nancy, Jean-Luc. "Cut Throat Sun." Translated by Lydie Moudileno. In Arteaga, *An Other Tongue*, 113–23.

Neely, Carol Thomas. "Women/Utopia/Fetish: Disavowal and Satisfied Desire in Margaret Cavendish's *New Blazing World* and Gloria Anzaldúa's *Borderlands/La Frontera*." In Siebers, *Heterotopia*, 58–95.

Nietzsche, Friedrich. *On the Genealogy of Morals*. Translated by Walter Kaufmann and R. J. Hollingdale. New York: Random House, 1967.

Olalquiaga, Celeste. "Pain Practices and the Reconfiguration of Physical Experience." In Burns et al., *When Pain Strikes*, 255–65.

Orellana, Sandra L. *Indian Medicine in Highland Guatemala: The Pre-Hispanic and Colonial Periods*. Albuquerque: University of New Mexico Press, 1987.

Parra, Antonio. "Flamenco: A Joyful Pain." *Pain: Passion, Compassion, Sensibility*. London: Wellcome Trust, 2004. CD-ROM.

Passman, Kristina M. "Demeter, Kore and the Birth of the Self: The Quest for Identity in the Poetry of Alma Villanueva, Pat Mora, and Cherríe Moraga." *Monographic Review/Revista Monografía* 6 (1990): 323–42.

Paz, Octavio. *El Laberinto de la Soledad*. Mexico City: Caudernos Americanos, 1947.

Pérez, Domino Renee. "Caminando con La Llorona: Traditional and Contemporary Narratives." In Cantú and Nájera-Ramírez, *Chicana Traditions*, 100–13.

Pérez, Emma. *The Decolonial Imaginary: Writing Chicanas Into History*. Bloomington: Indiana University Press, 1999.

Pérez, Laura E. *Chicana Art: The Politics of Spiritual and Aesthetic Altarities*. Durham, N.C.: Duke University. Press, 2007.

————. "Writing on the Social Body: Dresses and Body Ornamentation in Contemporary Chicana Art." In *Decolonial Voices: Chicana and Chicano Cultural Studies in the Twenty-First Century*, edited by Arturo J. Aldama and Naomi H. Quiñones. Bloomington: Indiana University Press, 2002. 30–59.

Pérez-Torres, Rafael. "Feathering the Serpent: Chicano Mythic 'Memory.'" In *Memory and Cultural Politics: New Approaches to American Ethnic Literatures*, edited by Amritjit Singh et al. Boston: Northeastern University Press, 1996. 291–319.

BIBLIOGRAPHY

————. *Mestizaje: Critical Uses of Race in Chicano Culture*. Minneapolis: University of Minnesota Press, 2006.

————. "Placing Loss in Chicano/a Narrative." *Literature and Psychology* 49.1–2 (Spring–Summer 2003): 110–18.

Pollock, Della. *Telling Bodies, Performing Birth: Everyday Narratives of Childbirth*. New York: Columbia University Press, 1999.

Popul Vuh. Translated by Albertina Saravia. Mexico City: Editorial Porrua, 1965.

Price, Janet, and Margrit Shildrick. "Bodies Together: Touch, Ethics, and Disability." In Corker and Shakespeare, *Disability/Postmodernity: Embodying Disability Theory*, 62–75.

————. *Vital Signs: Feminist Reconfigurations of the Bio/logical Body*. Edinburgh: Edinburgh University Press, 1998.

Price, Janet, and Margrit Shildrick, eds. *Feminist Theory and the Body: A Reader*. New York: Routledge, 1999.

Price Herndl, Diane. *Invalid Women: Figuring Feminine Illness in American Fiction and Culture, 1840–1940*. Chapel Hill: University of North Carolina Press, 1993.

Raiskin, Judith. "Inverts and Hybrids: Lesbian Rewritings of Sexual and Racial Identities." In *The Lesbian Postmodern*, edited by Laura Doan. New York: Columbia University Press, 1994. 156–69.

"Rest in Peace Gloria." Available: http://gloria.chicanas.com.

Rocha, Arturo. *Nadie es ombligo en la tierra / Ayac xictli in tlalécpac: Descapacidad en el México antiguo, Cultura náhuatl*. Mexico City: Miguel Ángel Porrúa, 2000.

Romo, Tere. "Mestiza Aesthetics and Chicana Painterly Visions." In *Chicano Visions: American Painters on the Verge*, edited by Cheech Marin. Boston: Little, Brown, 2002. 23–31.

Ruiz de Alarcón, Hernando. *Treatise on the Heathen Superstitions That Today Live Among the Indians Native to This New Spain*. 1629. Translated by Michael D. Coe and Gordon Whittaker. Albany: State University of New York Press, 1982.

Ruth, Sheila, ed. *Issues in Feminism*. 4th ed. Mountain View, Calif.: Mayfield, 1998.

Sahagún, Bernardino de. *Historia General de los cosas de Nueva España*. Mexico City: Editorial Porrúa, 1975.

Saldívar, José David. "Border Thinking, Minoritized Studies, and Realist Interpellations: The Coloniality of Power from Gloria Anzaldúa to Arundhati Roy." In Alcoff et al., *Identity Politics Reconsidered*, 152–70.

Saldívar-Hull, Sonia. *Feminism on the Border: Chicana Gender Politics and Literature*. Berkeley: University of California Press, 2000.

Sánchez, Rosaura. "Reconstructing Chicana Gender Identity." *American Literary History* 9.2 (Summer 1997): 350–63.

Sandahl, Carrie. "Ahhhh Freak Out! Metaphors of Disability and Femaleness in Performance." *Theatre Topics* 9.1 (1999): 11–30.

Sandoval, Chela. *Methodology of the Oppressed*. Minneapolis: University of Minnesota Press, 2000.

Scarry, Elaine. *The Body in Pain: The Making and Unmaking of the World*. New York: Oxford University Press, 1985.

Schiebinger, Londa, ed. *Feminism and the Body*. New York: Oxford University Press, 2000.

Sedgwick, Eve. *Tendencies*. Durham, N.C.: Duke University Press, 1993.

———. *Touching Feeling: Affect, Pedagogy, Performativity*. Durham, N.C.: Duke University Press, 2003.

Shildrick, Margrit. *Embodying the Monster: Encounters with the Vulnerable Self*. London: Sage, 2002.

———. *Leaky Bodies and Boundaries: Feminism, Postmodernism, and (Bio)ethics*. London: Routledge, 1997.

Siebers, Tobin. "Disability as Masquerade." *Literature and Medicine* 23.1 (Spring 2004): 1–22.

———. "Disability in Theory: From Social Constructionism to the New Realism of the Body." *American Literary History* 13.4 (Winter 2001): 737–54.

———. "Disability Studies and the Future of Identity Politics." In Alcoff et al., *Identity Politics Reconsidered*, 10–30.

Siebers, Tobin, ed. *Heterotopia: Postmodern Utopia and the Body Politic*. Ann Arbor: University of Michigan Press, 1994.

Singer, Linda. *Erotic Welfare: Sexual Theory and Politics in the Age of Epidemic*. Edited by Judith Butler and Maureen MacGrogan. New York: Routledge, 1993.

Slade, Carole. *St. Teresa of Avila: Author of a Heroic Life*. Berkeley: University of California Press, 1995.

Sloane, Johanne. "Spectacles of Virtuous Pain." In Burns et al., *When Pain Strikes*, 119–28.

Snyder, Sharon, Brenda Jo Brueggemann, and Rosemarie Garland Thomson, eds. *Disability Studies: Enabling the Humanities*. New York: Modern Language Association, 2002.

Soto, Sandra K. "Cherríe Moraga's Going Brown: 'Reading Like a Queer.'" *GLQ* 11.2 (2005): 237–63.

Steele, Cassie Premo. "Mutual Recognition and the Borders within the Self in the Writing of Cherríe Moraga and Gloria Anzaldúa." In *Critical Studies on the Feminist Subject*, edited by Giovanna Covi. Trento, Italy: Universita degli Studi di Trento, 1997. 229–43.

———. *We Heal from Memory: Sexton, Lorde, Anzaldúa, and the Poetry of Witness*. New York: Palgrave, 2000.

Szasz, Thomas S. *Pain and Pleasure: A Study of Bodily Feelings*. 2nd ed. New York: Basic Books, 1957.

Tafolla, Carmen. "La Malinche." In *Infinite Divisions: An Anthology of Chicana Literature*, edited by Tey Diana Rebolledo and Eliana S. Rivero. Tucson: University of Arizona Press, 1993.

BIBLIOGRAPHY

Talamantes y Baez, Melchor. *Panegírico de la Gloriosa Virgen y Doctora, Santa Teresa de Jesus*. Mexico City: Cofradía del Escapulario de la Santísima Madre y Señora del Carmen, 1803.

Teresa de Jesús, Santa. *Obras Completas*. Madrid: Aguilar, 1988.

Thomson, Rosemarie Garland. *Extraordinary Bodies: Figuring Physical Disability in American Culture and Literature*. New York: Columbia University Press, 1997.

Thomson, Rosemarie Garland, ed. *Freakery: Cultural Spectacles of the Extraordinary Body*. New York: New York University Press, 1996.

Tibol, Raquel. *Frida Kahlo: An Open Life*. Translated by Elinor Randall. Albuquerque: University of New Mexico Press, 1993.

Tompkins, Ptolemy. *This Tree Grows Out of Hell: Mesoamerica and the Search for the Magical Body*. New York: HarperCollins, 1990.

Torres, Edén. *Chicana Without Apology*. New York: Routledge, 2003.

Vasconcelos, José. *La raza cósmica*. 1925. Mexico City: Colección Austra, 1966.

Velasco, Juan. "The 'X' in Race and Gender: Rethinking Chicano/a Cultural Production Through the Paradigms of Xicanisma and Me(x)icanness." *The Americas Review* 24.3–4 (1996): 218–30.

Vercoe, Caroline. "Agency and Ambivalence: A Reading of Works by Coco Fusco." In Coco Fusco, *The Bodies That Were Not Ours and Other Writings*. London: Routledge, 2001. 231–46.

Weiss, Jeffrey S. *Picasso: The Cubist Portraits of Fernande Olivier*. Princeton: Princeton University Press, 2003.

Weitz, Rose, ed. *The Politics of Women's Bodies: Sexuality, Appearance, and Behavior*. New York: Oxford University Press, 1998.

Wendell, Susan. *The Rejected Body: Feminist Philosophical Reflections on Disability*. New York: Routledge, 1996.

Wiegman, Robyn. "The Possibility of Women's Studies." In *Women's Studies for the Future*, edited by Elizabeth Lapovsky Kennedy and Agatha Beins. New Brunswick, N.J.: Rutgers University Press, 2005. 40–60.

Williams, Raymond. *Marxism and Literature*. Oxford: Oxford University Press, 1977.

Yang, Mimi. "Pain and Painting: Frida Kahlo's Visual Autobiography." *Auto/biography Studies* 12.1 (Spring 1997): 121–33.

Yarbro-Bejarano, Yvonne. "Gloria Anzaldúa's *Borderlands/La frontera*: Cultural Studies, 'Difference,' and the Non-Unitary Subject." In *Contemporary American Women Writers: Gender, Class, Ethnicity*, edited by Lois Parkinson Zamora. New York: Longman, 1998. 11–31.

———. "The Multiple Subject in the Writing of Ana Castillo." *The Americas Review* 20.1 (1992): 65–72.

———. *The Wounded Heart: Writing on Cherríe Moraga*. Austin: University of Texas Press, 2001.

INDEX

ADA (Americans with Disabilities Act), 15*n*10
agency, 5, 18, 21–22, 49*n*14, 53, 80, 90, 103, 106–7, 126, 135*n*12, 138*n*16, 165, 187, 195, 208–9
Aguilera, Carmen, 138–39*n*17
Aguirre Beltrán, Gonzalo, 115*n*1, 130, 132–33
AIDS, 31, 56, 122, 140, 146, 152, 175, 183
Alarcón, Francisco X., 202
Alarcón, Norma, 23–24, 31, 45–46, 47, 48, 52, 74*n*35, 104, 104–5*n*25, 198*n*3
Alcalá, Rita Cano, 56*n*20
Alcoff, Linda Martín, 21–22, 26, 27, 166–67, 180–81*n*22, 185*n*26
Aldama, Frederick Luis, 185*n*27
amputation, dismemberment, 31, 32, 45–46, 49*n*14, 52, 58, 69, 79–81, 86, 100, 102, 116, 118, 138–39, 141, 143, 144, 156–57*n*3, 163–64*n*12, 192, 193–95, 213*n*12. *See also* Coyolxauhqui; Kahlo, Frida; Teresa of Avila, Saint
Anaya, Rudolfo, 39*n*5, 55*n*18
Anzaldúa, Gloria, 8–10, 9*n*7, 10–13, 14–16, 20, 31–32, 45, 77–113, 162; *Borderlands/La Frontera*, 4, 8, 12*n*9, 17, 40*n*6, 42–43, 58*n*22, 66, 71, 77–78, 82–86, 87–88, 93, 100–2, 103; borders, 20, 42–43, 77, 82–

84, 87–88, 95, 96*n*18, 103, 180–81*n*22; "*Cihuatlyotl*, Woman Alone," 79–81, 102; Coatlicue states, 94–96, 128, 153, 154, 165; critical reception of, 31, 77, 81–85; death, 12, 31, 77; genre, use of, 9, 74–75, 87, 88*n*8, 95–96*n*18, 101; goddesses, use of, 24*n*15, 55–56, 58, 71, 94–95, 104–5*n*25; "Holy Relics," 100–1, 102; indigenous cultures, use of, 40*n*6, 41–42, 45*n*13, 55, 58, 71, 91–92, 93–96; interviews, 12, 75, 85–89, 93*n*12, 95–96*n*18, 105; *Making Face, Making Soul*, 49–50, 198; *mestiza* consciousness, 8, 31, 64–65*n*28, 78, 79, 81–85, 87, 89–90, 94, 103, 104, 141*n*19, 198; nepantla, 95–96*n*18; new tribalism, 12, 155, 180; *nos/otras*, 81; "now let us shift," 12, 78, 84*n*6, 90, 107–8, 111, 112–13, 194–95; pain and illnesses, 4, 9, 10, 12, 14–15, 31, 77–91, 92–93, 94–96, 101–2, 104–5, 107, 114, 154–55, 195; "prieta, la," 4, 89, 108, 146; "Re: you & disability studies," 15*n*11; shape-shifting, 71, 74, 87, 158*n*5; spirituality in, 31, 57, 88–89, 91–92, 109–13; *This Bridge Called My Back*, 8, 36, 37. *See also* "Rest in Peace Gloria"; *This Bridge*

229

INDEX